PRESIDENTIAL
SECLUSION

PRESIDENTIAL SECLUSION

THE POWER OF CAMP DAVID

CHARLES FERGUSON

PB Prometheus Books

Essex, Connecticut

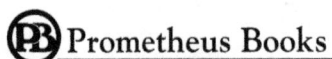

Prometheus Books

The Globe Pequot Publishing Group, Inc.
64 South Main Street
Essex, CT 06426
www.GlobePequot.com

Copyright © 2025 by Ferguson Hovey Enterprises, LLC

British Library Cataloguing in Publication Information available

Library of Congress Cataloging-in-Publication Data available

ISBN 9781493091461 (cloth) | ISBN 9781493091478 (epub)

Contents

PREFACE

You may wonder: why am I able to tell the story of such a historic location and the events and decisions that happened within? It is a valid question. Naval Support Facility, Thurmont—the official installation name given to Camp David by the US Navy—employs a chaplain as part of the permanent staff. In January 2017 after a comprehensive interview and selection process, I was picked to become the tenth chaplain at Camp David. Before my first day in February 2018, I began immersing myself in the history of the presidential retreat, reading a comprehensive list of related books. Not only did I serve as the chaplain to the permanent staff and the First Family and their invited guests, but I also acted as the official historian, making the stories of Camp David come alive to those permitted past the secret gates of this presidential retreat. Never knowing who might visit my office to ask questions about events that occurred within the gates, I continually sought information so that I was always prepared to discuss the rich history with whomever asked, for as long as they wanted to hear me regale stories of previous presidents and their guests.

Experiencing the same sense of awe as every other guest passing through the gates, I felt the "Spirit of Camp David" from the first day of work until I completed my tour of duty in 2021. Rather than letting the daily routine of arriving become just another mundane task, my work as the historian ensured that my sense of awe never faded. I saw the mystique wash over the faces of those arriving for the first time and that kept me continually energized and curious as to the significance of the retreat.

As I came to learn, many legends of dubious provenance were floating around among the staff, so it made sense to conduct detailed research on the tall tales to confirm or deny their validity. What appeared at first to be a short-term project developed into a larger one involving presidential libraries and museums, reading newspaper clippings at the Frederick County Library, and searching for memoirs and interviews of First Family members and other administration officials who recorded their memories of time spent on the mountain. I also listened to the stories of people who returned to Camp David and tracked down those tales to see if they could be corroborated. The legends remain among those who spent time on the mountain, and I've committed to keeping them among those who tell tall tales. However, some are relayed here because they add color to Camp David's character ... or they are too good to leave out.

In the following pages, you'll learn how Camp David frequently figures in world-changing events. Stories spanning multiple presidents are told as close to the corresponding administrations as I could place them. The journey will introduce you to a president seeking a secret place to escape the stress of running a world war, the first visit by a foreign leader, tales of US Marines guarding the perimeter, cordial meetings between Cold War foes, bitter enemies forging peace, determinations changing the core beliefs of the US financial system, and decisions leading to direct combat operations. These are set alongside the various activities the presidents and First Families undertook to relax, and they also give a glimpse into who these larger-than-life figures were away from the ever-present eyes of the world focused on the eighteen acres of the White House complex.

Most of those who read these pages will never find themselves inside the gates of Camp David. I routinely mentioned to staff and guests that they walked in the footsteps of history, an opportunity not available to everyone. I am grateful to the Navy for offering me such a rare and unique experience outside the typical duties of a chaplain. Because I lived the history for more than three years, spending so much time immersed in the stories of this magical place, I wanted to let those who lived at the center of history tell in their own words their experiences of the Spirit of Camp David and how their relationship with the retreat shaped their thoughts and actions. I hope these pages make you feel as if you are walking through the cool shade of the majestic oak and maple trees in the August heat and humidity; enjoying the warmth of a roaring fire in the living room of Laurel Lodge; riding horseback in late October among the leaves that paint the mountain with a blaze of vibrant reds, yellows, and oranges; or just sitting in the still quiet by the fish pond of Aspen Lodge lost in thought and meditation.

These chapters won't answer all your questions about this secluded retreat, nor will you hear all the stories. Many secrets remain locked in the participants' memories. In fact, due to release timelines from the presidential libraries and how every person who walks the secluded paths can describe their personal encounter with the Spirit of Camp David, new information emerges every year. While the stories I tell here are important to shine a light on the decisions made and the people involved, the hidden tales are just as important, for they provide the mystique comprising the soul of Camp David. I hope you come away from this journey with an understanding of the unique and significant history of this little-known place and with a fuller appreciation of the Spirit of Camp David.

ACKNOWLEDGMENTS

As with any writing project, there are many people supporting the name on the cover. Without people behind the scenes, this book would never exist.

I am singularly grateful for my partner not only of this book but also in life, my wife Lisa. She knew the stories I told on tours at Camp David deserved a much larger audience, and she planted the seed that grew into this book. Providing more than just the original idea, she served as a sounding board and ruthless editor who made this book readable and intriguing, even giving the book its title. Beyond her creative ability, she stands beside me motivating me to more ambitious goals and projects, and I am excited for the next adventure together. Life is better with you by my side.

To the First Families, White House staff, and their guests, Camp David is for you and is a special part of the White House experience. Seeing the Spirit of Camp David reflected in your eyes as I gave tours made me realize how important it was to give the public a small glimpse inside the gates of your exclusive retreat.

I am indebted to my editor, Jonathan Kurtz, and the entire team at Prometheus for seeing something in the proposal and shepherding the project to completion. Ann Wambach's superb editing made the story come to life, and Alden Perkins guided the project through production. All the mistakes are mine, not theirs. I want to say a special thank you to the National Book Network team for their care and hard work in getting this book to the readers. They work a stone's throw from Camp David, and it was fate that paired this book with them.

The librarians and archivists at the National Archives, the presidential libraries, and the White House Library, were indispensable in suggesting books, helping me decipher and find aids, and pointing me in the right direction during my research. And a huge thank you to the staff at Catoctin Mountain Park for steering me to records within the National Park Service, as well as for maintaining a beautiful drive into work every day for more than three years.

I am grateful to the many staff members of Camp David and the White House Military Office I served alongside and who shared stories they heard from guests—many of those stories making their way into this book. Your behind-the-scenes service to the guests keeps the Spirit of Camp David alive.

Gina Panettieri and Rob Brancatelli provided valuable advice and insight for the early manuscript.

A special thank you to Brian Andrews and Jeffrey Wilson for taking my calls to mentor me in the publishing world and for providing unparalleled advice. You are talented writers, incredible mentors, and amazing friends.

Finally, thank you, dear reader, for giving Camp David a few hours of your time.

INTRODUCTION

YOUR EXCITEMENT IS PALPABLE. PERHAPS YOU ARE A FRIEND OF THE First Family or someone with significant responsibility within the current administration—or you have a rare skill that is required to accomplish a critical task. Maybe you are someone in the military, or you are a family member of someone working on the secluded mountain and you have received a coveted invitation to the personal retreat of the president. Following specific instructions, you turn off a highway in a rural area in the state of Maryland, onto a winding road leading through a national park atop a peak in the Catoctin Mountains. In the summer, the dense forest lining the sides of the road forms a canopy overhead and offers a cool break from the summer heat surrounding your vehicle. At just the right time in October, the weather is picture-perfect, and the forest is on fire with the colors of autumn leaves before they fall and blanket the roads and trails. In the winter, you might time your visit such that the roads are clear, but ice still clings to the trees creating a crystalline tunnel the sun refracts into colorful rainbows. Snowflakes provide a protective blanket from the cold wind and reflect sunbeams onto your face.

Eventually you reach the signs prohibiting entry and second-guess if you really should enter this last bastion of privacy for the president, First Family, and guests. For most people, it's a once-in-a-lifetime opportunity to retrace the footsteps of history and walk the same trails as Franklin Delano Roosevelt, John F. Kennedy, and Ronald Reagan—to be so close to world-changing events that you sense the ghosts of the past. You feel the ability of the mountain to remove the weight and worry of the world as you ascend its peak, something once described by Nikita Khrushchev as the "Spirit of Camp David." As with most spiritual experiences, it is difficult to assign one definition because words are not always adequate for moments that resonate deeply in the soul.

While the Spirit of Camp David feels unique to each person who arrives through the heavily secured gates, I'm sure it means something entirely different for those who arrive by Marine One. When reading the recollections of the Camp David guests of the president, that spirit is often characterized by a relaxation and ease that allows these people to genuinely flourish as individuals while maintaining focus on changing the world from atop this unique and secret mountain retreat. It's a spirit that becomes part of the soul and shapes how you see the world, and you realize how a location can bond people across myriad differences. It's a place with a personality that infuses its guests with the realization people are more alike than society might indicate, and with time and effort challenges and obstacles can be overcome together.

The main character of this book isn't a single president, an event, or a memory of this most exclusive resort. Neither is it the staff in the background who attend to the First Family and their guests, providing five-star service to those who make significant global decisions during their short stays atop the mountain. No, the center of this book and the history within the gates of Camp David is the mountain itself. The mountain and its spirit are so interwoven with the First Family that it's hard to determine where one ends and the other begins. Without the mountain, there would be no underlying feeling of awe and awareness of history atop the Catoctin Mountains. Yet, without breathing in the spirit of hope and renewal, Camp David would have never lasted beyond the death of Roosevelt.

The Spirit of Camp David is mystical; indeed, much about the presidential retreat is retold as legend and myth. Partly because of the secrecy surrounding its operations, which allows complete seclusion for the president and invited guests, it is quite literally the last bastion of privacy for the First Family—one reason there are so few books and histories on this subject. While many members of the First Family mention Camp David in their memoirs and, with significant effort, you can find items among the archives at the presidential libraries, there is only one comprehensive history book on Camp David. Released in 1995, *The President Is at Camp David* by W. Dale Nelson offers a foundational history of Camp David. I owe gratitude to Nelson for his work, and I have built upon it here.

The mystique also lies in the magnitude of decisions and events occurring on top of a nondescript mountain overlooking rural Maryland, near the Appalachian Trail and Pennsylvania. Local residents take pride in sheltering the First Family, regardless of political persuasion, when they rest in their neighborhood. Past Camp David employees guard their personal interactions as closely as possible owing to a sense of duty to their presidents, reminiscing only with other mountain alumni about the stories.

Were it not for the continued use by the First Family, Camp David would indeed host tours and land a prominent spot on the listing of National Register of Historic Places. It would merit inclusion from its beginnings alone, with the use and war planning by Franklin D. Roosevelt. When you add in visits from Winston Churchill, Nikita Khrushchev, Leonid Brezhnev, Anwar Sadat, Menachem Begin, astronauts returning from the moon, and fifteen consecutive presidents, a rich tapestry of history is woven within the gates of Camp David. The purpose of this book is to let those who designed and wove that tapestry tell the story in their own words. Throughout the following pages, you will find the central feature in every event, every story, and every decision is Camp David. Many individuals breathe life into the Spirit of Camp David, and with each administration a new and different vision of Camp David's utility emerges. However, the mystical power of the retreat to bring people together—secluded from the distractions and pressures of the outside world—to relax, rejuvenate, be themselves, build relationships, avoid wars, and solve big problems never diminishes. It is a power that continually convinces those who entertain the idea of closing the retreat to reconsider that notion because it's difficult to put a price on the benefits of the only seclusion provided to those living in the White House. Camp David's story begins with a president seeking to escape the pressures of running a country at war to somewhere safe, secure, and secret.

Chapter 1

Shangri-La

Serving seven years as assistant secretary of the Navy under Josephus Daniels during Woodrow Wilson's administration, Franklin D. Roosevelt strengthened his strong affection for the Navy. Roosevelt bragged about reading almost ten thousand naval books in his life and even suggested leaving his post as assistant secretary to serve as a naval officer during World War I. So, it was not surprising that President Roosevelt preferred to escape the pressure and stifling summer weather of Washington, DC, aboard the presidential yacht USS *Potomac*. Roosevelt would use the *Potomac* to sail the Chesapeake Bay, venturing up and down the Atlantic Seaboard enjoying the benefits of the salt air and open spaces, away from the confines of the White House. He continued this escape routine even after Japan's December 7, 1941, attack at Pearl Harbor because on the Eastern Seaboard the war seemed distant despite the assault being on American territory. This false sense of safety would soon dissipate.

On April 14, 1942, the USS *Roper* (DD 142) sank U-85 off the coast of North Carolina. This was the first sinking of a German submarine by the United States during World War II, but the presence of German U-boats off the Eastern Coast of the United States had been known for months. Whatever secrecy the US government desired morphed into an open secret as the Eastern United States began to see allied shipping ablaze off major ports and realized the war had finally come to the United States mainland. German U-boats commenced attacking allied vessels in January 1942 in response to the United States declaring war against Germany the previous month. The first sinking occurred in Canadian waters on January 11, when U-123 sank the British freighter *Cyclops* killing eighty-seven of 182 passengers and crew.[1] For a variety of reasons, the United States was slow to respond to the U-boat threat as the attacks grew, with a peak number of forty-eight attacks in March 1942.[2] Finally organizing to decisively deter the threat, the Navy implemented a defensive plan with sixty-five anti-submarine ships in April, and the attacks and sightings of burning ships off the coast quickly abated.

From the sighting of the first burning of hulk off the coast, the White House appreciated the danger of the U-boat attacks. Roosevelt's advisors and Secret Service detail knew that allowing the president to escape Washington, DC, at sea was not a wise choice. It would destroy the war effort to have the president's yacht sunk off the coast by a lucky U-boat crew. Not even keeping the yacht close to shore along the Potomac River or within the security of the Chesapeake Bay would satisfy those charged with protecting the president. Roosevelt, fully understanding the potentially dire consequences, readily took their advice and directed a search for a land-based retreat to replace his frequent journeys aboard the USS *Potomac*.

Precedent existed for a land-based presidential retreat near Washington, DC. Jefferson escaped to his home in Monticello; Presidents Lincoln, Buchanan, Hays, and Arthur retreated to the Old Soldiers Home in the Petworth neighborhood of Washington, DC; and President Hoover built his personal retreat called Rapidan in the Shenandoah National Park. Closer to the White House, the president could easily visit Cleveland Park or the Naval Observatory to seek relief from the oppressive, swampy, summer heat. At 270 feet above sea level, Cleveland Park provided a marginal climate improvement from the White House's fifty-foot elevation. Roosevelt's own Hyde Park would serve well for a land-based retreat, but due to its distance from the White House, it did not make

---

1. https://www.newenglandhistoricalsociety.com/u-boat-attacks-of-world-war-ii-6-months-of-secret-terror-in-the-atlantic/.

2. https://www.newenglandhistoricalsociety.com/u-boat-attacks-of-world-war-ii-6-months-of-secret-terror-in-the-atlantic/.

sense for use during wartime, especially in light of the severe rationing of fuel everyday citizens endured to help the war effort.

In March 1942, Harold Ickes, secretary of the interior, took the lead on securing a site for the president's retreat. His latitude was broad as there were three general requirements for the site: relatively close to Washington, DC (less than about a three-hour drive to preserve precious, rationed fuel), secure from both safety and detection perspectives, and an altitude of at least 1,800 feet (to provide cool, clean air to help with Roosevelt's asthma). Roosevelt made it known he desired fiscal responsibility regarding the costs for construction/conversion of the site. The search was quick and thorough with several leading contenders rapidly emerging: Comers Deadening in the Shenandoah Mountains, Hoover's Rapidan, Sugarloaf Mountain in Maryland, as well as Trout Run near Thurmont, Maryland. While some of these met the broad requirements, they were eventually eliminated for a variety of reasons. Rapidan's rejection stemmed not only for political reasons due to Hoover's affiliation with the rival Republican Party, but also because "President Roosevelt was not a fly fisherman, and the damp valley aggravated his asthmatic condition."[3]

Sitting at an elevation of just 1,282 feet, Sugarloaf Mountain near Urbana, Maryland, was considered the front runner. A unique sight, the lone peak seen from miles around throughout Frederick County, the mountain was utilized by both Union and Confederate forces as an observation point in the Civil War and was purchased by Chicago lawyer Gordon Strong in the early 1900s. In 1924, Strong commissioned renowned architect Frank Lloyd Wright to design a combined planetarium and tourist attraction for the top of Sugarloaf Mountain. The project never came to fruition, though the spiral element of Wright's design for Sugarloaf can be seen in the Guggenheim Museum in New York City. For reasons entirely unknown, "under no circumstances would the owner make it available" to Roosevelt.[4] The steadfast refusal may have stemmed from political differences or because the owner was still holding out for Frank Lloyd Wright to complete his vision to develop the mountain.

3. Conrad Wirth, "Parks, Politics, and the People, Chapter 7," accessed at https://www.nps.gov/parkhistory/online_books/wirth2/chap7h.htm.
4. Wirth, https://www.nps.gov/parkhistory/online_books/wirth2/chap7h.htm.

Roosevelt's representatives looked elsewhere, and in 1946 Sugarloaf was placed in a trust, which still maintains the trails and facilities and was designated a National Natural Landmark in 1969.

As the search progressed, three sites emerged as front-running retreat locations. Comers Deadening in the Shenandoah National Park sat at an elevation of 3,300 feet and was only a two-and-a-half-hour drive from the White House. However, conversion to a presidential retreat would cost approximately $150,000 (roughly $2,566,000 in 2022 dollars), much more than Roosevelt would approve. The second contender was the yet-to-be developed camp site #4 in the Catoctin Recreational Demonstration Area, originally intended as a summer camp for girls but previously stalled due to World War II. It, too, carried a steep price tag of around $150,000; so, heeding the president's direction to remain fiscally considerate, the team reevaluated the existing third camp in the Catoctin Mountains.

The initial plan for developing the Catoctin Mountain Recreation Demonstration Area envisioned four camps. Each camp consisted of a main lodge for dining and gathering, a pool, and various sleeping cabins available for rent to the public. Designed for efficiency and because the country was still deep in the Great Depression and money was scarce, the camps would use reclaimed material from surrounding farms and native lumber for construction, while preserving the maximum number of trees and shrubs on site to ensure each camp matched the local landscape. The camps would utilize locally procured wood enhancing sustainability by securing as much naturally fallen lumber as possible. Ultimately, three of the four planned camps were constructed, all of which remain part of Catoctin Mountain Park: Misty Mount, Greentop, and Camp David.

Realizing the need to tighten the budget, the search team reassessed Camp #3 concluding it met the basic requirements. Completed in late 1938, the final design consisted of three lodging areas each containing six cabins of four beds, providing for a capacity of seventy-two campers and nine leaders. Constructed like many of the summer camps still in use today throughout the United States, these lodging units surrounded a common area containing the camp office, kitchen, recreation hall, recreation field, camp fire circle, swimming pool, craft area, nature lore building, central shower, and lodging for six staff members, one nurse, and four kitchen workers.[5] Converting Camp #3 to presidential use would not break the bank, costing only $25,000 ($448,000 in 2022 dollars). It provided extreme secrecy and security (especially with the Office of Strategic Services utilizing a nearby site), and the terrain would support those with mobility challenges. The fact that it was constructed by the Works Progress Administration and Civilian Conservation Corps under Roosevelt's New Deal was a bonus both politically and financially.

The search team presented the three finalists for a wartime retreat to Roosevelt for him to visit personally. At 3:45 p.m. on April 22, 1942, the presidential motorcade made its way through Frederick, Maryland, where keen-eyed residents did a double take as the motorcade sped by, and they recognized the president as he passed through the small town. After a two-hour drive, the party arrived at Camp #3. Camp workman William G. Renner recalled the president as he exited his limousine first setting eyes on the rustic camp atop the Catoctin Mountains. Inspired by British author James Hilton's novel *Lost Horizon*, Renner said Roosevelt exclaimed, "This is a Shangri-La."[6] Hilton had sent Roosevelt a copy of the novel in October 1937 prompting a personal thank-you note from Roosevelt to Hilton expressing a desire for more people to read the book. In fact, Roosevelt used the book as partial inspiration for his speech at the 1938 Democratic Convention in Chicago.[7] In May 1942, after hearing of the Doolittle Raid, Hilton wrote Roosevelt to explain his inspiration for the name Shangri-La came "at a certain corner of Paternoster Row, near St. Paul's Cathedral" in London.[8]

Today, the name Shangri-La conjures images of peace, harmony, an idyllic life, leisure, and paradise, within a distinctly Far Eastern context. Shangri-La is the place we all want to find and never leave, the place to rest the longing of our souls. This imagery comes directly from James Hilton's work, *Lost Horizon*. Published in 1933 as the first mass-market paperback in the United States, it became one of the most popular

---

5. Megan Weaver Tooker and Adam Smith, "Camp David Historic Resources Survey," 16.

6. W. Dale Nelson, *The President Is at Camp David*, 6.

7. Barbara M. Kirkconnell, "Catoctin Mountain: An Administrative History," 74.

8. Kirkconnell, 74.

novels of the twentieth century. The story details the travels of a group of British expatriates evacuated from India hoping to reach present-day Pakistan. However, a mysterious pilot hijacks the plane and takes them on a different route whereupon they crash in a mountain range and are eventually rescued by a resident of Shangri-La, a place where one can live a long life of leisure and soul-nourishing rest while exploring paradise—a fitting name for a place where the president can relieve the stress of the job and reenergize and nourish the soul and hopefully extend life. When Roosevelt proclaimed Camp #3 as a Shangri-La, it settled the question of where he would establish his new, secret retreat.

After selecting the retreat site, things moved quickly. Just three days later, Director of the National Park Service Newton Drury forwarded a memo to the president outlining the proposed conversions, including floor plans for Roosevelt's lodge and a renovation cost estimate. Roosevelt took a personal interest in the conversion of Camp #3 to his own personal Shangri-La. Visiting Shangri-La on April 30, Roosevelt sketched a vision for his cabin that would enlarge and screen in the porch and add a paved terrace, a corridor for the four bedrooms, and two bathrooms, plus a kitchen and pantry.[9] A passionate amateur architect, "President Roosevelt took great pleasure in going up to Shangri-La during construction, and it wasn't uncommon for the telephone to ring and the operator to say the president was leaving in a half hour for Shangri-La and would like me to join him,"[10] said Drury. In fact, his pride in the future retreat and the name Shangri-La led to him bringing close friend Queen Wilhelmina of the Netherlands, exiled in the United States due to the war, to inspect the progress where she, the president, and construction manager Conrad Wirth "sat on a car robe spread out on the ground right in front of the lodge under construction to have lunch and look out over the beautiful rolling Maryland farmland."[11]

Soon after his April 30 visit, Roosevelt approved the plan for converting the camp and authorized a budget of $15,000 ($270,000 in

---

9. Nelson, 6.

10. Wirth, https://www.nps.gov/parkhistory/online_books/wirth2/chap7h.htm.

11. Wirth, https://www.nps.gov/parkhistory/online_books/wirth2/chap7h.htm.

2022 dollars). This small budget kept the camp fiscally responsible and deflected criticism of discretionary spending during wartime. He did his best to ensure the top line of $15,000. When the initial budget crossed his desk at $18,600, Roosevelt annotated to transfer $3,000 of the cost to the Works Progress Administration and to put the Secret Service in tents rather than spend money on constructing a more permanent presence.[12] Ultimately, the project cost $28,800 ($518,000 in 2022 dollars), still fiscally responsible, but it seems Roosevelt's aides never told the president the budget-busting cost of converting Camp #3 for presidential use.

Some presidential requests would be included no matter the cost. As a child, Roosevelt watched an aunt die in a house fire and because he would forever live a life of limited mobility after his polio diagnosis, he developed a healthy fear of house fires. The nagging idea that a fire would take his life proved to be more than unfounded fear. On June 23, 1933, after only three months as president, while on a sailing trip off the coast of Maine aboard the *Amberjack II*, he found himself trapped below deck during a fire. With no Secret Service aboard, Roosevelt's son Jimmy and another individual sailing with the president, Paul Rust, leaped into action grabbing Roosevelt and tossing him up a hatch to safety topside. Others on deck "caught him as he came [up] and sat him aft by the wheel."[13] In a feat unheard of in our modern world of 24/7 news and the ever-present eye of phone cameras and social media, witnesses that day were able to keep the incident from the press. That or the press deferring to publish anything that might cause a scare related to presidential health decided not to print the story. The only news from that day on the wires discussed how the *Amberjack II* had a poor stove.[14]

Because of his close, personal experiences with fire, Roosevelt required two items at his cabin. First, there had to be a ready source of fire-fighting water. The design team accomplished this through the construction of a small pond just outside the front door of the president's lodge. Once the president began to use the lodge, industrious stewards

12. FDR-43: Cost Estimate for Shangri-La (Hi-Catoctin Lodge), April 24, 1942.
13. Robert F. Cross, *Sailor in the White House: The Seafaring Life of FDR*, 18.
14. Cross, 18.

would use the pond as a holding area for any fish they caught in nearby streams before cooking their catch for dinner. Second, Roosevelt directed that his bedroom wall adjacent to the patio have a cantilevered design, advanced engineering for the time, allowing it to fall away with adequate pressure from his wheelchair so he could escape to safety from any fire in his lodge and exit to the back patio while firefighters passed water from the fishpond in the front.[15]

Due to Roosevelt's personal involvement in the construction plans for Shangri-La, at the end of 1942 his secretary, Grace Tully, knowing his pride in designing the retreat, inquired about the whereabouts of Roosevelt's original sketches. Luckily, these initial conceptual designs remained within the National Park Service because someone had the foresight to maintain these small artifacts of history. The park service created a portfolio bound in blue leather with gold letters and entitled "A Summary of the Development of 'Shangri-La': The President's Lodge on Catoctin Recreational Demonstration Area Mountain, Maryland." It contained the drawings as well as the area's history and chronology of the construction. Harold Ickes, secretary of the interior, presented the portfolio to Roosevelt on February 19, 1943, in recognition of the president's personal design contributions to the project.[16] The portfolio is on exhibit at the Roosevelt Presidential Library and Museum in Hyde Park, New York.

As construction progressed, security concerns began to occupy the thoughts of the Secret Service detail tasked with the president's safety. On May 14, Mike Reilly visited the site with Conrad Wirth to assess the security situation. Based on the visit, seeing many security gaps that caused a great deal of anxiety, Reilly ordered a nine-foot fence, complete with barbed wire, installed around the perimeter. The Army Corps of Engineers completed the work adding floodlights and guard posts at regular intervals around the perimeter to further strengthen security. Additionally, a warning system was installed to alert of any intruders who might slip by the Marines guarding the perimeter. Camp security

---

15. Nelson, 7.
16. Kirkconnell, 80.

personnel would also rely upon instruction from Captain C. T. Farber of the British Army, "recognized as the world's foremost expert of jujitsu."[17] On May 28, the electrical power of the site went out, increasing security concerns. Five days later, investigators discovered the main power line had been cut by a stray bullet from a nearby Army camp, proving the need for the additional security measures requested by Reilly.[18]

With the conversion of Shangri-La to presidential use completed on July 1, 1942, Roosevelt officially opened and christened the retreat "USS Shangri-La" on July 5, 1942, with five guests in tow.[19] Whenever he used Shangri-La, Roosevelt's nautical background would appear as he termed each Shangri-La visit a "cruise," recording the date and type of cruise in a blue-bound logbook. The shakedown cruise, where the staff tested the systems and processes with real guests, occurred July 18 to 21 during the first overnight visit by Roosevelt, accompanied by Billy Donovan, head of the Office of Strategic Services, and Justice James Byrnes whom Donovan took next door to Greentop to observe Office of Strategic Services training.[20] Final trials occurred at the end of July with Roosevelt's full acceptance cruise on August 8. He would deem Shangri-La "Cruising with the Atlantic Fleet" during his last visit in 1942 and "recommissioned" in May 1943 with the new summer cruise season.[21] The nautical relationship to the retreat remains today as it is run by Navy personnel.

When completed, Shangri-La retained the look of a rustic, mountain summer camp with large, central buildings surrounded by smaller living quarters. Constructed by reclaiming materials from three smaller cabins, the president's three-bedroom lodge was complete with an office, dining room, kitchen, and sunroom overlooking the valley below. The construction team added a stone patio off the back of the lodge allowing the president and his guests to take advantage of summer weather to dine and lounge amid the tall pines and oaks of the Catoctin Mountains. Shangri-La kept most of the twenty-four lodging cabins, converting

---

17. Kirkconnell, 78.
18. Nelson, 7.
19. Nelson, 8.
20. Nelson, 9.
21. Kirkconnell, 79–80.

them into sleeping quarters for presidential staff, though they did not offer many amenities. Each guest cabin contained two beds, two wardrobes, and screen windows and doors so fresh mountain air would naturally cool the cabins and slowly air out the musty smell that accumulated while the cabins sat empty.

Shangri-La centered on the presidential lodge. The closer the guest cabin was to the president, the higher the influence in the president's circle. One hundred meters away from the president stood the office, dining, and conference lodge that provided meals to presidential guests as well as a place for the president and his staff to work away from his residence. Most notable was the structure closest to the presidential lodge: a luxurious cabin for his beloved dog Fala. No staff member held the president's heart above his trusted furry member of the family. Five hundred meters from the front door of Roosevelt's personally designed cabin was a twenty-five-meter pool, filled with mountain water to offer escape from the frequently oppressive humid heat of a Maryland summer. In keeping with the rustic feel, the footpaths were dirt and crushed rock following natural paths created by the foliage and marked with stones painted white every few meters. Hidden among the trees and just off the major footpaths lay lodging, recreation, and dining facilities for the Marine guards and the Navy mess stewards responsible for cooking, cleaning, and taking care of the expansive resort and the president's every need.

Roosevelt and his team imprinted their personality beyond the design and construction of the buildings. They renamed the buildings from the bland naming convention of A-1, B-3, C-6, etc., describing the area of the camp and the building number. The president's lodge became "Bear's Den," with the pool named "Bear's Wallow." Those working the president's communications worked in "One Moment Please." Instead of tents, Secret Service started out staying at the Cozy Inn in Thurmont, eventually staying overnight at Shangri-La in "221B Baker Street," an homage to Sherlock Holmes. The stewards' quarters received the name "Little Luzon" as they all hailed from the Philippines. Roosevelt named the bathhouse "Hickory Limb"; the mess hall, "Breadbasket"; the medical lodge, "Pillbox"; and the main entrance earned the moniker "Tell It to the

Marines."[22] The lighthearted naming convention provided insight into the president's sense of humor as well as the casual, relaxed atmosphere he desired while at his retreat.

While visiting Shangri-La, Roosevelt took his relaxation seriously doing what he needed for self-care, specifically focusing on his stamp collecting and card playing—either solitaire in the sunroom of Bear's Den or gin rummy with members of his staff. Sometimes while relaxing to escape the pressure of the world at war, he would ignore wartime messages until he completed his card game.[23] Notable in his card playing was the uncanny ability of his secretary Grace Tully to win at any card game. So much so, Roosevelt installed a sign warning: VISITORS WILL BEWARE OF GAMBLERS (ESPECIALLY FEMALE) ON THIS SHIP.[24]

During Roosevelt's visits to Shangri-La, he would often receive significant news. The first such report occurred in November 1942 when he received word of the successful landings in Morocco and Algeria at the beginning of Operation Torch. A visit on July 10, 1943, coincided with the invasion of the Italian island of Sicily. In late July 1943, Roosevelt heard of Mussolini's resignation while at his mountain retreat. During an August visit that same year, six of eight German saboteurs, who previously came ashore from the German U-boats off Long Island, were executed in a Washington, DC, jail. Coincidentally, or perhaps not, Sam Rosenman, the White House Counsel whose advice to Roosevelt sealed the Germans' fate was with Roosevelt during that visit to Shangri-La. The next afternoon, Captain John McCrea, Roosevelt's naval aide, arrived with news of significant allied losses in the battle of Guadalcanal, which began only two days earlier.

Staffing the mountain retreat posed some small problems, as there was no way to hire so many individuals without attracting attention or while striving to keep those costs under control. To solve this, sailors onboard the USS *Potomac* received a new assignment: to serve as the

---

22. Michael Giorgione, *Inside Camp David*, 30.
23. Winston Churchill, *The Hinge of Fate*, 797.
24. Nelson, 18.

retreat staff whenever the president visited his new mountain retreat and to provide caretaking duties throughout the year. The arrangement made sense because if the president was at Shangri-La he couldn't be on the USS *Potomac*, so using those sailors would not take them away from any other more important duties onboard the ship. Neither would it utilize additional military personnel who could be useful in other parts of the world. The task of overseeing this new retreat fell upon William Rigdon, the Naval aide to Roosevelt who also oversaw operations of the presidential yacht. Additionally, US Marines would serve as the security force, arriving just prior to a visit to guard not only the perimeter of Shangri-La but also to keep the bridges along the route free from any possible saboteurs. This allowed the Secret Service to focus on personal protection for the president on the motorcade to the retreat, as well as staying close to him while inside the gates of Shangri-La. While the sailors would reside at Shangri-La when serving the president, the Marines would stay at Misty Mount, a small camp at the base of the Catoctin Mountains. This arrangement worked well and is the reason the retreat remains a Navy-controlled facility eighty years later.

Over the three remaining years of his presidency, Roosevelt visited his private retreat in near absolute secrecy. Known as Shangri-La only to those within the White House circle of trust, as early as 1942 rumors had spread of a secret retreat for the president in the mountains outside Washington, some saying he would venture to Rapidan and others spinning tales of a luxury retreat similar to that of Hitler's in Bavaria.[25] The White House staff remained tight-lipped and allowed those ideas of Roosevelt visiting those rumored sites as they weren't near the actual location and would keep people looking in the wrong directions. However, on October 15, 1943, a report appeared across the United Press wires by reporter Merriman Smith describing Roosevelt utilizing a secret retreat in the Catoctin Mountains, the exact location undisclosed.[26] The National Park Service confirmed that Roosevelt utilized the secret retreat but deferred details to the White House. This prompted a flurry of activ-

---

25. Nelson, 19.
26. Nelson, 19.

ity from the Secret Service who sought advice on if the reporting violated the Censorship Act, so they could silence any follow-ups on the subject, to which a veteran reporter suggested there was no violation because "they make no mention of any particular trip of the president."[27]

During the most notable visit during his presidency, Roosevelt started a tradition that continues eighty years later: inviting foreign leaders to the mountains to discuss weighty matters in a relaxed and inviting atmosphere. From the beginning, Roosevelt knew the relational power and value of getting away from distractions and the public would allow decision-makers to relax and be themselves, and through strengthening relationships, better decisions and policies could be explored and implemented.

On May 14, 1943, the presidential motorcade left Washington, DC, for Shangri-La accompanied by Sir Winston Churchill, the British prime minister with whom Roosevelt had developed a close friendship, who was in America for the Trident conference discussing the planning of the war. During their stay, the duo visited a local establishment in Thurmont, Maryland, called the Cozy Inn, where Churchill partook of beer and selected tunes on the jukebox. As the limousine departed to return atop the mountain, it stopped briefly at a traffic light, and residents recounted their surprise upon recognizing the passengers, though Churchill flashing a *V* for victory also aided in the recognition.[28]

Camp legend tells a story that during this visit, Roosevelt and Churchill sat on the porch of Laurel, the president's dining cabin, and outlined the broad strokes of freeing Europe from Hitler's grasp. Churchill preferred attacking the soft underbelly of Europe through Italy—utilizing territory recently liberated in North Africa, while Roosevelt favored crossing the English Channel, striking German forces head-on. Both ideas would come to fruition with the invasion of Italy in July 1943 and the landings at Normandy in June 1944. The relaxed

27. Nelson, 19.

28. David Kidd, https://www.governing.com/context/how-thurmont-coexists-with-presidents-and-camp-david (retrieved December 28, 2021).

atmosphere and lack of onlookers at the retreat had allowed both men to put aside their egos and see the benefit of both of their visions in how the war should progress and set the stage for victory in Europe.

Two bizarre accidents at Shangri-La occurred during separate presidential visits in which Roosevelt escaped near death. One evening, as was customary, the president and a guest played cards in the main room of Bear's Den. A chandelier crafted from an old wagon wheel hung directly above the table with wrought iron lights affixed. In the dead of night, the chandelier "slipped out of its suspended iron rim" and crashed onto the table below where hours before the president had sat.[29] Surprisingly, no one heard the crash, and National Park Service employee Conrad Wirth recalled, "Roosevelt was not told of this, nor have I seen the story published heretofore."[30] Some things are best left with a sense of relief at no disaster when the issue can be resolved quietly. The staff repaired the table and ensured the offending chandelier was securely bolted together for future use.

The second near-death experience occurred one morning while Roosevelt took a drive outside the confines of his retreat. Reluctant to give up his driver's license and eager to drive himself, Roosevelt, accompanied by a Secret Service agent, routinely and stealthily drove himself around the mountain roads surrounding Shangri-La. On one such ride, he turned onto a private road and continued along until they arrived at the caretaker's cottage and faced "a small woman carrying a shotgun, who absolutely refused to believe" they were who they claimed to be.[31] Unable to produce written permission to drive on the property, the woman took aim at the pair demanding they leave, a warning the president gladly heeded. The next morning, the owner of the property, Mr. Charles Paine, received a summons to the White House, two hours away, where staff angrily recounted the events of the previous morning. After apologizing to the president in person, Mr. Paine "wrote him a permit to use the road through his place."[32]

---

29. Wirth, https://www.nps.gov/parkhistory/online_books/wirth2/chap7h.htm.
30. Wirth, https://www.nps.gov/parkhistory/online_books/wirth2/chap7h.htm.
31. David Jones, "A History of Camp David," 8.
32. David Jones, 8.

Roosevelt formed the character and personality of Shangri-La in many ways. Not only did he select the site, but he also personally designed the main presidential cabin, a design which mostly remains eighty years later. Roosevelt kept information about the place as hush-hush as possible because he wanted privacy and relaxation above all else. This also made an invitation to the retreat special, proving someone's importance to the president. Perhaps most importantly, Roosevelt understood the power of seclusion and nature to break down barriers so people, including the president of the United States, could relax, be themselves, and accomplish world-changing things through strong relationships and few distractions.

The fictional Shangri-La from *Lost Horizon* positively affected the characters visiting there, as did Roosevelt's version of the idyllic retreat. Roosevelt could relax and recover from the demands of running a country as well as the concerns of a war raging across the globe. And the cool, mountain air undoubtedly alleviated his asthma, allowing respite from a climate that took its toll on a wheelchair-bound president, possibly even extending his life, if ever so slightly. It also allowed Roosevelt the space to look at the world from a fresher perspective with a clear mind and heart and, at least in one aspect of war planning, changed the course of history.

On April 12, 1945, the future of Shangri-La plunged into uncertainty. Having not been used as extensively during 1944 in favor of other locations, possibly due to security concerns now that his retreat had received coverage in the press, the president was staying at Warm Springs, Georgia, a place long visited by Roosevelt after his polio diagnosis. First visiting Warm Springs in 1924 and eventually building a cabin in 1932 that would be dubbed the Little White House, he would frequent the small resort for its literal warm, rather than hot, spring, in hopes it would improve his paralysis. On his sixteenth visit to Warm Springs as president, Roosevelt suffered a stroke and died. Vice President Truman ascended to the presidency without any real knowledge of Shangri-La, and no one knew if it would match his liking, or if he would even decide to visit Roosevelt's secret mountain hideaway.

CHAPTER 2

Voice of the President

NOT ONLY DID FRANKLIN ROOSEVELT ESTABLISH SHANGRI-LA AS A presidential retreat, but he also instructed his staff to devise a way to keep him in close contact with world events. In the twenty-first century, Americans are accustomed to instantaneous communications. We have access to the breaking news of the day in the palm of our hand, and it is difficult to imagine a time when the president of the United States was not within arm's reach of a phone with which to respond to any number of crises throughout the world. Before World War II, the presidency was not as ever-present as it is today. Presidents really could get away from the pressures of the office or at least have a buffer before a crisis or other important work event broke through time and distance to reach them on their vacation. Even with war raging across Europe in 1939 to 1941, the need for omnipresent presidential communications, while identified as desirable, remained a low priority. Despite efforts to shorten the delays in receipt of time-sensitive matters, the Japanese attack on Pearl Harbor accelerated such thinking, forcing planners to develop ways to keep the commander in chief connected with every war detail across the globe, regardless of the time of day or his proximity to Washington, DC.

This desire to connect the president to the world around the clock had started before Pearl Harbor. In fact, during the middle of 1941, "General Frank Stoner, the then head of Army Communications, had detached [Colonel William] Beasley from Fort Monmouth and sent him to Washington, DC, to survey the communications situation in the

Nation's capital, and with an eye to the White House."[1] Before completing a full assessment of the communications needed for the government, war came to the United States prompting the Army to assign Colonel Beasley directly to the White House because of his expertise in communication systems. His first mission entailed upgrading the White House communications equipment and procedures to include those of the Secret Service. Beasley's first major upgrade involved installing mobile radios in presidential automobiles as well as establishing a base station to keep the vehicles in contact with the White House.

It did not take long for the White House to realize communications support not only kept the president informed, but it also enhanced his security during wartime. To support the wartime communication needs of the president, the War Department commissioned the White House Signal Detachment on March 25, 1942. Working directly for the White House and under the direction of Colonel Beasley, the detachment assisted Secret Service communications to protect the president of the United States. Given the importance of the new detachment, Colonel Beasley's direction was simple, "You're working for the president. He is to have everything he needs, and it must be the best."[2] The War Department backed up their words with action as the new team received the highest priority in purchasing equipment and then quickly setting up the needed communications. Their role rapidly expanded to include communications at all out-of-town trip locations as well as setting up the highly secret Map Room in the White House basement, where a world map on the floor allowed Roosevelt to track the locations and movements of Allied Forces and provided him with a valuable resource in making strategic decisions.

To ensure security of the communication system, the Signal Detachment created their own communications network, which designated the White House agencies that received access.[3] Possessing a reliable means that would enable Roosevelt to maintain situational awareness of the war

---

1. George McNally, *A Million Miles of Presidents*, 18.
2. McNally, "The White House Signal Team," 25.
3. According to McNally in "The White House Signal Team," visiting foreign leaders, including Queen Wilhelmina of the Netherlands, received communication support.

while traveling, the Signal Detachment unleashed their collective imagination. Knowing Roosevelt enjoyed trips to his home in Hyde Park, New York, and the soothing baths of Warm Springs, Georgia, made maintaining communications with the White House from those distances a logistical and engineering challenge. How would they make the large communication suite needed for receiving and transmitting voluminous messages mobile and relatively economically feasible? Presidents routinely utilized trains for cross-country travel and attaching a communication suite to said train would not cause too much additional logistical cost to maintain a mobile communication center. The ever-ingenious Signal Detachment converted a train car for presidential communications allowing Roosevelt to resume long-distance trips fully connected to a war raging on the other side of the globe.

As they fulfilled the communications requirements for the White House the need for their expertise arose at another local site: Shangri-La. Despite manning shortages due to rapidly expanding responsibilities, the Detachment accepted their new mission and quickly set about establishing a second presidential communications hub. To run the cables supporting communications on the mountain, the Detachment blasted into the solid rock of Catoctin Mountain ensuring the cables lay at a depth safe from tampering and the elements—rain and snow being the main culprits of equipment disruptions. However, the rain constantly thwarted any progress made in establishing the communications system. Those laboring to set up the new site complained the weather never wanted to cooperate, leading the men to describe the rain as "one day from the sky and two from the trees" with the crews constantly working to repair cables soaked by the seemingly incessant water or charred and melted by frequent lighting strikes atop the Catoctins.[4] Undeterred, the crew completed their mission, and, once finished, the site at Shangri-La included a full communications center, telephone switchboard, voice radio, teletype, and radio relay capability.

As typical with those military members serving at the mountain retreat, the Signal Detachment spared no expense of personnel or finances

---

4. McNally, "The White House Signal Team," 27.

to act upon the president's request or wishes. During one presidential visit to Shangri-La, Harry Hopkins wanted to hear Hitler's speech that was scheduled to occur in a few hours. Whether it was a lack of foresight to request capability to hear the speech, late intelligence indicating Hitler would soon say something significant, or just a last-minute idea to hear what Germany was thinking, whatever the reason for the late request was of no consequence. The president asked, so they delivered. Soldiers from the Signal Detachment scoured the retreat looking for a short-wave radio on which to tune in the requested speech, to no avail. "Finally, in one cabin a table-style broadcast receiver was found. A quick check revealed a short-wave band. The switch thrown and the set tuned. German speech issued from the speaker. With ten minutes to go, two soldiers quickly strung an antenna outside the Roosevelt lodge. . . . Then, tenderly the set was carried to the president's study where . . . the 'Boss' and Mr. Hopkins listened while a stenographer recorded the frenzied phrases."[5] In this moment the signal detachment set the standard of keeping the president constantly connected to events around the world no matter the location.

Despite their success, as the war wound down, so too did the size of the military as the country reaped the peace dividend that coincided with the idea that wars were no longer necessary. With this drawdown, the Signal Detachment at the White House faced deactivation in 1946. The military aide to the president assigned George McNally the demoralizing task of returning the communications facilities to their pre-war configuration, even if that meant complete dismantlement, placing the ingeniously crafted railroad-communications car in mothballs, sending the military men home to life as civilians or on to other assignments, and consigning the small detachment to a quiet and unheralded demise. However, since no agency would step into the void and take the responsibility of ensuring reliable communications for the president, the detachment remained—albeit with a laughable footprint of just twenty personnel.

Yet, that small group of communications personnel, which, as they did during the war years, punched well above their weight, and it did not go unnoticed. The White House could not ignore the value provided

5. McNally, "The White House Signal Team," 28.

by them, so as often happens to success in the military, their mission expanded in 1946 to include sound pickup and reproductions, installing public address systems, operating motion picture projectors, and coordinating with television and radio broadcasters to become "The Voice of the President," a moniker that remains today. As once again war broke out a scant five years after the great conflagration, this time on the Korean Peninsula, the detachment's size tripled. By 1954, the detachment changed its name to the White House Army Signal Agency, reflecting its expanded mission and size while also indicating its impending permanence and its importance to the mission of the president in a more complex world. As more personnel from other services joined the agency, its name changed again in 1962 to the White House Communications Agency to demonstrate how all branches of the military participated in this vital presidential mission.

Today, the White House Communication Agency continues as "The Voice of the President," providing the president and vice president continuous, reliable, secure communications from anywhere in the world. Whenever you see the president on a screen or hear his voice, members of the White House Communication Agency are ensuring the president's message reaches the world under any circumstance or from wherever the president and other key administration officials find themselves.

CHAPTER 3

Uncertainty

Upon each new presidential inauguration, military members managing and operating Shangri-La are keenly in tune with the transition and anxiously await word of the new president's intentions regarding use of the camp. Present-day military members don't worry over a possible divestment and closure of the retreat, but they do agonize over small details required to provide the highest level of service to the president, First Family, and their invited guests. How much use will the president require? What amenities do the president and family expect or desire? Will there be advance notice for visits to the retreat? Will they enjoy the retreat and use it on a regular basis?

While it seems surprising today, President Harry Truman never visited Shangri-La before assuming the presidency. From the time Roosevelt first set eyes on the Catoctin mountains, a visit to Shangri-La occurred only through presidential invitation, just like today, making an invitation to the president's retreat a sign of one's personal importance to the president. As vice president, Truman wasn't the first name on Roosevelt's contact list. In fact, Roosevelt reluctantly invited Truman on the 1944 ticket as his running mate, and after the election Truman stayed on the sidelines. The Office of the Vice President looked much different during the 1940s than it does today. Eighty years ago, the vice president garnered votes for election and performed ceremonial tasks that did not appeal to the chief executive of the government. Most of those day-to-day duties focused on events inside the Capitol—helping to whip up votes and voting to break ties in the Senate. In fact, after the 1944 election, Truman was invited to the White House only once, for breakfast with Roosevelt in the garden, an occasion which for much of the White House staff marked the first time they had laid eyes on the vice president. Shangri-La was Roosevelt's retreat, and no one knew if Truman would use the retreat or return the camp to the National Park Service.

Not knowing what the retreat was like, or if it was even worth the expense, President Truman indicated a desire to declare Shangri-La a historical site due to its importance during World War II. Many planning meetings were held there, and in June 1944 during a visit to Shangri-La, Roosevelt learned of the successful landing on Normandy. Combined with Greentop's role in training Office of Strategic Service agents, the entire Recreation Demonstration Area in the Catoctin Mountains deserved historical protection. It all hinged on whether Truman desired to keep Shangri-La for his own use or if he sought a different retreat in the local area. Would the magic of the location work on someone who had no say over its initial construction and purpose?

Truman made his first visit to Shangri-La in September 1945 and was disappointed. A Missourian used to wide open spaces, the abundance of trees, despite offering respite from the summer heat, depressed the new commander in chief. The gloominess and poor first impressions extended beyond the president. In fact, the entire First Family expressed a desire to relax anywhere other than Shangri-La. Truman's wife, Bess, made her first visit a month later in October 1945 and left disappointed, not visiting again until May 1946. After her first visit, their daughter Margaret commented, "Shangri-La was damp and cold most of the time. I thought it was a terrible place and went there as little as possible."[1]

Within the first two visits by Truman, Lieutenant Commander William Rigdon, Naval aide to the president, responsible for planning presidential travel and in charge of Shangri-La and the presidential yachts, as well as offering advice on naval topics as requested, noticed the disappointment and asked, "Is there anything that we can do up here that would make you like the place better?"[2] This tactful question

---

1. Nelson, 23.
2. Rigdon, oral history from Jerry N. Hess, July 16, 1970.

allowed Truman to voice his displeasure and he stated, "I feel cooped up in this lodge. I look out the window and there's nothing but trees."[3] It was a problem with a straightforward solution, but as often happens in significant decisions, multiple people take credit for the action, especially when it involves keeping the president happy. Admiral Robert Dennison, Truman's senior naval aide, recalled being the one to broach the subject with Truman, "The cabin was a miserable place because there was no outside terrace. The trees were so grown up you couldn't see anything. You looked into a dense bank of foliage. You couldn't breathe in it."[4] He asked the president for permission to change things and open up the view, to which the president gave his approval.

As the military commander in charge of operating Shangri-La, Rigdon arranged for dozens of sailors from the USS *Williamsburg* (the new presidential yacht) to clear the slope behind the president's lodge with axes and for bulldozers to open up a view into the valley to the east of the retreat, allowing sight lines as far away as Keysville, Maryland, the birthplace of Francis Scott Key. Following that tiresome job, "[the President] didn't seem so hemmed in up there, he went more frequently, and so did Mrs. Truman."[5] Beyond merely cutting trees to create a magnificent view of the valley, the industrious sailors "put in a terrace so you could sit out there and look over this beautiful valley. . . . It was delightful."[6] Their work is a legacy as the spectacular view from the back of the lodge into the valley remains today. Things looked dramatically better from the president's lodge, as well as for the future of the camp.

Removing the trees and opening up the view from the president's lodge brightened Truman's time at Shangri-La, but he never grew fond of the retreat, preferring instead to escape to Key West or aboard the USS *Williamsburg*. Over his nearly eight years in office, he only visited the retreat ten times. However, Truman winterized the buildings allowing use of the retreat year-round instead of just a summer retreat as was the

---

3. Rigdon, oral history, July 16, 1970.
4. Robert Dennison, oral history from Truman library, interviewed by Jerry N. Hess, October 6, 1971.
5. Rigdon, oral history, July 16, 1970.
6. Dennison, oral history, October 6, 1971.

case for Roosevelt. During his occasional visits, Truman would enjoy the time outside and take thirty-minute walks with Lieutenant Commander Rigdon, frequently abandoning the main paths to explore the various trails throughout the compound. During these walks, the two men discussed all manner of topics ranging from work and world affairs to those of a friendly, personal nature providing Truman a brief, yet valuable, respite from the burdensome weight of the presidency and a fleeting moment of life as a normal person.

Following his first visit, Truman allowed members of his staff to utilize Shangri-La when he wasn't there, a practice many of his successors continued. Truman recognized the need of all senior White House officials to have a place to relax, be themselves, and let off some steam away from the press and other prying eyes in the Washington, DC, social circles. While no comprehensive records exist concerning the use of the facility by staff, anecdotal evidence suggests the camp wasn't idle. In fact, Truman's selected aides took a liking to the private retreat, with some members of the president's staff occupying the compound almost every weekend. So much so, Rigdon spent most weekends on the mountain overseeing the care of invited guests. Those coming to Shangri-La without the president first obtained approval through the naval aide and agreed to follow a short set of rules: "There must not be any 'wild parties' or other unbecoming conduct on the part of anybody at the camp. Excessive drinking or gambling for high stakes is absolutely forbidden. . . . It is not desirable that the camp be discussed as to its location, facilities, or any phase of its operation."[7] Opening up the power and beauty of the retreat to a wider audience not only ensured its survival, but it allowed Shangri-La's magnetic personality to seep into senior White House staff, especially those who would work in successive administrations, creating a powerful legacy of exclusivity beyond just the president and First Family.

Summer 1946 saw memorable visits by the First Family. Both President and Mrs. Truman arrived at the retreat for a lunch accompanied by Bess's mother. Desperately needing a break from the Washington

---

7. Memo from James Vardman to Truman, dated September 5, 1945, located in Papers of Harry S. Truman Official File, OF 101-H (Shangri-La).

heat, despite the installation of air conditioning in the White House a few months prior, Truman wrote to Bess on June 24, 1946, asking if she would like to spend the Fourth of July weekend on the mountain. He reasoned, "I've signed a bill giving it [a holiday] to all the government employees, so why not the top employee take one too?"[8] After this visit, Bess's impressions were improved from her previous memories of a dull, damp, and dreary run-down camp. She wrote a cheerful letter to her daughter Margaret claiming, "The most peaceful Fourth I have any recollection of."[9] Despite this one positive visit, the depressing first impression remained the more powerful memory whenever the Truman family thought about Shangri-La.

On another weekend that summer, Truman made a visit to the historical military site in Gettysburg, starting a tradition among presidents to travel to the famous battlefield just fifteen miles away. The site of a key battle of the American Civil War, the land upon which the battle raged in July 1863 earned designation as Gettysburg National Military Park in 1895. Long considered hallowed ground by both sides who fought among the farmland, Gettysburg quickly became a historic treasure, eventually coming under the care of the National Park Service in 1916.

During pauses in the construction of what would become Shangri-La, work crews, having grown up hearing stories from parents and grandparents who fought in the legendary battle, eagerly assisted in a restoration project at Gettysburg National Military Battlefield. These young men, some veterans themselves, set about retrieving aged rail fences from deep in the forests to create a more realistic appearance for the battlefield so visitors could better appreciate the scale and conditions men on both sides of the conflict faced during the three-day battle.[10] Tranquil and dotted with memorials erected by veterans of the bloody battle and their units, the battlefield provides miles of reflection regarding the horror of war. It is only fitting that those with the power to send young men and women into battle spend time among the ghosts of

---

8. Robert H. Ferrell, *Dear Bess*, 529.

9. Margaret Truman, *Bess W. Truman*, 287.

10. NPS website: www.nps.gov/cato/learn/historyculture/ccc.htm accessed June 16, 2020.

battles past to inform their policies and decisions. During Truman's visit, he surprised the press assigned to follow his every move by giving the park ranger a break so he could show off and guide the press tour himself.[11]

Escaping to Shangri-La also afforded the president a treat other areas could not allow for security reasons: The president could drive himself around the camp and surrounding roads. "Shangri-La was the only place I knew where [Truman] could drive his own vehicle. He and Mrs. Truman could go for rides in the jeep up there."[12] Never far from protection, the president and Bess would sit together like a normal married couple up front, relegating the Secret Service and Rigdon to the back seat as they explored the surrounding landscape from the road. Rigdon recalls Truman "could ride for a whole afternoon and maybe not even meet another car."[13] Savoring the idea of traffic-free driving without worries about his safety, Truman often commandeered a jeep dragging Rigdon—and Bess if she was there—along on an expedition to the countryside. Pushing the boundaries of freedom allowed by the Secret Service, Truman himself occasionally drove the entire trip from Washington to Shangri-La. Presidents freely driving cars outside the security of the White House grounds or Shangri-La would soon end, as a tragic event would highlight the importance of presidential seclusion and safety.

Soon after Truman took office, uncertainty over the future of Shangri-La and the surrounding camps sparked a battle between the District of Columbia Society for Crippled Children and the Department of the Interior over the use of Greentop, the pre-war summer camp for disabled children in Maryland and Washington, DC, located next to and built one year before Shangri-La. Encouraged by Truman's aversion to Shangri-La, forces assembled to restore the rest of Catoctin Mountain to recreational use. On January 16, 1946, Mrs. Jewell Gaffney, the executive secretary for the Society, penned a letter to the White House concerning the use of

---

11. Nelson, 27.
12. Rigdon, oral interview, July 16, 1970.
13. Rigdon, oral interview, July 16, 1970.

the "Little White House" on Mt. Catoctin—a name used by the public for Shangri-La. Quoting a statement from President Truman that the area "would be made available to Marylanders for recreational purposes," she added her plea to that of the Maryland League for Crippled Children asking that the National Park Service again permit use of Greentop for their summer camp.[14]

One month later, on February 12, Matthew Connelly, secretary to the president, responded to Mrs. Gaffney informing her, "Camp #2, [also known as Greentop] which was used as a camp for crippled children from 1938 to 1941, is now occupied by the US Marine Corps."[15] He further offered the use of Misty Mount for their summer camp site. One week later, Mrs. Gaffney retorted that Misty Mount presented difficult terrain and would severely limit the number of campers, but they would study his proposal. She then asked a masterful question, "Matt, under these conditions, do you think we would be justified in asking the Capitol Park Service to seek appropriate funds for building adequate camping facilities on a level site on the Catoctin Mountain that would be large enough for present purposes and make some provision for future expansion?"[16] After forwarding her letter to the Department of the Interior, on March 19, 1946, Mr. Connelly politely informed Mrs. Gaffney that there would be no funds for her proposal and that Misty Mount remained the only possible solution.[17]

Unknown to the White House, there was a multifront campaign to reallocate Greentop for summer camp use for disabled children and for the public at other times of the year. Other groups knew the magical power of the mountain location in providing rest and rejuvenation, and they were not going to let the opportunity pass them by. On April 20, 1946, Clinton Anderson, secretary of agriculture, wrote Matthew

14. Letter from District of Columbia Society for Crippled Children to White House, dtd January 16, 1946, located in Papers of Harry S. Truman Official File, OF 101-H (Shangri-La).

15. Letter from Matthew Connelly to Jewell Gaffney, dtd February 12, 1946, located in Papers of Harry S. Truman Official File, OF 101-H (Shangri-La).

16. Letter from Jewell Gaffney to Matthew Connelly, dtd February 19, 1946, located in Papers of Harry S. Truman Official File, OF 101-H (Shangri-La).

17. Letter from Matthew Connelly to Jewell Gaffney, dtd March 19, 1946, located in Papers of Harry S. Truman Official File, OF 101-H (Shangri-La).

Connelly asking for the return of Greentop on behalf of the Maryland League for Crippled Children. He described Greentop as having "everything needed to make a good camp for the children."[18] Ensuring a response to his letter, he stated, "It is my understanding that the Marines are taking it over to make a summer resort for the Commandant of the Marine Corps. I do not believe this is quite fair to the crippled children of Maryland. It does not belong to the government; it belongs to them . . . Find out who gave the Marine Corps authority to take over [Greentop] as a summer home for General Vandergrift."[19] Highlighting a possible underhanded theft of the camp for someone's personal use reanimated the discussion regarding the future of Greentop.

On April 30, 1946, Matthew Connelly asked the new secretary of the interior, Julius Krug, to look into the matter and provide a memo, presumably to back the assertion Greentop stay closed to the public. Secretary Krug responded to Matthew Connelly on May 15 describing how Greentop could house only ninety-six individuals while the Maryland League requires space for two hundred, and they returned their camping permit in favor of utilizing a site at Hopewell Village in Pennsylvania.[20] Secretary Krug also noted Greentop's conversion for their use as temporary until the Maryland League either found or developed an adequate camp.[21] He also addressed use of the camp by General Vandegrift and the Marines "for the express purpose of providing security for the President during his visits to the Catoctin area and as a rehabilitation center for disabled Marines. Some alterations have been made . . . to provide suitable quarters for General Vandegrift during his inspection of the rehabilitation center."[22] Not a categorical denial of a Marine Corps plan

18. Letter from Clinton P. Anderson to Matthew Connelly, dtd April 20, 1946, located in Papers of Harry S. Truman Official File, OF 101-H (Shangri-La).

19. Letter from Clinton P. Anderson to Matthew Connelly, dtd April 20, 1946, located in Papers of Harry S. Truman Official File, OF 101-H (Shangri-La).

20. Memo from Julius Krug to Matthew Connelly, dtd May 15, 1946, located in Papers of Harry S. Truman Official File, OF 101-H (Shangri-La).

21. Memo from Julius Krug to Matthew Connelly, dtd May 15, 1946, located in Papers of Harry S. Truman Official File, OF 101-H (Shangri-La).

22. Memo from Julius Krug to Matthew Connelly, dtd May 15, 1946, located in Papers of Harry S. Truman Official File, OF 101-H (Shangri-La).

to take Greentop for the commandant yet this squashed any plans the Marines held for permanent use of Greentop. Secretary Krug ended the letter with a hope Greentop would expand to meet the Maryland League's needs in the future.

Sensing a lack of resolve on the government's part, and with firm dedication of purpose, the campaign to restore Greentop to its rightful use caught fire when the Rotary Club of Baltimore joined the fray. The Baltimore chapter adopted a resolution on April 26, 1946, calling for the return of Greentop to the Maryland League for Crippled Children. The Rotary Club mailed the resolution to Secretary Krug and various congressmen, most notably Thomas D'Alesandro (father of the first female speaker of the United States House of Representatives, Nancy Pelosi) of the Third Congressional District of Maryland, leading to various letters from local politicians to both the secretary of the interior and President Truman in May 1946. Congressman Beall of the Second District of Maryland is quoted in the Frederick, Maryland, newspaper saying, "What could be a better shrine than for the crippled children of Maryland to be allowed to again use their camp."[23] A full-court press underway, would the White House cave or continue to aver and hide behind security concerns for a little-used presidential retreat? If Truman wasn't interested in going to the retreat, why keep the nearby camps closed to the public?

As the debate lingered, more voices joined the children's side with the Maryland Rotary Clubs of Bel Air, Sykesville, and Rockville echoing the calls for returning Greentop to its "original" use. In September 1946, Senators Millard Tydings and George Radcliffe penned letters to the administration regarding Greentop to include resolutions from two Rotary Clubs. Both received a reply from the superintendent of the National Park Service on October 2 stating, "We have not been informed by the White House of any plans for a change in the usage of this facility, but we shall be pleased to advise you when we receive this information."[24]

---

23. *The News*, Frederick, Maryland, May 25, 1946.

24. Letter from Irving C. Root to Millard E. Tydings, dated October 2, 1946. Letter from Irving C. Root to George L. Radcliffe, located in Papers of Harry S. Truman Official File, OF 101-H (Shangri-La).

Desiring a quick resolution, he copied the replies to Matthew Connelly at the White House.

Persistence paid dividends. On December 10, Matthew Connelly informed Congressman D'Alesandro, "The status of the camp remains unchanged at the present time, but arrangements are being made for the return of [Greentop] to the National Park Service in time to permit the crippled children to use it during the summer of 1947."[25] After almost a year of steady pressure from multiple individuals, the administration relented returning Greentop to the National Park Service for use by the Maryland League for Crippled Children after May 1, 1947. Security forces would now reside within Shangri-La, which remained closed to the public. In a gesture of goodwill and no hurt feelings, in 1948 Truman invited Greentop campers for a tour of his retreat, though, unsurprisingly, Truman was absent.

"Absent" is the best word to describe Truman's relationship with Shangri-La. It was always viewed as Roosevelt's retreat, and, as with any vice president ascending to the presidency, Truman sought ways to get out from under the large shadow Roosevelt cast. That combined with a claustrophobic feeling from the trees, which form a key part of the magical seclusion of the mountaintop, Shangri-La would never win out against Key West as the ideal rest spot for President Truman and his family. However, despite everything stacked against its survival, Shangri-La cast a strong enough spell on Truman to earn a stay of execution. Sitting mostly ignored for eight years by the person for whom it existed, when given a bit of a chance to show its worth, the retreat's privacy and relaxed atmosphere shined brightly when the president was in residence. Truman saw something Roosevelt missed, but most succeeding presidents quickly realized: the healing power of the retreat was valuable to everyone in the administration. Truman's contribution to form the character of the retreat was allowing others to share in the magic. Expanding the vision of who deserved to experience the power of Shangri-La set the stage not only

---

25. Letter from Matthew Connelly to Thomas D'Alesandro, dated December 10, 1946, located in Papers of Harry S. Truman Official File, OF 101-H (Shangri-La).

to keep the retreat available for future presidents, but it also showed a glimpse of what could happen when people who didn't like each other gathered on the mountain. If the mountain could overpower Truman's first impression, it could win over even the coldest of hearts.

The battle over Greentop served public notice that the president's retreat resided within the Catoctin Mountains and prompted a number of written requests from Boy Scouts, church groups, and everyday citizens passing through the area to tour the compound and see the president's mountain hideaway. These were accompanied by renewed requests from local newspaper reporters to visit the facility now that the war was over and security could relax. However, all requests to tour the facility received the reply that "in order to ensure the maximum privacy for the President and members of his family, visitors are not permitted."[26] The reason for keeping people away shifted from security to presidential privacy, a better reason to keep people away. To sneak a peek inside the fence knowing security would not be as tight following the war, two reporters from the *Baltimore Sun* rented a plane and flew over the retreat in September 1945, publishing photos informing the world of the retreat.[27] Soon after, the White House invited select reporters inside the fencing to see the facility. Now that the president's movements weren't a national secret, the press began to send reporters to Thurmont whenever the president left Washington for his mountain retreat, with the Cozy Inn just off Highway 15 evolving into the preferred gathering location for press for the next five decades.

After reelection in 1948, the First Family made a short move across Pennsylvania Avenue to the Blair House until 1952, while the entire White House underwent much-needed repairs. Years of neglect and hurried repairs/construction projects since the War of 1812 led to fears of the White House collapsing due to inadequate structural integrity. Despite many warning signs, it wasn't until June of 1948 when Margaret, the president's daughter, had a leg of her piano bench go through

---

26. Letter from Robert L. Dennison to Mr. Frederick Schafer, dated January 25, 1950, located in Papers of Harry S. Truman Official File, OF 101-H (Shangri-La).

27. Nelson, 26.

the floor and, subsequently, the ceiling of the family dining room that people took notice of the decaying residence. Architects determined the building was in danger of collapsing, so the First Family was advised to move out during the needed renovations. Despite having to move out of the White House to a much smaller house with few amenities, their aversion to Shangri-La ran so deep the family did not increase their use of the spacious retreat.

On November 1, 1950, Truman was at Blair House preparing to deliver a speech at Arlington National Cemetery to dedicate an equestrian statue on the grave of Sir John Dill, a British Army officer who helped solidify the "special relationship" between the United States and Great Britain. Two activists for Puerto Rican independence, Oscar Collazo and Griselio Torresola, attacked Blair House from Pennsylvania Avenue. Hearing gunshots and noise below, Truman looked out and even raised a second-floor window to observe the commotion. The Secret Service immediately ordered him to back away and take cover.[28] Secret Service and Capitol Police quickly ended the attack, killing Torresola and injuring Collazo, who later received a death sentence. (Truman reduced the sentence to life in prison, and President Carter later released Collazo in 1979.) This attack claimed the life of Leslie Coffelt, a White House police officer, who while mortally wounded by Torresola, returned fire killing Torresola. This tragedy marked the first death of someone protecting a president. Donald Birdzall of the Capitol Police and police officer Joseph Downs also suffered wounds during the attack. While this attack on their temporary home did not inspire the Trumans to increase their use of Shangri-La, it did enhance the nervousness among the Secret Service when the president was outside the White House and lead future presidential advisors to strongly suggest escaping to the seclusion and security of the mountaintop retreat.

28. John W. Snyder, oral history, April 2, 1969, by Jerry N. Hess.

CHAPTER 4

Cold War Diplomacy

Eisenhower differed from Truman on many levels. Regarding Shangri-La, whereas Truman found the retreat lacking in amenities and more rustic than he preferred, Eisenhower deemed the mountain camp luxurious for his tastes. Shangri-La never received accolades for decor and elegance, but if you've spent a few years sleeping on battlefields saving democracy, you judge your accommodations differently than others. Perhaps because of the perceived luxury of the facilities, President Eisenhower utilized the mountain more than his predecessors, eventually escaping the White House to both the presidential retreat and the home he built just up the road in Gettysburg, Pennsylvania. But preferring his home in Gettysburg, Eisenhower spent more time at the farm than the secluded mountain retreat. Keeping work and family as separate as possible, Eisenhower frequently traveled up the mountain for meetings with his staff or foreign dignitaries allowing his family time alone while he continued working in a relaxed atmosphere. Evan Aurand, President Eisenhower's naval aide recalled, "It was the President's idea, doing this kind of informal diplomacy at Camp David. . . . The formal state dinner thing, he never felt accomplished a damn. . . . When you think about it, there are very few presidents that I know who are willing to take the risks of personal diplomacy of this kind."[1]

Before making his first visit in May 1953, people thought Eisenhower would close Shangri-La as a cost-cutting measure. Why keep a

---

1. Evan P. Aurand, oral history by John T. Mason Jr., on May 1, 1967, 50–51.

symbol of luxury on the expense ledger when recouping savings in a peace dividend? In April 1953, the Navy conducted an austerity review of the presidential yachts and Shangri-La. While Shangri-La ultimately survived the austerity review, Eisenhower gave up the presidential quarters at Key West and reduced the number of personnel supporting the retreat.

Family mattered to Eisenhower, so he honored his grandchildren through small gestures during his time as president. One such way was naming presidential perquisites after his beloved grandchildren. Shortly after taking office, two yachts, the *Lenore II* and the *Margie*, were acquired (of course they survived any austerity measures), which he rechristened the *Barbara Anne* and *Susie E.* after his granddaughters.[2] That left his grandson, David, without a presidential amenity named in his honor. In 1953 Eisenhower decided to change the name of Shangri-La to Camp David keeping with the original intent for the retreat. The name change wasn't publicized before it occurred. In fact, the staff at the retreat were surprised by notice of the president's wishes learning of the new name just hours before a presidential visit. Such short notice, in fact, the newly minted entrance sign's paint was still wet as the presidential motorcade rolled through the gate.[3]

Eisenhower intended it to be a temporary renaming. He anticipated his successor would revert the name back to Shangri-La or pick a name of his own choosing. In fact, Kennedy renamed the yachts *Barbara Anne* and *Susie E.* to *Honey Fitz* and *Patrick J.* after his grandfathers.[4] Had Kennedy utilized Camp David more during his time in office, it too may have received a Kennedy family name. Remarkably, no one since Eisenhower ventured to change the name, and after President Carter's term the name is etched in history.

On July 5, 1953, the worshippers of Trinity United Church of Christ received an unexpected visitor when President Eisenhower, accompanied

2. Judith Martin, "All the President's Yachts," *Washington Post*, April 2, 1977.

3. Rigdon, *Sailor in the White House, 214.*

4. Judith Martin, "All the President's Yachts," *Washington Post*, April 2, 1977.

by the officer in charge of Camp David, Lieutenant Hugh Culbreath, left the confines of Camp to worship.[5] While Eisenhower wasn't the first president to venture down the mountain during a visit, he was the first to attend church in the town of Thurmont. The town's residents were not surprised as the previous day they had spotted Secret Service agents discreetly looking around to ensure the president's security. As with any small town there are no secrets, so word quickly spread of the comings and goings of the Secret Service. Because Eisenhower preferred to worship without much fuss, the fact the church gave no special recognition toward his presence pleased him and paved the way for future visits.[6]

Eisenhower's wife Mamie finally visited the retreat in late 1953, and much like Bess Truman, her first impression was one of disappointment. The weather and the remoteness of the retreat didn't bother her. Holding a contrarian view to that of her husband, the rustic and run-down feel of the accommodations turned her nose. Distraught regarding the quality of lodging, she made it known "she would not go back to the rustic, rather shabby place unless it was modernized."[7] Her staff sympathized but made it clear there wasn't any money in the White House budget to renovate or modernize the mountain retreat. However, one intrepid staffer suggested that since the Navy operated the facility perhaps the Navy budget could fund the necessary improvements. This was all it took for Mamie to "pass a hint along to the Commander-in-Chief."[8] Aiming to keep his wife happy, construction in Gettysburg proceeded with occasional visits to Camp David until their house in Gettysburg was completed. As with the renovations at the Gettysburg home, and following the lead of her inaugural gown choice, pink played a prominent role in the decor of their cabin at Camp David—a design choice of the past that does not remain today.

Vacationing in Colorado on September 24, 1955, Eisenhower scared the nation when he suffered a heart attack. Once cleared for travel, he spent months recovering at his Gettysburg farm. In early November,

---

5. George Wireman, *Gateway to the Mountains*, 221.
6. Wireman, 221.
7. Stephen Ambrose, *Eisenhower: Soldier and President*, 313.
8. Ambrose, *Eisenhower: Soldier and President*, 313.

he informed his staff he intended to hold a cabinet meeting later that month, well before anyone expected him to hold such meetings. Because the farm was not suitable for such a large gathering, he invited his cabinet to Camp David for the day. Many members of his cabinet had not seen him since the heart attack, and definitely not in a working capacity, so "everybody in the room was studying Eisenhower intently, looking for a change in his appearance and in his actions."[9] They wanted to see firsthand Eisenhower's condition and if he could handle the rigors of the office. His presence and demeanor cast aside any lingering doubts, with the end of the meeting sealing his leadership in their minds. As they rose to leave the meeting, Eisenhower asked them to stay for a moment. He mentioned that for weeks after his heart attack, he didn't see any newspapers until recently when someone showed him an editorial expressing surprise "the cabinet had been able to work so well together while he was not with them."[10] He expected nothing less because he picked a cabinet that didn't need him hovering over their every decision. He also noted one good thing arising from the heart attack was it gave his cabinet "this chance to prove itself, although he did not particularly care for the circumstances that provided the grounds of proof."[11]

On July 12, 1957, Eisenhower, accompanied by a Secret Service agent, boarded an Air Force Bell H-13J helicopter as part of a nuclear emergency evacuation drill called "Operation Alert" requiring travel to an undisclosed location. In this first-ever helicopter ride by a sitting president, Eisenhower flew to Camp David. The ride to the mountain was uncomfortable due to the heat and cramped nature of the cockpit, which barely held the pilot, Secret Service agent, and Eisenhower. To further sour Eisenhower's mood, six other larger and faster helicopters participated in the exercise, lifting off after the president's ride but arriving at Camp David much earlier. According to Virgil Olson, soon to be the first Marine Corps presidential pilot, "When the President arrived, he was sweating from an uncomfortable ride and annoyed to find us on

9. Sherman Adams, *Firsthand Report: The Story of the Eisenhower Administration*, 191.
10. Adams, 192.
11. Adams, 192.

the ground, with the engines of our helicopter already turned off and cooled down."[12] This marked the one and only time the Air Force lifted a president via helicopter. The Army and Marine Corps shared the mission until 1976 when the Army disbanded the Executive Flight Detachment to cut costs, leaving the Marine Corps as the sole provider of presidential helicopter travel.[13]

On March 22, 1959, Eisenhower again visited Trinity United Church of Christ for Palm Sunday with a guest of his own, British prime minister Harold Macmillan. The church visit is credited to the simple question of a local resident, Carole Wireman. Two weeks prior to the visit, a newspaper article appeared in the *Frederick News* announcing the upcoming visit between Eisenhower and Macmillan. Ten-year-old Carole suggested it would be a nice gesture to invite the two leaders to church. Despite expecting a polite declination of the invitation, Carole convinced her father to write the letter to the White House. A few days later, the predicted response arrived expressing the president's regrets and thanking the Wiremans for their invitation.[14] However, two days later Secret Service agents visited the family informing them both leaders would attend church the next morning, and the agents, alongside a representative from Scotland Yard, needed to see the church.[15]

As a gesture of thanks, President and Mrs. Eisenhower contributed an arrangement of lilies for the church's Easter celebration the following week. This prompted a handwritten letter to the president from Carole after the Easter service thanking him for attending the Palm Sunday service and for the "lovely" lilies saying the president "made me a very happy girl indeed, by accepting my father's invitation which I asked him to write for me."[16] She went on to say, "I would like to visit your farm sometime

12. Roger Conner, https://airandspace.si.edu/stories/editorial/ike-and-first-presidential-helicopters, retrieved August 7, 2020. Published July 12, 2010.

13. Conner, https://airandspace.si.edu/stories/editorial/ike-and-first-presidential-helicopters, retrieved August 7, 2020. Published July 12, 2010.

14. Letter from Thomas Stephens to George Wireman, dtd March 19, 1959, located in Dwight D. Eisenhower's Records, President's Personal File, Box 60, PPF 1-F-127.

15. Wireman, 223.

16. Letter from Carole Wireman to President Eisenhower, dtd March 31, 1959, located in Dwight D. Eisenhower's Records, President's Personal File, Box 60, PPF 1-F-127.

but I guess this is impossible."[17] So honored, the congregation memorialized the visit and installed a plaque upon the pew the two leaders shared.

Taking a page from Roosevelt, Eisenhower invited world leaders to Camp David to discuss important and weighty matters in a relaxed atmosphere. His most famous foreign guest visited in September 1959 when Soviet Premier Nikita Khrushchev arrived as part of his tour across America. The two-week visit to America included time in Washington, DC; New York City; Hyde Park, New York, to visit Eleanor Roosevelt; Los Angeles; San Francisco; Des Moines, Iowa; and Pittsburgh. Khrushchev observed American farming and industry alongside government and diplomacy. At the end of this whirlwind tour, Khrushchev flew with Eisenhower to Camp David for two days of talks in the comfortable setting of the Catoctin Mountains.

Relaxation amid such a massive undertaking and discussion of weighty matters of the Cold War is paradoxical. This was the largest visit to Camp David in its short history—both in magnitude of foreign impact and numbers of people. Only five US officials and five Soviet officials stayed the night, but the support staff was enormous with hourly helicopter flights between Camp David and the Pentagon ferrying those not staying the night. Additionally, the influx of over 250 members of the press was too large for Thurmont's hotel accommodations, so the White House Press Corps set up at the Gettysburg Hotel with the remaining US and international press members renting every available hotel room in Gettysburg. The White House wire photographers remained close by in Thurmont at the Cozy Inn.[18]

Khrushchev remained skeptical regarding Camp David, and with little public information on the facility, he reached out to his embassy for further information, to little avail. According to his memoirs, Khrushchev felt embarrassed he lacked the necessary intel on Camp David and thought it was a place to keep those of questionable motives quarantined, much like some of the camps for dissidents in the Soviet Union. Because

---

17. Letter from Carole Wireman to President Eisenhower, dtd March 31, 1959, located in Dwight D. Eisenhower's Records, President's Personal File, Box 60, PPF 1-F-127.
18. Press list from Dwight D. Eisenhower Library, Box 21, James C. Hagerty Papers.

of the initial apprehension, his staff demanded to tour the president's "dacha" before agreeing to the visit. Once the misunderstanding was cleared, the Soviet government newspaper *Pravda* would state the retreat was "created for fruitful reflections by nature itself."[19] John Eisenhower recalls Khrushchev's change in tone, "The Russians were always afraid for their lives when they came over here. Then, when he found out what a nice place Camp David was, Khrushchev was delighted."[20] Both leaders stayed in the presidential lodge, Aspen, even holding one-on-one meetings without interpreters, relying on Khrushchev's broken English. The talks, not formal negotiations, sought "a better understanding of the motives and position of each and thus to the achievement of a just and lasting peace."[21] Eisenhower embarked on the meetings with a list of talking points including the Berlin Wall and "when he came back from Camp David he thought he'd gotten most of what he wanted, had a pretty good understanding with Khrushchev on most of those points."[22]

Absent advisors, Khrushchev and Eisenhower's conversations were friendly, seeking to bridge the public differences between the two nations. Eisenhower reflected that when alone Khrushchev "was very convivial with me, especially eager to be friendly. He kept belittling most of our differences and gave every indication of wanting to find ways to straighten them out through peaceful compromise. . . . But when Menshikov and Gromyko were with us, Khrushchev acted differently . . . he became much more reserved and guarded."[23]

The two Cold War leaders spent a great deal of time discussing tensions between the two countries and ways to thaw the relationship, as well as trying to impress the other and show off the power of their respective countries. Taking every advantage of hosting the talks in the United States, Eisenhower put Americans and America center stage, especially American technology. Having sent Khrushchev on a tour of

19. Nelson, 43.

20. John S. D. Eisenhower oral history by Carol Hegeman on January 26, 1984, 16.

21. Joint United States-Soviet Communique, September 27, 1959, Edward Beach and Evan Aurand Records, Box 17, Eisenhower-Khrushchev Conference at Camp David-Press.

22. Clyde A. Wheeler oral history by Mack Teasley on November 15, 1990, 23.

23. Adams, 454–455.

the country, Eisenhower didn't feel the need to press the advantages of America during the Washington and Camp David talks, letting the whirlwind tour speak for itself . . . with one exception. Knowing helicopters were a novelty in the Soviet Union, he flew Khrushchev as much as possible, to impress him with something not yet available in the Soviet Union.

While at Camp David, it was the Soviet leader's turn to try to impress the Americans as best he could without the backdrop of his home country. Khrushchev repeatedly highlighted military accomplishments such as breaking into American communications and the fact he had all the nuclear bombs and missiles he would need alongside the best nuclear submarines. When Eisenhower inquired about Khrushchev's thoughts on American homes and automobiles, the Soviet dismissed them with a mocking wave of his hand, calling them superfluous and opining the sheer number of cars "represented only a waste of time, money, and effort."[24] Shocked at the response, Eisenhower questioned his counterpart on the interconnected road system in America, as surely this would impress his guest. Khrushchev replied such a system was unnecessary because Soviets lived together and liked each other unlike Americans who "do not seem to like the place where they live and always want to be on the move going someplace else." As if this wasn't disconcerting enough, Khrushchev stated that the sheer number of individual homes in which Americans lived expended too many resources through construction, heating, and landscaping compared to the Soviet style of family housing.[25]

Time at Camp David rarely was all work and no play or just boasting about respective nations, and together the two leaders watched movies, such as film of the submarine USS *Nautilus* traveling under the polar ice cap;[26] enjoyed the two-lane bowling alley, specifically the automatic pin-setting feature that piqued Khrushchev's interest[27]; and walked around getting to know each other. Of note, on September 26, Eisen-

---

24. Ambrose, *Eisenhower: Soldier and President*, 493.
25. Ambrose, *Eisenhower: Soldier and President*, 493.
26. News conference transcript from September 25, 1959 (7:35 p.m.), by James C. Hagerty, Box 21.
27. News conference transcript from September 26, 1959 (1:47 p.m.), by James C. Hagerty, Box 21.

hower and Khrushchev boarded the helicopter for a short trip to Eisenhower's farm in Gettysburg to show the Soviet premier how Eisenhower lived. This side trip left a lasting impression on the agrarian-minded leader. While there Khrushchev met Eisenhower's grandchildren and commented, "I jokingly told the President that I found it easier to come to an agreement about his return visit [to Moscow] with his grandchildren than with the President himself."[28]

Despite initial wariness, Eisenhower's faith in the retreat's magic was well placed as the leaders deemed the talks productive. The relaxed atmosphere prompted Khrushchev to use the phrase the "Spirit of Camp David" when describing the ease with which leaders could connect on a personal level and discuss important matters atop the mountain. Eisenhower's naval aide Evan Aurand recalled, "I think when Khrushchev talks about the 'Spirit of Camp David,' he was really impressed with the easiness with which the President talked. And they often got off and talked without interpreters."[29] While Khrushchev motivated his political allies upon his return home by alluding to poor treatment and threatening to stop the visit because he disliked interactions with everyday Americans and the nature of questions from certain members of the press, he wasn't totally displeased with America. He praised the workers he met in San Francisco and the farmers in Iowa. Apparently, his helicopter rides left such an impression that on October 6, 1959, the US Embassy in Moscow received word "the Soviets were ready to buy three of these helicopters [the type he rode during his US visit]."[30] Regardless of how both leaders played the outcome of the meeting at Camp David, it began to thaw the Cold War. The thaw, however, quickly refroze on May 1, 1960, as Francis Gary Powers floated to the ground after ejecting from his U-2 inside Soviet airspace.

Changing the name from Shangri-La isn't the only legacy of Eisenhower's use of Camp David. While in office, Mamie gave the retreat a homey

---

28. Khrushchev remarks at Luzhniki on September 28, 1959. Box 9, OSS: International Trips Series.

29. Evan P. Aurand oral history by John T. Mason Jr., on May 1, 1967, 12.

30. Memo for the President from Christian Herter, dated October 8, 1959. Dwight D. Eisenhower's papers Dulles-Herter Series, Box 12.

touch as well as changing the guest cabins' names from those selected by Roosevelt to the current scheme of local tree names—with the exception of the president's lodge named "Aspen" in honor of Mrs. Eisenhower's home state of Colorado.[31] In 1957, the cabins were showing their age and required extensive repairs, as buildings designed for use by a single administration had stretched into a second decade of presidential service. Basic utilities broke down with alarming frequency, but the crisis escalated when pipes burst in multiple cabins creating uninhabitable conditions due to flooding and lack of heating. As part of the repairs and renovations, a barracks for junior personnel was constructed to provide necessary lodging to support a permanent, 24/7 presence to support the president on short notice.

Early in his administration, Eisenhower eyed the large open field off the back patio of Aspen with a vision of something special. An avid golfer with a cabin named after him at Augusta National Golf Club, Eisenhower inquired, "Could we fit in a golf hole?" No request or musing of the president goes unexplored so of course the staff said yes. Still in operation, but renovated over the years, a four-hole pitch and putt was installed in late 1954 and was highlighted in a *Sports Illustrated* article in January 1955. Designed for play in a counterclockwise direction, over four tee boxes ranging in distance from 80 to 140 yards, the player would hit from each tee and then hole out on the green. To ensure he could enjoy his beloved golf when unable to play his favorite courses at Burning Tree or Augusta National (which he visited twenty-nine times while in office), Robert Trent Jones maximized the tight space designing the chip and putt with an Augusta-inspired green.[32]

After Truman's ambivalence regarding the private retreat, Eisenhower's use of Camp David saved the retreat from becoming a footnote of history and a difficult-to-maintain site of obscure presidential history. It was not just his more frequent use of the retreat to relax, recover, and rejuvenate, it was also his observation there was something deeper under

---

31. Memo from Evan P. Aurand to Mrs. Eisenhower, November 17, 1958. Retrieved from Dwight D. Eisenhower library on August 6, 2020.

32. Herbert Warren Wind, "A First Look: World's Most Exclusive Golf Course," *Sports Illustrated*, January 24, 1955, 22.

the surface that held a power his predecessors didn't fully appreciate. Much like his work with Allied Forces during World War II, Eisenhower found the strengths of Camp David and used this to his advantage against his enemies. Inviting Khrushchev to chat in a relaxed atmosphere after a whirlwind tour of the United States was a stroke of genius, which, until the U-2 incident, set both countries on a path of cooperation over conflict. Because Eisenhower saw the true power and character of the humble retreat, he set the stage for its continued use to gather friends and enemies together over their shared humanity, because it is those commonalities that change the course of history toward peace and justice.

When Eisenhower left Camp David for the last time as president, he didn't know his successor would soon request his presence on the mountain.

CHAPTER 5

Marines Land

WHEN CONSIDERING THE PLAN FOR A PRESIDENTIAL RETREAT AWAY from the White House, one major concern revolved around who would guard the area—not just who would provide physical protection but also who would turn away prying eyes and maintain privacy for the president and guests. The Navy would supply the stewards and maintenance personnel and keep a skeleton caretaking crew on site if needed. Secret Service couldn't patrol the perimeter as their mission kept them alongside the president, not set up on permanent duty at a place whose usage wasn't consistent. This left the logical choice between the Army and the Marine Corps.

The Army demurred providing personnel for security due to a variety of reasons, leaving the Marine Corps as the best choice for protecting the president at Camp David. Because there was a ready source of Marines in Washington, DC, it made economic and practical sense to utilize their fully trained guard force. Marines were experienced standing guard and acting as ceremonial guards. These Marines possessed the necessary training, and their use wouldn't raise any suspicion or concern. Any history of Camp David could not claim completeness without discussing the camouflaged sentries keeping the perimeter and president secure for eighty years. Frequently overlooked, the Marines at Camp David are more than a historical footnote.[1]

---

1. Gratitude to Jared Gastrock and Corporal White for directing me to the 8th and I alumni website for some of the stories in this chapter (www.8thandi.com).

But the Marines were not the first military personnel to establish a semipermanent presence on the mountain. In fact, it was a group of British sailors who established the first beachhead atop the Catoctin Mountains.

Months before America's entry into the war, World War II came to Catoctin Mountain. Between June and November 1941, sailors from the Royal Navy utilized the Catoctin camps for rest while their ships underwent repairs in Baltimore, Maryland, under the lend-lease program between America and Great Britain. This program was of mutual benefit to both countries as war raged across Europe. While the program sent more goods and materials to European Allies than the United States received in return, it did provide the United States with critical parts for defense manufacturing while British minesweepers provided coastal protection as they came to the United States for repairs in shipyards along the East Coast, including Baltimore.

Because Baltimore was "overcrowded with industrial defense employees and men from nearby military bases who overtaxed public services and crowded restaurants, grocery stores and recreational services"[2] the British sailors had no place for relaxation while their ships underwent repairs. The secretary of the Navy, Frank Knox, requested use of space in Catoctin from Harold Ickes, secretary of the interior, for a mountain retreat for the British sailors. Ickes approved the request, granting permits for the use of cabins and services at Catoctin Recreational Demonstration Area, even cancelling all other short-term reservations, with the first group arriving on June 5, 1941.[3] Under the agreement, the Navy provided food and transportation with the Park Service providing the lodging, specifically at Greentop and the short-term lodge that previously served as a boarding house before acquisition by the park.

Unknown to the local community at the time and of no concern to the British sailors enjoying the peace and relaxation afforded by the tranquil setting of the Catoctin Mountain, this secret wartime use of the relatively new retreat facilities and the formation of strong bonds between the

---

2. Kirkconnell, 69–70.
3. Kirkconnell, 70.

military and the surrounding civilians laid a solid foundation of mutual trust and respect that would shape history for decades. The British sailors made good use of the retreat during the pleasant summer weather of 1941. Supervisors at Catoctin Recreational Demonstration Area arranged activities for the sailors to help pass the time. Not confined to the camps, the British sailors were outstanding neighbors exploring the surrounding area and towns and impressing the local residents "with the 'exemplary conduct' of the sailors [who] could easily get a ride on county roads with their thumbs and their accents."[4] Local clubs and organizations offered recreational and sporting opportunities, which the sailors "reciprocated by holding exhibition games of cricket, soccer, and rugby."[5] Between June 10 and November 8, 1941, the Royal Navy occupied various camps at Catoctin accounting for "6,383 camper days, and leaving many phone bills that arrived after they had gone."[6] The positive experience between the locals and secret Brits relaxing on the mountain proved a perfect test run for protecting the privacy of more famous visitors.

For the first couple of years, the procedure for protecting the president followed a similar pattern. At a set time before the president's departure from the White House, the Marines assigned to guard Camp David boarded a bus for the two-hour drive. Along the route, there were designated bridges requiring a security watch prior to the president's arrival, so Marines would leave the bus, secure the bridge, and ensure there were no explosive devices or untoward persons in the area. They would stand guard until after the president's arrival when the bus would come and retrieve the Marines, rejoining the rest of the detachment for guard duty. It didn't take long for the residents of Thurmont and the areas surrounding Camp David to realize what this signaled and to gossip about the arrival of the Marines.

With no place for the Marines to stay overnight while on guard duty, the Marines would sleep in nearby cabins at Misty Mount or

---

4. Kirkconnell, 70.
5. Kirkconnell, 70.
6. Kirkconnell, 70.

Greentop. They would catch a ride to and from their cabins to Camp David, spending the rest of the time training or resting when off the perimeter. When the goal was keeping the location of the president's retreat secret (Roosevelt) or when the visit frequency was low (Truman), it made sense that the guard force would stay elsewhere. However, when the president's visits become more frequent, as they did with Eisenhower, shuttling the guard force up and down the mountain is tedious and presents a vulnerability in protecting the president.

In the late 1940s or early 1950s, the Marines shifted their posture from one of on-demand protection, heading up the mountain only when the president was in residence, to a full-time presence. From then on, Marines would stand guard over Camp David 24/7, constantly improving their position and making the camp as safe and secure as possible against expected and unexpected threats. The first iteration of Marines to occupy a full-time presence at Camp David operated on a rotational basis. Marines would bus up from Washington, DC, between every two to four weeks for weeklong rotations onboard. Within each detachment was a set rotation to ensure the Marines rested, relaxed, ate, and trained while remaining alert for any dangers. This rotational model continued for a number of years.

Following the model of rotating Marines on and off the mountain at two-week intervals, the powers that be decided to permanently station Marines at Camp David. After the construction of suitable barracks and mess facilities, the Marines established their permanent beachhead in 1957. This presence continues today as Marines guarding the presidential retreat are permanently housed on the grounds.

Selected for training during their first months in the military at boot camp, present-day guards at Camp David undergo a number of schools on infantry tactics and guard fundamentals before arriving for duty. While there, their skills as guards and representatives to the public are honed. Once they are deemed ready and fully qualified for the assignment, the young Marines head up the mountain for more training, eventually entering the rotation silently and professionally.

In their role of guarding the president for eighty years, the Marines have not only played a significant part in the history of Camp David, but many have also settled down and provided color and legend to the local community. Stories abound in the Thurmont area of Marines helping the local citizens and becoming part of the community, some literally, with a number of Marines marrying locals. One such Marine, TJ Demmon, arrived at Camp David after a tour in Vietnam and frequented the Shamrock Restaurant, located just north of Thurmont on Highway 15. As a local Irish pub and the first restaurant in Frederick County, Maryland, to receive a liquor license, the Shamrock was a natural attraction for local service members.[7] Sometime during 1972, TJ developed an interest in Donna, one of the daughters of the owner. From that first meeting at the pub, TJ's career trajectory sharply turned, as he left the Marine Corps and married Donna in 1973 and then managed the Shamrock until the restaurant closed at the end of 2019.

TJ's story is one of many; his is just more well-known due to his connection with a popular local restaurant. Throughout the years, many Marines fell in love with the area, or a special individual in the area, and developed strong ties to the region. This isn't surprising, for when the president is not present, there is ample opportunity for these young men to spend time in the local restaurants and hangouts. Marines throughout the years hold fond recollections of the Cozy Inn, Thurmont Tavern, and popular spots in Gettysburg, Pennsylvania, just fifteen minutes north on Highway 15. A number of former guards in the area remain in contact with the current Marine guards passing along stories, both true and of questionable origin, maintaining a vibrant connection to history. One former Camp David guard served three consecutive terms as the mayor of Thurmont.

Legends survive whenever those before us regale their experiences, stories, and highlights. One legend frequently recalled from the early days on the mountain revolves around a friendly skunk. Many versions are told, but the core of the tale remains—young Marines were passing the time standing post in the wee hours of the night. During one two-week

7. Sue Gleiter, "Landmark Fitzgerald's Shamrock Restaurant Closes After 57 Years," *Penn Live Patriot News,* January 8, 2020, https://www.pennlive.com/life/2020/01/landmark-fitzgeralds-shamrock-restaurant-closes-after-57-years.html (retrieved April 7, 2021).

rotation in 1957, the Marines on duty noticed a skunk stalking the main·
guard post in the middle of the night. Curious as to its intentions, and
looking to alleviate some boredom, the Marines fed the confident skunk
some leftover food. The skunk obliged their generosity, encouraging the
Marines to continue this midnight ritual the remaining days of their
rotation, with the skunk returning from the forest darkness the same time
each night, scratching on the door for food and then well-fed, returning
home to sleep off its food coma. This particular detachment rotated off
the mountain forgetting, however, to inform the relief team about their
furry friend.

It didn't take long for this odd friendship to take an unexpected
turn. The first night with the new security team, the Marine standing
post heard scratching on the door. Not expecting anything to approach
his post, and not seeing any humans around, he was curious as to what
created the noise. Wary of the warnings accumulated over years of scary
movies and stories around campfires, the Marine opened the door expecting the worst. To his surprise, there stood the friendly skunk expecting
a nightly snack from the magic building that provided delicious food.
Here the stories diverge, obscuring truth from legend. Either the skunk
expressed anger at the lack of immediate food, causing a scene and baring
its teeth, or the mere presence of a skunk at the door startled the poor,
unsuspecting Marine causing fear and confusion. Whatever occurred,
the Marine drew his weapon reportedly firing at the hungry skunk. This
discouraged the skunk from any further forays to the guard post, but not
without leaving the lingering gift of spraying the cramped guard post . . .
and the Marine. In a futile effort to avoid the smell, the embarrassed
Marine stood outside the rest of the night until his relief arrived.

Despite the wooded location among curious wildlife, skunk stories are
rare. More common are the stories of Marines protecting the president
at all costs, regardless of who tries to gain access. Ron Burton and Bob
Capeci both related a story of someone following orders at all costs
and angering the head of the Secret Service detail enough to report the

Marine to the commanding officer.[8] A young Marine was assigned to guard a room with the express order to not let anyone enter who did not display the proper credentials. Early one morning, the head of the Secret Service detail approached the Marine. The Marine recognized him, snapped to attention, and greeted him by name. Assuming he was cleared, the agent continued toward the door, but the Marine quickly stepped in his path barring entry. The surprised agent demanded entry; he was the head of the Secret Service after all. Our rule-following Marine refused to move because the agent was not wearing the correct badge. No badge . . . no entry!

The Secret Service agent exploded, calling the sentry a variety of names, most derogatory and better left unprinted. To no effect, as the sentry refused to clear a path. Quickly shifting tactics, the agent tried to reason with the Marine, "You called me by name, you know who I am." "Without a badge I can't be sure you are who I think you are," quipped the erstwhile sentry. Ron Burton recalls a physical altercation as the agent tried to push past the Marine, never a smart idea, leading to a square hit on the head by the butt of the sentry's rifle. This prompted more rage and threats, eventually leading the agent to storm off to the commanding officer to have the Marine removed. Coming to his senses during the journey, the agent admiringly relayed the story to the commander and recommended a letter of commendation for the Marine with a personal apology for his actions toward the Marine.[9] For the past eighty years, this dedication to protecting the guests of the presidential mountain are why Marines form a key thread of Camp David's historical tapestry.

8. R. R. Burton, "Ceremonial Adventures: Marine Barracks, Washington, DC, 1955–1959," http://www.8thandi.com/cdburton.pdf (retrieved August 7, 2020), 12.

Bob Capeci, "Reflections on serving at Camp David," http://www.8thandi.com/mem5001capeci.pdf (retrieved August 7, 2020).

9. R. R. Burton, "Ceremonial Adventures: Marine Barracks, Washington, DC, 1955–1959," http://www.8thandi.com/cdburton.pdf (retrieved August 7, 2020), 12.

Bob Capeci, "Reflections on serving at Camp David," http://www.8thandi.com/mem50-01capeci.pdf (retrieved August 7, 2020).

CHAPTER 6

Tragedy

AT HIS FIRST PRESIDENTIAL PRESS CONFERENCE, PRESIDENT KENNEDY received a question regarding plans for the famed mountain retreat. One reporter inquired, "You have available, sir, to you at the Catoctin Mountains in Maryland a very fine weekend retreat that has been used by former Presidents. Sir, do you plan to use it, and if so, do you plan to rename it back to Shangri-La?"[1] Kennedy responded, "I don't plan to use Camp David very often. Now I will keep—I think the name should be kept Camp David, but I doubt if I will go there very often."[2] Keen observers of the Kennedys who noticed the couple searching for a weekend retreat near Washington before moving into the White House expected this tepid endorsement of a government-owned retreat. While not going so far as to suggest shuttering the retreat, Kennedy made it clear Camp David barely made it on his list for places to escape the pressures of the presidency. With four hundred acres of land and plenty of space to stable their horses just forty miles west of Washington, DC, Glen Ora would satisfy Jackie's desire to give the children a place away from the press and craziness of the White House while allowing time to indulge her equestrian hobby.[3]

---

1. Kennedy press conf February 8, 1961, 6. Retrieved August 8, 2020, from https://www.jfklibrary .org/asset-viewer/archives/JFKPOF/054/JFKPOF-054-004.

2. Kennedy press conf February 8, 1961, 6. Retrieved August 8, 2020, from https://www.jfklibrary .org/asset-viewer/archives/JFKPOF/054/JFKPOF-054-004.

3. In a coincidence of history, Glen Ora also touched on British Royal family drama as this is the place where Wallis Simpson, for whom King Edward VIII would abdicate the throne in 1936, met her first true love (Mark Meredith, "Glen Ora").

However, in early 1962, for reasons not fully detailed, Gladys Tartiere, the owner of Glen Ora, declined to renew the First Family's lease. Some said it was because the Kennedys requested to purchase the estate, prompting the owner to sever ties. Other rumors surmised the lease wasn't renewed due to needed additions to the house to maintain the office of the presidency or because the presidential visits drew ire and complaints from residents annoyed by the inconvenience of presidential security and the disruptions to the community. The loss of the lease incurred additional costs for the Kennedys from a stipulation in the contract requiring a return of the property to its original state. This included reversing the extensive changes that were made, as only the paneled library with rows of leather-bound first edition works survived Jackie's redecorations.[4] For whatever reason they lost the lease, the family was in search of a nearby location for rest and relaxation. They decided to build a new home, which they would name Wexford, but it would not be ready for occupancy until summer 1963. So, they looked north to the previously dismissed mountain retreat.

Despite his initial statement regarding Camp David, President Kennedy did make one visit in his first year. Two days after the embarrassing failure at the Bay of Pigs, on April 22, 1961, President Kennedy made the short helicopter ride to Camp David to meet its former resident and his predecessor. This visit would mark the first time a former president returned to Camp David for any reason. Arriving first, Kennedy greeted Eisenhower's helicopter when it landed from the short trip from Eisenhower's Gettysburg farm where he had retired. In this meeting, Kennedy did not seek advice from President Eisenhower, rather he wanted the frank opinion of General of the Army Dwight D. Eisenhower, the man who oversaw the invasion of Normandy. With near perfect timing, President Kennedy had signed legislation restoring Eisenhower's military rank on March 22, 1961, one month before the historic meeting at Camp David.

4. Mark Meredith, "Glen Ora," February 15, 2019, https://househistree.com/houses/glen-ora (retrieved July 28, 2020).

The two men did not see eye to eye. Eisenhower felt the young president had ignored most of the advice offered during the transition, but knowing the loneliness and difficulty of the job, Eisenhower did not hesitate to assist his president. During the meeting, Kennedy ruefully mentioned to Eisenhower, "'No one knows how tough this job is until after he has been in it a few months.' Eisenhower looked at Kennedy, then said softly, 'Mr. President, if you will forgive me, I think I mentioned that to you three months ago.'"[5] The sharp tone of the gentle rebuke was the result of Eisenhower's perception of Kennedy viewing the presidency as something, "one man could handle with an assistant here and another there. He [Kennedy] had no idea of the complexity of the job."[6]

Though a veteran of WWII himself, Kennedy sought advice on strategic thinking and evaluating military advice, especially during a crisis. Their luncheon conversation was a five-star general listening to his president's concerns and offering blunt advice where asked. General Eisenhower saw the main causes of failure as "gaps in our intelligence, plus what may have been some errors in ship loading, timing, and tactics."[7] Almost as if Kennedy expected another Cuban crisis, Eisenhower recalled, "He has the feeling that we can be faced with some similar situation over the next decade and thinks we should do our best to be prepared to meet it."[8] Eisenhower didn't offer any specifics on future actions but stated he would "support anything that had as its objective the prevention of Communist entry and solidification of bases in the Western hemisphere."[9]

Kennedy sought to prevent another Bay of Pigs incident and wasn't looking to place blame. According to Eisenhower, "The purpose of this scrutiny is not to find any scapegoat, because the President does seem to take full responsibility for his own decisions, but rather to find and apply

---

5. Stephen Ambrose, *Eisenhower: Soldier and President*, 553.

6. Ibid.

7. Notes by General Eisenhower on Luncheon Meeting, April 22, 1961, with President Kennedy at Camp David, Dwight D. Eisenhower's Post-Pres Papers, Augusta-Walter Reed Series, Box 2, 1.

8. Notes by General Eisenhower on Luncheon Meeting, April 22, 1961, with President Kennedy at Camp David, Dwight D. Eisenhower's Post-Pres Papers, Augusta-Walter Reed Series, Box 2, 3.

9. Notes by General Eisenhower on Luncheon Meeting, April 22, 1961, with President Kennedy at Camp David, Dwight D. Eisenhower's Post-Pres Papers, Augusta-Walter Reed Series, Box 2, 3.

lessons for possible future actions."[10] Eisenhower offered, "If there had been a good staff system there never would have been the Bay of Pigs fiasco."[11] Not satisfied with such a nonanswer, the press asked if he supported the president. Accepting his role as a retired commander in chief, Eisenhower replied, "I repeated a generalization that I had expressed on other occasions—that when it came to problems of foreign operations, then an American traditionally stands behind the Constitutional head, the President."[12]

Embracing the Spirit of Camp David, their meeting was not all work. The two leaders walked the trails sharing a bond only those occupying the presidency comprehend. After their walk, the leaders returned to Aspen facing a group of reporters assembled to probe details of their historic meeting. Eisenhower relished his advisory role saying, "It was rather fun to be in the position of not having to make a statement and having nothing to say."[13]

Without Glen Ora, and awaiting completion of Wexford, the Kennedy family finally utilized Camp David. Knowing the family valued horses and would want to ride while on the mountain, the staff ensured adequate stable facilities for the horses helping to entice the family to visit. Anticipating the needs of the First Family is the hallmark of an exceptional staff. Caroline's prized pony named Macaroni, a gift from Lyndon Johnson, would make the trip and stay onsite.[14] In fact, a quick Internet search for Caroline Kennedy on Macaroni provides a rare video from Camp David as she rides Macaroni from the stables near the field that

10. Notes by General Eisenhower on Luncheon Meeting, April 22, 1961, with President Kennedy at Camp David, Dwight D. Eisenhower's Post-Pres Papers, Augusta-Walter Reed Series, Box 2, 5.

11. Interview of Dwight D. Eisenhower with A Ross Wallen, Friday, November 27, 1964, for *The Pointer*, Dwight D. Eisenhower's Post-Presidential Papers, 1965 Signature File Series, Box 7, PR-3 Public Relations-Interview, 14.

12. Notes by General Eisenhower on Luncheon Meeting, April 22, 1961, with President Kennedy at Camp David, Dwight D. Eisenhower's Post-Pres Papers, Augusta-Walter Reed Series, box 2, 8.

13. Notes by General Eisenhower on Luncheon Meeting, April 22, 1961, with President Kennedy at Camp David, Dwight D. Eisenhower's Post-Pres Papers, Augusta-Walter Reed Series, box 2, 8.

14. YouTube video of Caroline riding Macaroni at Camp David: https://www.youtube.com/watch?v=HSBWWQNpKBQ.

doubles as the helicopter landing zone. After visiting, Jackie commented that if she had known what Camp David was like and how comfortable the retreat would make her feel, she never would have signed the lease at Glen Ora. Over the last year and half of his presidency, Kennedy visited Camp David eighteen times, with the family making several visits without the president in residence.

Kennedy's visits at Camp David looked like his visits to Glen Ora, visits full of family time, especially horseback riding. The president utilized the twenty-five-meter pool, sometimes swimming to relieve pressure on his back but more often lounging on the pool deck and socializing with his guests. Camp David's seclusion offered a place for the president to maintain the personal relationships he had developed over many years, without the press covering his every move. One such example is David Ormsby-Gore, then British ambassador to the United States and longtime friend of the president. Their discussions rarely centered on affairs between the two countries and were rather conversations you would expect between close friends as "the President felt no obligation either to transform all his personal relationships to an official level or to transfer all his professional relationships to the social level."[15]

Kennedy's relationship with Camp David, while short, demonstrated the power of the retreat to win over the hearts and minds of not just presidents, but also the entire First Family. The complete reversal of the Kennedy family's perception of the private retreat plays out with each successive administration. Even a wealthy family's access to secluded properties around the world is no match for the power of Camp David. There is something magical about true privacy, something in short supply for many people today . . . and even more so for the president and the First Family. So, when presented with a secluded retreat available to only the select few of the president's choosing, the choice of truly relaxing and letting life's pressures melt away, if for only a few days, becomes an easy decision. Camp David's ability to overcome its harshest critics, especially one who controls its fate, is remarkable and a testament to the basic human need to have a safe space to be unguarded with loved ones.

---

15. Theodore Sorensen, *Kennedy*, 378.

November 22, 1963, shocked the nation and devastated the crew at Camp David as they lost their president. The staff had developed a strong, loving bond with the family who many never expected would make the journey up the mountain to such a rustic retreat. The sudden loss of the president and subsequent transfer of power prevented the Kennedys from leaving their personal, permanent stamp on Camp David, though the echoes of tragedy would reverberate in the construction of a chapel twenty-five years later.

CHAPTER 7

Working Retreat

UNLIKE TRUMAN'S LACK OF KNOWLEDGE REGARDING SHANGRI-LA IN 1945, when Lyndon B. Johnson assumed the presidency on November 22, 1963, he was familiar with Camp David from making occasional visits as Kennedy's vice president. As with many presidents before him, Johnson toyed with the idea of closing Camp David as a cost-cutting measure. According to Lee White, associate special counsel at the time, "He wanted to close Camp David on the grounds that it was during that economy move where he turned off the lights in the White House. . . . He wanted to close Camp David just as he wanted to get rid of the yachts."[1] He only visited twice in his first year in office because it was not until after his inauguration in 1965 that he felt the retreat was truly his and he was comfortable to embark on routine usage.

Out of respect to his predecessor and the Kennedy family, Johnson took his time settling into the presidency. He waited until December 7, 1963, to move into the White House allowing Jacqueline Kennedy time to move without feeling rushed. It would take time for the memory of Kennedy's Camelot to fade. In fact, Lady Bird Johnson did not feel the presence of Camelot fade until the day Jackie married Aristotle Onassis. Camp David became a place to get away from the pressures of Washington especially as the protests against the war in Vietnam grew in numbers, frequency, and volume. Sometimes the protest chants in

---

1. Oral Interview with Lee White by Joe B. Frantz, February 18, 1971, p. 15, Lyndon B. Johnson library, http://discoverlbj.org/exhibits/show/loh/oh.

Lafayette Square reverberated loudly through the thick-paned windows of the White House and were heard by the First Family throughout the upper floors of the residence.

President Johnson made his first visit to Camp David as president on January 11, 1964, in true Lyndon Johnson fashion. That evening, while standing in a receiving line for the Democratic National Committee with the respective state chairmen and vice chairmen, President Johnson leaned over to Lady Bird and asked if she wanted to head to Camp David that night. She recalled Johnson saying, "'If you would, get your clothes packed and we will leave in twenty minutes.' He had sent someone else to phone Secretary and Mrs. McNamara who, happily, are used to spur-of-the-moment engagements. They came and brought their son Craig, and we flew off into the night."[2] That spur-of-the-moment visit included a trip to church on Sunday morning, late meals, and bowling—the First Family finding much-needed solace amid the demands of the presidency.

In July 1965 the president invited two guests rarely associated with each other: John Steinbeck and Billy Graham. The pairing stunned Lady Bird, "Sometimes I don't know whether his choosing of people to bring together is by innocence or design. They are both great workers in today's vineyards, to their rather different audiences, it seems to me."[3] As with most visits, bowling stood atop the activity list, with Lady Bird quickly changing into bowling attire upon arrival and heading straight for the lanes. Lady Bird remembered, during the weekend, John Steinbeck embraced a chance at relaxation, "with his cane and beard, and bright colored shirt that reminded me of the Virgin Islands . . . [he]was an exotic note among us plainer citizens."[4] Sunday, July 18, found all the guests gathered with some camp staff in Hickory for a religious service conducted by none other than Billy Graham. Later that afternoon, the guests were lounging around the pool as the Steinbecks regaled everyone "talking books and Russia, and what I used to call, in my university days, 'Life with a capital L.'"[5]

---

2. Lady Bird Johnson, *A White House Diary*, 41.

3. Lady Bird Johnson, 300.

4. Lady Bird Johnson, 302.

5. Lady Bird Johnson, 303.

Vietnam and recreation played major roles in Johnson's use of Camp David. He would use the retreat as a place to both get away from the pressures of the office and a location to ponder decisions on how to proceed in Vietnam. He would also convene key advisors for frank discussions regarding that conflict half a world away, as well as other issues facing the country. Willard Deason, a close personal friend, sums up Camp David's role in Johnson's decision making, recalling a trip the president took to "spend some time thinking about [a troop increase in Vietnam] at Camp David. . . . He went up there and he tried to relax, and he'd walk up and down the roads and take some of us with him walking . . . I could tell he was greatly troubled. He wasn't his same old humorous self that he normally was. But he was trying to make up his mind whether or not he would approve additional military men being sent to Vietnam."[6]

Despite the serene environment, even presidents lose their tempers amid the peaceful greenery of the mountain. On April 3, 1965, following a speech at Temple University in Philadelphia, in which he gently criticized American policy regarding Vietnam, Canadian prime minister Lester Pearson joined President Johnson for a coveted lunch invitation at the secluded retreat. Speaking the day before, Pearson described American motives as "honorable; neither mean nor imperialistic" and suggested "the US might suspend the [air] raids unilaterally; that in turn might bring the Communists closer to the bargaining table, or if it did not, would show the world that the Americans were sincere in their quest for peace, while their opponents seemingly were not."[7] Johnson's fury to the speech when alone with the prime minister burned so hot Pearson only told his cabinet a story rather than reveal the ire his speech provoked.[8]

According to Charles Ritchie, the Canadian ambassador to the United States and the only other Canadian in the room, Pearson's speech

6. Oral Interview with Willard Deason by Michael L. Gillette, April 6, 1988, Interview VII, 4 Lyndon B. Johnson library, http://discoverlbj.org/exhibits/show/loh/oh.
7. Charles Ritchie, "The Day the President of the United States Struck Fear and Trembling into the Heart of Our PM," *MacLean's*, January 1, 1974, https://archive.macleans.ca/article/1974/1/1/the-day-the-president-of-the-united-states-struck-fear-and-trembling-into-the-heart-of-our-pm (retrieved on March 19, 2021).
8. Robert Dallek, *Flawed Giant*, 259.

enraged the brash Texan leading him to unleash his fury behind closed doors. Before the speech, it seemed the prime minister was on decent terms with President Johnson, having previously visited the Texas ranch one weekend, a sure sign of Johnson's favor. Ritchie sets the background for the meeting's tone describing how "even when the sun of favor is shining there are outer limits for a foreigner to exchanges of thought with the Washington Higher Management. . . . The idea of learning anything from allies seems strange to official Washington thinking."[9] On the fateful April day, the president didn't greet them at the helicopter, as is custom, instead sending aides acting "like schoolboys escorting the victim to the headmaster's study for a sharp wigging."[10] In the moment, neither the prime minister nor his close aide recognized the dark clouds gathering for a storm.

As lunch began, there was no opportunity for routine conversation as the president made himself busy answering phone calls and receiving updates on bombings in Vietnam, ignoring his Canadian counterpart. Johnson bided his time between incoming calls making outgoing calls, "tidying up any telephone calls remaining at the bottom of his list—some fairly trivial ones that could have waited."[11] To fill the gap, the prime minister conversed with the First Lady about the flight over the fields of Gettysburg and his interest in the battle. Once lunch concluded, Prime Minister Pearson broached the subject of his speech, eliciting a "pause when darkest clouds lower pregnant with the coming storm."[12] Johnson deemed the prime minister's speech awful and led Pearson onto the terrace, leaving those inside to witness a presidential tirade through pantomime and occasional raging words that pierced through windows. After some time, Mac Bundy led Ritchie for a stroll through the tranquil paths, leaving the two leaders to sort out their differences. Returning, the

---

9. Charles Ritchie, "The Day the President of the United States Struck Fear and Trembling into the Heart of Our PM," *MacLean's*, January 1, 1974, https://archive.macleans.ca/article/1974/1/1/the-day-the-president-of-the-united-states-struck-fear-and-trembling-into-the-heart-of-our-pm (retrieved on March 19, 2021).

10. Ibid.

11. Ibid.

12. Ibid.

president's tongue lashing continued unabated, and more furious, and culminated with Johnson grabbing the prime minister "by the lapel of his coat—at the same time raising his other arm to the heavens."[13] Between waves of ire the prime minister found an opportunity to take his leave, accompanied by the president who offered a genial departure. As with his staff, foreign leaders never knew how President Johnson would react to any situation.

Never hosting high-level summits, Camp David provided a space where close friends and advisors joined Johnson in a relaxing atmosphere where he could be himself and ponder looming decisions regarding Vietnam and his political future. Friend June White recalls, "His forms of relaxation included going out on the *Sequoia*, going to Camp David, and going to the ranch . . . I think he was in a sense always thinking ahead, too, and probably recharging his batteries, in a sense. He would bowl a lot, which was good for him, of course, the exercise. He was a good bowler."[14] Her reflections comport with many other oral histories describing Johnson's love for bowling at the Camp David lanes. Another old friend, Arthur Krim describes his first visit to Camp David, "The next day [Saturday] was spent in various activities, swimming, bowling, and walks and driving around the compound and having relaxed conversations. . . . He did everything quickly to diminish the awe of being in the presence of the President of the United States on occasions such as this."[15]

Saturday, April 24, 1965, started full of promise. The president and First Lady flew to Norfolk, Virginia, in support of their daughter Luci, chosen queen of the annual Azalea Festival, where the president would place the ceremonial crown on her head. Following the day's ceremony and celebration, the family flew to Camp David for a relaxing weekend. However, as the president is never off duty, world events have a way of scaling the mountain. When Johnson finally returned, he took a call from

---

13. Ibid.

14. Oral Interview with June White by Michael L. Gillette, February 17, 1976, Interview I, 29 Lyndon B. Johnson library, http://discoverlbj.org/exhibits/show/loh/oh.

15. Oral Interview with Arthur Krim by Michael L Gillette, May 17, 1982, Interview II, 2 Lyndon B. Johnson library, http://discoverlbj.org/exhibits/show/loh/oh.

Tom Mann, undersecretary of state for economic affairs, and learned of severe trouble brewing in the Dominican Republic. Amid conflicting and confusing reports arriving from various sources, the president learned of an overthrow of the acting president Donald Cabral. Worried something larger loomed, Johnson ordered the US Navy's Atlantic fleet to move ships toward Santo Domingo in preparation for imminent evacuation of American citizens, especially as the embassy began fielding numerous calls from concerned American expats, culminating in an evacuation operation on April 27.

On March 31, 1968, Johnson shocked the political world announcing he would not run for reelection "because he hoped he could therefore remove his personality from the issue and perhaps could work then in a calmer atmosphere toward a rational solution of Vietnam."[16] But, for some close friends, such as William S. White, it was not shocking because "he had told me in great confidence at Camp David nearly eighteen months before that he doubted he would run again. Indeed, he had about decided he would not for those very reasons."[17] Camp David provided a place for Johnson to let his guard down, be himself, and have deep, meaningful conversations with trusted friends and advisors, even if those chats led to his stepping away from the presidency.

A few weeks later, Johnson flew to Camp David with advisors "to get away from the noise and carbon monoxide of downtown Washington" and to discuss Vietnam—in particular an exit strategy. The evening of April 8, 1968, found the president relaxing and preparing for meetings the following morning. After greeting his team at the helicopter pad, he hosted them at breakfast discussing "the latest exchanges with Hanoi."[18] Post-lunch discussions focused on the difficulty of negotiating with Hanoi amid their broken promises. Vowing not to let down their guard, the team sent word to the negotiators their primary objective was to make arrangements "for prompt and serious substantive talks looking

16. Oral Interview with William S. White by Dorothy Pierce McSweeny, March 10, 1969, Interview II, 11 Lyndon B. Johnson library, http://discoverlbj.org/exhibits/show/loh/oh.

17. Oral Interview with William S. White by Dorothy Pierce McSweeny, March 10, 1969, Interview II, 11 Lyndon B. Johnson library, http://discoverlbj.org/exhibits/show/loh/oh.

18. Lyndon Johnson, *The Vantage Point*, 500.

toward peace in Vietnam, in the course of which an understanding may be reached on a cessation of bombing in the North."[19]

One form of respite from presidential rigors Camp David provided was a place for President Johnson to practice his faith without disrupting public worship. Johnson routinely invited Dr. George Davis of the National City Christian Church to Camp David on Sunday afternoons to conduct church services. Not to impinge on the normal worship services of the congregation, "He never asked me to leave my own service or my own worship to conduct a special service for him. It was always at a time when it would not interfere with my own church obligations."[20] Dr. Davis recalls the president pondering decisions regarding education and poverty; "I asked Mr. Busby if he could think of any particular scripture that might be pertinent, and he recalled to my mind this scripture that Johnson had loved specially, having to do with the implications toward education over ignorance and caring for those who were hungry and so on, so I used that as the background for my brief message that day."[21] Dr. Davis wasn't the only pastor to make the journey to Camp David to attend to the spiritual needs of the president. Billy Graham served as a spiritual advisor to President Johnson—as he was for Presidents Truman to Obama—as well as being a close friend of Johnson. In that dual role, Billy Graham made multiple trips to Camp David, leading worship for the president on two or three occasions.[22]

Johnson, as with previous presidents, took advantage of Camp David's informal atmosphere and relaxed setting to invite foreign leaders to Camp David seeking to form strong relationships and cementing alliances through breaking bread and leisure activities. Camp David uniquely facilitates what Keith Waller, the Australian ambassador to the United States from 1964 to 1970, describes as, "a great deal of what

19. Lyndon Johnson, 501.

20. Oral Interview with Dr. George Davis by Dorothy Pierce McSweeny February 13, 1969, Interview I, 7–8 Lyndon B. Johnson library, http://discoverlbj.org/exhibits/show/loh/oh.

21. Oral Interview with Dr. George Davis by Dorothy Pierce McSweeny, February 13, 1969, Interview I, 12 Lyndon B. Johnson library, http://discoverlbj.org/exhibits/show/loh/oh.

22. Oral Interview with Billy Graham by Monroe Billington, October 12, 1983, Special Interview, 2 Lyndon B. Johnson library, http://discoverlbj.org/exhibits/show/loh/oh.

one might call high level diplomacy depends on the development of the personal relationship. You must have mutual trust and confidence. You must have the sense of being at ease, and this can often be achieved more readily if you're away from the formal atmosphere of the White House."[23] During his time in office, Johnson developed a particularly strong bond with the Australian prime minister Harold Holt. According to Ambassador Waller, "I think it was with Harold Holt that he was most intimate [of the three prime ministers Waller served]."[24] Upon the drowning death of Prime Minister Holt in December 1967, Johnson traveled halfway around the world to mourn the loss of a friendship partly forged atop the mountain.

As with most presidents, Johnson worked constantly. Relaxation for a president looks much different to those on the outside. Jack Brooks described Johnson's, and really any president's, difficulty with typical relaxation: "He had so much to do and was working so hard that if some people would relax a little too much he'd look like he wanted to say, 'Well, by God, if you were working as hard as I was, you wouldn't be quite that relaxed!'"[25] Camp David provided a place to work at his own pace. According to Lady Bird Johnson, "He took people with whom he was doing business, and he did business. But he did it at his own pace, in a leisurely fashion, with a lot of jokes and anecdotes and maybe afternoon naps."[26]

Being himself at Camp David included torturing the staff with odd, and conflicting, requests. Much like his trend at the White House, Johnson would rage against the pressure and temperature of the shower in Aspen. He was known for installing a shower with multiple showerheads with extreme pressure in the White House, causing stress among the plumbers in Washington, DC, because he could never find satisfaction

23. Oral Interview with Sir Keith Waller by Joe B. Frantz, December 1, 1969, Interview I, 10 Lyndon B. Johnson library, http://discoverlbj.org/exhibits/show/loh/oh.

24. Oral Interview with Sir Keith Waller by Joe B. Frantz, December 1, 1969, Interview I, 10 Lyndon B. Johnson library, http://discoverlbj.org/exhibits/show/loh/oh.

25. Oral Interview with Jack Brooks by Joe B. Frantz, February 1, 1971, Interview I, 36 Lyndon B. Johnson library, http://discoverlbj.org/exhibits/show/loh/oh.

26. Oral Interview with Lady Bird Johnson by Michael L Gillette, February 20–21, 1981, Interview XX, 16 Lyndon B. Johnson library, http://discoverlbj.org/exhibits/show/loh/oh.

in the plumbing no matter the adjustments.[27] It wasn't just plumbers and other tradesmen suffering from changing standards and moods. Doris Kearns described the ever-changing mood within the White House: "Since Lyndon Johnson's White House completely resonated with his personal moods and activities, it seemed to me at such times that I was at the center of government and power, of history itself. Moments later, the ambience could tilt toward absurdity when personal idiosyncrasy sent the very staff that had just been hard at work on matters of high policy off on a desperate search for huge quantities of a specific brand of peanut brittle, which Lyndon Johnson needed within a half an hour."[28]

Camp staff were not immune to ever-changing requirements with each visit revealing the water was too cold, then too hot, or of unsatisfactory pressure for Johnson's current liking. The staff on the mountain never knew if adjustments from the previous visit would satisfy the president on his subsequent visit. "Aware that the slightest mishap could send Johnson into a fury, the domestic staff spent hours anticipating his most trifling whims."[29] Based on the ever-changing nature of requests nullifying the previous request, it would seem Johnson's way of keeping the staff on their toes was a peculiar, long-term practical joke only the president found humorous.

For long-time friends, Johnson would meet them after arrival and in their words, "impress us with his informality and the extent he would go to make his guests, such as us, comfortable. Starting with the fact that it was the first time we drove in one of those golf carts with him when he would always be the driver."[30] Unfortunately for guests, golf carts were not the only form of transportation the president utilized at Camp David. Rumors abound of President Johnson grabbing advisors and friends for high-speed drives around the winding, hilly roads of his retreat. Even staying within the bounds of the retreat, the speed of the drives in open-top convertibles caused white knuckles among passengers

27. Kate Andersen Brower, *The Residence*, 125.

28. Doris Kearns, *Lyndon Johnson and the American Dream*, vi.

29. Kearns, vii.

30. Oral Interview with Arthur Krim by Michael L. Gillette May 17, 1982, Interview II, 1 Lyndon B. Johnson library, http://discoverlbj.org/exhibits/show/loh/oh.

and Secret Service alike. If he couldn't drive in public, he would certainly take advantage of the relative safety of the secure retreat and indulge in a favorite pastime the office denied him.

While he invited many close friends and advisors, Johnson preferred to keep their presence at his retreat as discreet as possible. As with other administrations, his did not readily divulge the guest list of those attending Camp David, typically only releasing the names of foreign dignitaries and members of the staff in attendance, rarely publishing the names of his close friends who either met him at the retreat or flew with him from the South Lawn of the residence. In fact, Johnson's desire for secrecy included devising elaborate ruses to shield guests from the ever-present eyes of the White House Press Corps. Joseph Laitin, who worked in the White House Press Secretary's office recalled, "I discovered later, the president didn't want them to see who he was taking with him to Camp David, and when [the press] would go down there [South Lawn], they thought they were beating the system, you see, by watching with binoculars. But the fact is that the passengers were getting on from the other side of the helicopter, and they couldn't see who was getting in."[31]

Johnson participated in a Camp David first; he sat for his official portrait at the retreat. This is the only portrait sitting on record at the presidential retreat, and the finished results of which infuriated President Johnson, calling Peter Hurd's work, "the ugliest thing I ever saw."[32] Johnson's protests regarding the portrait resulted in it not hanging in the National Portrait Gallery until after his death.[33] Perhaps if the president had put more interest in the process, the result would have appealed more to his vanity.

According to Hurd, "The sittings were nonexistent except for one weekend, which I spent at Camp David going back and forth to the

31. Oral interview with Joseph Laitin by Michael L. Gillette, June 19, 1967, Interview IV, 14. Lyndon B. Johnson library, http://discoverlbj.org/exhibits/show/loh/oh.
32. Zoe Sayler, "The Presidential Portrait That Was the 'Ugliest Thing' L.B.J. Ever Saw," *Smithsonian Magazine,* February 16, 2018 (retrieved from www.smithsonianmag.com on August 27, 2020).
33. Ibid.

White House, where I was a small pea in a big pod over the weekend."[34] It was a busy weekend where the president "literally began to doze as he began to sit the one-half hour that I was allotted in the little sideroom in [Aspen]."[35] Hurd suggested stopping because of the president's catnap, but because Johnson had promised his wife he'd sit for the portrait he wouldn't leave. In fact, Mrs. Johnson and her office had arranged for the accomplished Hurd to complete the portrait. At the end of the sleepy half-hour, Johnson glanced at the initial sketch noting, "Looks like an old drunk to me."[36] This single sitting occurred in 1965 with the portrait finally debuting in 1967 after an estimated four hundred hours of work for the final product. Despite the president's reaction, David C. Ward, former senior historian of the National Portrait Gallery praises the work, "It's a really good portrait. . . . The fact that you've got Lyndon Johnson in this fictitious space, elevated above the entire landscape of the nation's capital, I think that's interesting. . . . That's what Johnson was. He was master of the Senate and then an extremely important president."[37] Despite Johnson's original protests, the portrait is now on view in the National Portrait Gallery.

Johnson knew what Camp David could offer him as president: solitude, escape, privacy, and a place to let his guard down. He took full advantage of the rejuvenating power of this private retreat. He frequently took the short helicopter ride up the mountain to clear his head and think through the challenges of Vietnam and the Gordian knot conflict he inherited from Kennedy. Because of modern communications he was able to balance relaxation and war planning just as Roosevelt had. The irony was his decisions regarding Vietnam fueled the protests making him and his family escape to the mountain as much as possible. Regardless of the reason for escape, the secluded mountain retreat remained true to its purpose and welcomed the First Family with open arms to get what they

---

34. Oral interview with Peter Hurd by Elizabeth Kaderli, April 6, 1969, Interview I, 12. Lyndon B. Johnson library, http://discoverlbj.org/exhibits/show/loh/oh.
35. Oral interview with Peter Hurd by Elizabeth Kaderli.
36. Oral interview with Peter Hurd by Elizabeth Kaderli.
37. Zoe Sayler, "The Presidential Portrait."

needed from walking and soaking up the solitude and privacy provided by the dense, green canopy of trees that have witnessed all the emotions of presidents before and since. Camp David's character as a place of refuge left a lasting impression on the Johnson family beyond their time in the White House.

Lady Bird Johnson's memoirs provide wonderful glimpses into the effect of Camp David on any First Family. Recording her impressions of the retreat on May 13, 1967, she reflected on what she would miss about Camp David: "The two 'Martians' in their silver suits and helmets, stiff and silent, who startle you when you first step off the helicopter (they are firefighters) . . . the cool, green tunnel that leads through the woods to Aspen . . . the drifts of snow, still there in late March . . . ham and grits and hot cakes, all for breakfast. Mamie and Dwight Eisenhower's bold signatures in the guestbook and those of many famous guests . . . But mostly just the carefree mood of being there—a spirit of release and relaxation—quite unattainable, somehow, in the White House."[38] Words of praise for a staff and locale true to its purpose.

---

38. Lady Bird Johnson, 519.

CHAPTER 8

Hideout

WATERGATE DEFINED RICHARD NIXON'S PRESIDENCY, SO IT'S NATURAL to associate his presidency with that seminal event in American history. While Watergate plays in the background at Camp David, his legacy on the mountain looms large as one of expansion and upgrades.

Having visited as Eisenhower's vice president, Nixon was familiar with Camp David and its offerings. He noticed needed repairs and issues plaguing the aging buildings and systems supporting the site. Never expressing an interest in shutting the retreat down or converting it from presidential use, Nixon's administration embarked on an extensive construction campaign throughout the retreat. Despite such a massive construction and remodeling spree upgrading the thirty-year-old retreat, the presidential cabin, Aspen, remained untouched. The only upgrade Aspen received during the Nixon administration was the addition of a pool off the back patio, allowing the First Family to enjoy a refreshing swim on a warm, sunny, summer day. A few steps down from the main patio and shaped like a peanut with a slate deck surrounding it, the pool had its own shower house and sauna. Diligent staff anticipated any use of the pool and ensured the chairs were clean and towels were always at the ready for whenever the president decided on a swim, no matter the time of day. Building a pool for the First Family further enhanced their privacy and ability to relax together without having to walk or drive a golf cart across the retreat. To ensure continuous availability, the pool contained powerful heaters that allowed a warm swim on a cold, snowy day if desired.

Named Laurel during the Eisenhower administration, the lodge designated for the president's office, conference room, and formal dining area, built for summer campers in 1938, was inadequate for hosting large gatherings, especially meetings for foreign dignitaries. To alleviate this concern, a new, larger cabin was constructed close to Laurel. The new cabin contained a professional-grade kitchen allowing larger, more complex menu execution alongside an expanded dining room and living room, complete with fireplace, to meet the social needs of hosting foreign heads of state. Taking the name Laurel, the lodge contained a presidential office alongside an improved conference room able to host bilateral meetings or convene the entire Cabinet. The old Laurel, renamed Holly, remains as a secondary location for senior staff workspaces and additional entertaining space.

Recognizing the allure of the mountain retreat in hosting foreign leaders for important decision making in a relaxed, friendly atmosphere, Nixon's administration approved the construction of two premier cabins named Birch and Dogwood. Larger than any other guest cabins, yet smaller than Aspen, these cabins allowed more room for dignitaries such as visiting heads of state, the vice president, members of the president's family, close friends, etc. With a stroke of design brilliance, both cabins contain identical floor plans equidistant from the front door of Aspen. At first glance, it is easy to assume constructing twin guest cabins as a cost-saving measure. However, the equality arose from a hallmark of diplomacy. With two identical cabins, if two foreign leaders were in attendance neither would feel less important or less valued. Little did Nixon know in a few short years, the equality of the cabins would play a significant role cementing Camp David's place in history.

Camp David intersects with larger world events in interesting and unexpected ways. Nixon's presidency played out in more ways than just Watergate and Vietnam, both of which loomed large. His time in office enjoyed the fruits of Kennedy's promise to put a man on the moon by the end of the decade, with every moon landing occurring during Nixon's administration. Just as John Glenn had received an invitation to Camp David from President Kennedy in 1961, Nixon extended invitations to some of those astronauts who walked on the moon. Following their return from the moon, after completing quarantine, astronauts from Apollo 13, 14, 15, and 16 received presidential invitations for themselves and their wives to spend a few nights at Camp David away from the glare of the public eye.

Astronauts arrived at Andrews Air Force Base and, after a day of receptions and meetings in DC, boarded a helicopter for the ride to Camp David with a late evening arrival and the second day spent relaxing at the presidential retreat. After the second evening, the group boarded the helicopter and returned to Andrews Air Force Base to meet their return flight to Houston. While at Camp David, the families enjoyed all the amenities: walking along the trails, shooting skeet, swimming, movies in the theater, staying in the guest cabins, and dining on specially cooked meals from the highly trained Navy staff. This was a well-deserved break for those returning from humanity's longest expeditions.

Nixon first visited as Eisenhower's vice president during the summer of 1960 to prepare his acceptance speech for the Republican nomination for president. Appreciating the restorative power and seclusion of the retreat to hash out elaborate plans, President Nixon utilized the retreat more than his predecessors. "In the mountains, Nixon was forever plotting, planning revolutions great and small, sometimes to build a better world, more often just coups against his own staff and Cabinet."[1] Even before Watergate drove Nixon to Camp David in hopes of escaping the crush of questions from reporters, his pace of use set a record. In fact, his presidential visits totaled more than that of all the previous five presidents combined—and tripled Eisenhower's visits. In just five years, Nixon's 161 total visits set a record until President Reagan discovered the mountain.

Serving as Eisenhower's vice president had bonded the two gentlemen, so March 28, 1969, just two months into Nixon's presidency, Eisenhower's death hit hard. Immediately after the public announcement, Nixon rushed to Bethesda Naval Hospital to offer Mamie Eisenhower his respects. From there, he headed back to the White House and boarded a helicopter

---

1. Richard Reeves, *President Nixon: Alone in the White House*, 97.

for Camp David to craft his eulogy for Eisenhower's funeral. While at Camp David, Nixon drafted a proclamation honoring his former boss and letting federal employees take the rest of the day off in mourning. Mrs. Eisenhower, hearing Nixon was at Camp David, shared about her conversation with Nixon, "That was [Eisenhower]'s favorite spot in the world and she was so glad the President was there.... They had a fairly long and good chat, which obviously affected him emotionally."[2]

The last two weeks of October 1969 saw consecutive Camp David weekend visits by Nixon as he prepared the most important speech of his nascent presidency. Over the weekend of October 24, he worked "twelve to fourteen hours a day writing and rewriting different sections of the speech" that would define his strategy going forward in Vietnam.[3] By the following Friday, Nixon said, the speech "had gone through twelve drafts, and I was ready to take it to Camp David for a final review."[4] All through Halloween night, Nixon worked on the speech and called his chief of staff at 8 a.m. proclaiming, "The baby's just been born!"[5] Nixon would deliver the speech on November 3, telling America and Vietnam the fight would continue until a fair peace for South Vietnam was negotiated and called on the "silent majority" of Americans to continue supporting the Nixon doctrine. Not prone to humility, Nixon's evaluation of his speech was thus: "Very few speeches actually influence the course of history. The November 3 speech was one of them."[6]

Reflecting on his first year in office, Nixon opined, "the biggest surprise of the first year for Pat and me was that we had not been prepared for the paradoxical combination of loss of privacy and sense of isolation that we experienced in the White House."[7] A common refrain from all presidents, even from those who previously served one heartbeat away from the office as vice president. As nothing prepares one for the weight

---

2. Haldeman, *The Haldeman Diaries: Inside the Nixon White House,* 45.
3. Nixon, *RN: The Memoirs of Richard Nixon,* 408.
4. Nixon, 408.
5. Nixon, 409.
6. Nixon, 409.
7. Nixon, 434.

and loneliness of the job, Camp David stood as a refreshing island of respite amid chaos and always searching eyes. Nixon explained, "For all its cosmopolitan self-confidence, Washington is a parochial city preoccupied by politics and gossip—which at times in Washington are the same thing. Like other presidents before and after me, I felt a need to get out of the White House and out of Washington in order to keep some sense of perspective."[8]

The glaring eyes of the press corps—and now social media—disrupted the lives of the First Family. Protests against the Vietnam War prevented Nixon's daughter Julie from attending her graduation from Smith College in Northampton, Massachusetts, on June 6, 1970. Choosing not to disrupt the ceremony with the presence of the First Family, the Nixon clan gathered at Camp David to privately celebrate multiple graduations. Using a robe borrowed from George Shultz, Bebe Rebozo staged a mock graduation ceremony with a commencement speech written by Pat Buchanan to celebrate Julie's graduation from Smith College, David Eisenhower's from Amherst College, Susan Eisenhower's high school graduation, and John Eisenhower's twenty-sixth anniversary of graduating from West Point. A poor substitute for the real thing, Julie confessed, "Despite all his attempts to make the party a gala celebration, most of us were unable to forget why we were not in Massachusetts."[9]

On August 13, 1971, Nixon gathered "fifteen economic experts, White House staff members, and a speechwriter . . . some arriving by secret routes lest news of the meeting itself trigger a wave of international speculation" for talks that would permanently reshape the global economy.[10] Nixon's memoirs quote Herbert Stein's impressions of the gravity of the meeting: "The tense psychological condition in the country, the remoteness and beauty of the Camp David setting, the orderly and disciplined conduct of the business there, and the surprising and sweeping character of the decisions taken make the August 13–15 meeting one of the most

8. Nixon, 434.
9. Ambrose, *Nixon: Volume 2*, 362.
10. Nixon, 518.

dramatic events in the history of economic policy."[11] Nixon embargoed all of the attendees from speaking of the meeting until after his announcement of their agreed way forward, an announcement scheduled for Sunday evening so the markets would see the new economic landscape prior to opening Monday morning.

Nixon worked odd hours preparing speeches and remarks, and the announcement floating the dollar was no exception. Waking at 3:15 a.m. on Saturday, Nixon began the outlines of his speech using stationery by his bedside. Covering three sheets of paper in an hour, he woke Haldeman at 4:30 a.m. to read a draft of the speech and changed the delivery to be Sunday evening rather than Monday. After reading his notes into a dictation machine for transcription by Rose Mary Woods, he walked out of Aspen as the sun rose, "scaring the hell out of a Navy chief petty officer coming out of the presidential sauna."[12] Amused, the president greeted the wayward, embarrassed sailor who responded, "Good morning, ma'am, I mean sir!" to which Nixon handed him the dictation tapes for delivery.[13] No word of the sailor's fate, though it's a safe bet his employment at the retreat was short-lived as any staff intrusion of the president's privacy, real or perceived, did not bode well for one's career plans.

On Sunday, August 15, Nixon instituted a 10 percent credit for new equipment investments, repealed the 7 percent automobile excise tax, and set a tax break for individuals. He also ordered a $4.7 billion reduction in government spending and a temporary 10 percent import tax. Nothing too dramatic or earth-shattering during the first half of his announcement. Nixon then revealed why his advisors submitted to a gag order during their meeting. He announced a ninety-day wage and price freeze for the country followed by the action that would reshape the global economy: he would end the gold backing of the dollar, and from that day the dollar would float like any other currency.[14] The gamble paid off, as on Monday, August 16, the markets responded favorably, and the dollar remains the standard currency throughout the world.

---

11. Nixon, 519.
12. Reeves, 359.
13. Reeves, 359.
14. Ambrose, *Nixon: Volume Two*, 458–459.

Sensing a reelection victory, in September 1972, Nixon summoned Caspar Weinberger to Camp David outlining a broad vision to realign the executive branch of the federal government following his reelection. He would reduce the cabinet to eight departments, four new and four traditional: Economic Affairs, Human Resources, Natural Resources, Community Development, State, Defense, Justice, and Treasury.[15] Nixon was only getting started in reshaping the executive branch, he wanted "to tell all hands that everybody should resign November 8, but no one should plan a vacation. That the period of November 7 to December 7 should be the most intensive month ever."[16] It was to be an intense month centered at Camp David.

Following his reelection, Nixon flew to Camp David on November 13 digging in with a number of assistants to reorganize government and analyze the election results down to the state and local level. While staying in contact with Secretary Kissinger regarding Vietnam, Nixon crafted the general vision of the plan as the White House staff fleshed out the reorganization. "The living room of Aspen Lodge became the White House in voluntary exile. . . . The president would sit for hours with Haldeman, or Haldeman and Ehrlichman, tossing around names, deciding who was in and who was out. Then Haldeman or one of his aides would order Cabinet members or staffers to come up one at a time, some to be fired, some to be promoted."[17] During the extended visit, Haldeman fielded calls from senior officials curious to their roles and status in the new organization, with Haldeman demurring until their summons atop the mountain to learn their fate. Those deemed worthy to remain needed to pass one final test, "check off and sign a five-page, fifteen-item list"[18] detailing the expectations of their continued employment at the pleasure of the president.

Amid the churn of reorganization, the First Family left the mountain the weekend after Thanksgiving for shopping in New York City. Upon his return, Nixon gathered the press camped outside the gate, bringing

15. Reeves, 612.
16. Haldeman, 507.
17. Reeves, 546.
18. Reeves, 546.

them into the helicopter hangar for a twenty-minute discussion regarding his two-week isolation on the mountain. "I find that up here on top of a mountain it is easier for me to get on top of the job, to think in a more relaxed way at times. . . . My study of elections in this country, and of second terms particularly, is that second terms almost inevitably are downhill. . . . The only way that historical pattern can be changed is to change not only some of the players but also some of the plays."[19] Nixon would stay two more weeks, coming down the mountain to accept "fifty-seven resignations and retirements. He had made thirty new appointments, many of them younger men, such as [Egil] Krogh, inserted into departments as the president's watchdogs."[20]

Beyond Watergate, Nixon's presidency is known for foreign policy inroads, specifically his historic trip to China, the first by a sitting president. China wasn't the only focus of Nixon's charms during his administration. In June of 1973, Nixon hosted Soviet leader Leonid Brezhnev for the Washington Summit to discuss nuclear control issues, among other items. Unlike the previous visit of Khrushchev, Brezhnev's visit was strictly a working visit with no public appearances, much less a tour of the United States. Even the arrival and departure from Andrews Air Force base were closed to guests, as only those Air Force personnel on duty and the press were allowed to view events that usually would be dripping with pomp and circumstance. The only public appearance of Brezhnev was a televised address to the nation the night before his departure.

After arriving at Andrews, Brezhnev spent two days at Camp David relaxing and adjusting to the time difference. As the president was in Florida on the day of Brezhnev's arrival, Nixon phoned the Soviet leader in the afternoon welcoming him to the United States. Nixon recalled, "I had never heard him sound so friendly and completely uninhibited as he did on the phone that afternoon. . . . He said that he appreciated my thoughtfulness in providing a place as private and comfortable as Camp David,

---

19. Reeves, 549.
20. Reeves, 550.

and that he regretted that his wife had not been able to take the trip with him."[21] The gesture set a positive tone for the remainder of the visit.

Seeing firsthand Khrushchev's appreciation of the location's power to thaw relations between adversaries, Nixon tapped into the Spirit of Camp David as part of the Washington Summit. Nixon hosted Brezhnev at Camp David to show the Soviet leader his country "dacha" and conduct talks on a personal level in a relaxing setting. Nixon would eventually host a staggering eleven foreign leaders at Camp David, but this visit was special beyond the goals of the summit. Typically, when leaders visited Camp David they received blue jackets with their names and a presidential seal embroidered on the jackets. Either because they wanted to impress the Soviet premier or because Brezhnev made an odd request to see if it would be granted, there was a large surprise awaiting Brezhnev just outside of the newly constructed Laurel: a brand-new, blue Lincoln Continental with "black velour upholstery and 'Special Good Wishes— Greetings' engraved on the dashboard."[22]

Brezhnev wasted no time breaking in his newest gift. Gesturing for Nixon to take the passenger seat, the two world leaders embarked on a driving tour of the grounds. What Nixon and his Secret Service detail most likely assumed would be a leisurely drive on enclosed mountain roads became a test of nerves with Brezhnev driving through the camp at high speeds. One particular curve on a hill, specifically marked "dangerous curve slow down," caused white-knuckle consternation among Nixon's protective detail. Nixon said, "Even driving a golf cart down it, I had to use the brakes in order to avoid going off the road at the sharp turn at the bottom. Brezhnev was driving more than fifty miles an hour as we approached the slope. I reached over and said, 'Slow down, slow down,' but he paid no attention. When we reached the bottom, there was a squeal of rubber as he slammed on the brakes and made the turn."[23] All passengers survived the premier's driving, and Brezhnev left Camp David pleased with the performance of his new car, stating, "This is a very fine

21. Nixon, 877.
22. Nixon, 880.
23. Nixon, 880.

automobile. It holds the road very well."[24] Later shipped by air to the Soviet Union, one had to wonder if there was an ulterior motive gifting the vehicle and how many listening devices lurked within the gift.

In August 1972, the United States Attorney for the District of Maryland opened an investigation into corruption within Baltimore County. This investigation spread, eventually enveloping Vice President Agnew for receiving kickbacks while a government official. As controversy deepened, Agnew arranged a plea agreement, pleading nolo contendere to tax evasion. He received a $10,000 fine and three years of probation and resigned the vice presidency the same day, October 10, 1973. The next day, Nixon traversed the mountain with a list of four finalists for vice president, with a potential announcement for each candidate: John Connally, Nelson Rockefeller, Ronald Reagan, and Gerald Ford. Nixon evaluated the recommendations: "Rockefeller and Reagan were in a virtual tie for first choice; Connally was third; Ford was fourth. Ford, however, was first choice among members of Congress, and they were the ones who would have to approve the man I nominated."[25] Nixon established four criteria for his vice president: "qualification to be president; ideological affinity; loyalty; and confirmability."[26] (Those qualities would prove desperately needed less than a year later.) The following day, October 12, Nixon made his choice informing the world through a televised address at nine o'clock that evening.

Watergate had come to dominate Nixon and his presidency and was deeply intertwined with Camp David. As the walls closed in, Nixon increasingly escaped to the retreat to avoid the press and distractions of the scandal. Camp David not only allowed retreat, but also, as with President Johnson, a place to strategize about Vietnam, among other topics, because despite a personal political scandal, the business of governing a country continued.

---

24. Nixon, 880.
25. Nixon, 925.
26. Nixon, 926.

As the scandal deepened and Nixon spent more time at Camp David, he lost trust in several advisors. Two figures closely linked with Watergate who remained loyal to Nixon despite the approaching end of the presidency stand out because of the way their tenures in the administration ended. On the night of Saturday April 28, 1973, the First Family gathered in Laurel and discussed the mounting pressure on the president, coming to a tearful conclusion to sacrifice certain members of Nixon's inner circle in a desperate move to stave off the inevitable. Sunday, April 29, 1973, saw both H. R. Haldeman, the chief of staff, and John Ehrlichman, the White House domestic affairs advisor, summoned to the retreat. Shortly after noon, President Nixon called his chief of staff, requesting his and Ehrlichman's presence at Camp David at 1:30 p.m. to meet with them separately. Soon after that call, Haldeman received a message from Ron Ziegler, the press secretary, informing him it was time for both men to offer their resignations and to expect the president to ask for such on the mountain.

Once he arrived, following a quick discussion with Ziegler, Haldeman said he was ready to see the president and headed to Aspen. According to Haldeman, Nixon "was in terrible shape. Shook hands with me, which is the first time he's ever done that. Told me to come look at the view out the window, then stepped to the door and said, 'Let's go outside and look at the flowers and all.'"[27] Stating, "This was the hardest decision I had ever made," Nixon asked for Haldeman's resignation.[28] Instead of fighting the decision, even if Nixon was the guilty one, Haldeman agreed it was the correct action because, "He's got to stay in the office, he's got to pull things back together and move them upward."[29]

Ehrlichman stood next in the guillotine line arriving at Aspen shortly after Haldeman's departure. Ehrlichman found Nixon on the patio gazing out over the valley below the Catoctins. Offering another rare handshake, Nixon lamented the difficulty of this day and the gut-wrenching discussion with his family the previous evening reminiscing about his

---

27. Haldeman, 672.
28. Nixon, 847.
29. Haldeman, 672.

longtime aide. Knowing the inevitable result of the moment, Ehrlichman "put his arm around [Nixon's] shoulders and said, 'Don't talk that way. Don't *think* that way.'"[30] Nixon offered financial support for attorney fees in the upcoming criminal investigation, something Ehrlichman knew he could not accept. Ehrlichman only asked that the president explain the situation to Ehrlichman's children and then took his leave of the man he so admired.

Completing their resignation letters, the duo returned to Aspen together around 5:30 that evening for the president and secretary of state, Bill Rogers, to read over the letters before official acceptance. Ehrlichman requested the president inform the world that both he and Haldeman resigned, unlike the firing of John Dean, so they might escape the same disgrace Dean suffered in the public's eye. Satisfied with their letters, Nixon bid farewell to his two friends, again letting emotions bubble to the surface. In Nixon's words, "I tried to make it up to them the next night by saying in my speech what I deeply believed: 'Today, in one of the most difficult decisions of my presidency I accepted the resignations of two of my closest associates in the White House—Bob Haldeman, John Ehrlichman—two of the finest public servants it has been my privilege to know.'"[31]

Watergate never faded to the background, staying at the forefront of the public's opinion of Nixon despite every attempt to shake the weight over the next year. Making the decision to resign on August 1, 1974, Nixon spent the last weekend of his presidency, August 3 and 4, at Camp David. He took his family up the mountain to prepare them for what was to come. In the days before his last trip to Camp David, his chief of staff, Alexander Haig, seemed to convince Nixon to resign on Friday, August 2. However, discussions with his family prompted Nixon to change his mind and he released the infamous June 23 tape, and he said, "If it was as bad as I expected, then we could resume the countdown toward resignation."[32]

---

30. Nixon, 847.
31. Nixon, 848.
32. Nixon, 1061.

On a hot, humid August 3, the Nixon family boarded Marine One for their final trip to Camp David. Quickly heading to the pool to cool off, Nixon said they "sat on the terrace, looking out across the wide valleys. On evenings like this it was easy to see why Franklin Roosevelt had named this place Shangri-La, and I think that each of us had a sense of the mystery and the beauty as well as the history and the tragedy that lay behind our weekend together in this setting."[33] Throughout the weekend, Nixon's family urged him to force an impeachment fight, and, if he must give up, wait until the release of the tapes on Monday. Nixon decided to take their advice, "It's fight or flight by Monday night!" Releasing the Oval Office tape only worsened the political environment leaving an ominous pall over the administration. Finally realizing there remained only one option that would provide any control of the narrative, Nixon resigned the presidency at noon on Friday, August 9, 1974.

If any president needed a place to escape Washington, DC, and the craziness surrounding the presidency, it was Richard Nixon. He took full advantage of the private retreat visiting 161 times in his five years in office. Camp David was one place where he and his family could go and not have to deal with questions surrounding Watergate because the retreat's mission is to be whatever the president needs at the moment. Even before Watergate, Nixon understood the importance of such a place and approved the largest expansion and renovation of the retreat in its history. Today Nixon's legacy can be seen in photos at Camp David of the presidents after him: Carter walking with Sadat and Begin near the premier cabins; Clinton at a family Thanksgiving meal in Laurel; George W. Bush planning a response to September 11, 2001, in the conference room Nixon built; and Obama playing with his children at the Aspen pool. It's only fitting that a man with such a large personality and shadow over the presidency would still lurk in the background of the line of his successors.

---

33. Nixon, 1061.

CHAPTER 9

Recovery

GERALD FORD ASSUMED THE OVAL OFFICE, AND THE EVER-PRESENT elephant in the room of government mistrust as the aftermath of Watergate loomed over his every action. The press displayed skepticism for the Office of the President because of the way Nixon and his aides treated the press corps. This mistrust and wariness between the fourth estate and the president arrived at Camp David.

For years, reporters would distantly follow the president to Camp David, only allowed through the intimidating fence line in certain situations with an express invitation from the president, usually to cover the arrival or departure of foreign leaders or because the administration wanted to allow an interview for a specific purpose or particular journalist. Reporters covering the president would drive up from Washington upon hearing of the president heading toward Camp David. They would stay in Thurmont idly waiting for breaking news or the rare unscheduled presidential trip into town from the mountain. Most reporters stayed at the local motel, the Cozy Inn—since closed, demolished, and replaced by a car dealership, a tragic loss of living presidential history.

The summer of 1972 saw Camp David's staff construct a place for members of the White House Press pool to witness the arrival and departure of the president, as well as providing a trailer just outside the perimeter to file stories with their respective news agencies. For arrivals or departures, select members of the press would stand at a small niche in the perimeter fenced area. This cramped space accommodated photographers with a limited view of the landing zone through a small window the press dubbed "the duck blind."[1] Further driving press relations into the ditch, after installing the press trailer and in keeping with the tradition of naming buildings after local flora, the administration derogatorily named the trailer Poison Ivy.

Soon after Ford took office, the press noticed efforts to reach out and improve the relationship between the White House and the press corps. During a press conference, a young member of the press corps suggested one way the president could bridge the gap between the press and administration would be to rename the Camp David press trailer something less abrasive than Poison Ivy. Ford considered the suggestion, and by late October 1974, the press trailer had received a new name, Honeysuckle. A sweet-smelling plant of no danger to humans, honeysuckle is highly invasive and takes over a forest by choking out native flora. Even when searching for détente with the press, the White House still looked for ways to have the last laugh and assert its dominance. The young reporter who had suggested the name change to repair relations was Helen Thomas, who would serve the press corps with distinction and become synonymous with White House reporting, eventually receiving her own seat at the front of the Press Briefing Room in the West Wing and the honor of asking the first question during press availabilities.

Maintaining his goal of improving relations with the press, President Ford invited Harry Reasoner, then of ABC News, to Camp David for an exclusive interview. While not the first time press walked the hallowed grounds, it marked the first televised interview inside the perimeter. Throughout the day of October 26, 1974, President and Mrs. Ford sat with and walked the trails of Camp David with Reasoner, answering his questions on film. The interview explored the president's thoughts on adjusting to life in the White House for him and his family and his political ambitions while serving in the House of Representatives. The interview was intended to show a day in the life of the president at Camp David, while simultaneously providing a glimpse behind the veil of secrecy high atop the Catoctin Mountains.

1. Helen Thomas, *Front Row at the White House: My Life and Times*, 91.

The interview highlighted the allure, character, and charm of Camp David for those who were able to visit the retreat. President Ford said, "I think, Harry, number one it is a nice place to bring your family out and get kind of a family atmosphere. . . . But it is also a good place to work."[2] Later in the interview, Reasoner surmises the possibility to run the country from the retreat, prompting Ford's response, "You actually can. There are some very appropriate security measures, and also communications . . . It is a place where in any emergency the president could —actually operate in that capacity."[3] Strolling the retreat from the Camp commander's house toward Aspen Lodge as the last few leaves clung to their branches waiting for one strong wind to blow them away, President Ford described various uses of the compound. "There is an excellent place for a cabinet meeting, or a larger conference, good accommodations for feeding as many as one hundred people or more. So, it is a place where you could really bring the Government and operate it pretty efficiently."[4]

As the two approached Aspen, Reasoner correctly surmised the large cabin overlooking the valley served as the president's residence. Ford proudly noted, "It is the nicest place on the Camp David site. It is a place where you can really live as a family" and could accommodate his entire family, but his grown children preferred separate cabins nearby.[5] During this part of the interview Betty Ford joined them with their dog Liberty, who lovingly said hello to the reporter, prompting Reasoner to mention Camp David would be paradise for a dog. Betty confirmed his observation relaying Liberty was fresh off a losing chase of one of the resident deer.

Reasoner recalled that urbanite President Kennedy enjoyed the surroundings and relayed a conversation where Kennedy admitted thinking about Camp David during construction of Wexford, "Why build a

2. Ron Nessen Files at Gerald R. Ford Presidential Library, Box 25, folder "10/26/1974—Harry Reasoner, ABC News," 1.

3. Ron Nessen Files at Gerald R. Ford Presidential Library, Box 25, folder "10/26/1974—Harry Reasoner, ABC News," 6.

4. Ron Nessen Files at Gerald R. Ford Presidential Library, Box 25, folder "10/26/1974—Harry Reasoner, ABC News," 7.

5. Ron Nessen Files at Gerald R. Ford Presidential Library, Box 25, folder "10/26/1974—Harry Reasoner, ABC News," 9.

weekend house when we have this for free?" President Ford echoed the sentiment, "It is so beautiful I don't see any reason why we should have any other spot. There is tennis, a little three-hole golf course. There is a swimming pool. It is a total complex, and it is so comfortable and so beautiful, and it is so handy with all the facilities that you need as president. I really don't think we ought to go beyond it."[6]

Demonstrating that even the president cannot always command the airwaves, the carefully planned interview and its glimpse inside the security perimeter did not air as planned. The White House desired images of Ford in a relaxed setting and encouraged the interview, eagerly anticipating its broadcast, something rare in the history of Camp David. Ultimately, the network pulled the plug because of the proposed air date. Even after sending Reasoner up the mountain, William Sheehan, then president of ABC News, declined to air the program as scheduled on November 2, 1974, three days ahead of the 1974 mid-term elections, feeling "some of the president's statements went beyond a tour guide's comments and could be considered political."[7] CBS turned down the first interview opportunity when approached by the White House staff a week prior. ABC moved the broadcast to two weeks after the election, however the program was preempted due to the priority of football games that ran over schedule. The public lost a wonderful opportunity to witness the power of Camp David, even if from the distance of a television screen. Through the power of the Internet, however, the video is now available as part of a C-SPAN program from October 2007 about Ford's presidency.

The mention of Liberty chasing deer during the interview is ironic considering some behind-the-scenes machinations the previous month. On September 2, 1974, a photograph appeared throughout the country with the First Family feeding a deer a bottle of milk at Camp David.[8]

---

6. Ron Nessen Files at Gerald R. Ford Presidential Library, Box 25, folder "10/26/1974—Harry Reasoner, ABC News," 10.

7. Les Brown, "ABC Delays Ford Film, Cites Election," *New York Times*, October 31, 1974, https://www.nytimes.com/1974/10/31/archives/abc-delays-ford-film-cites-election-800000-for-realidades.html (retrieved on April 3, 2021).

8. With President Ford wearing an outfit of questionable fashion taste—checkered trousers and white shoes with black socks.

The heart-warming photo inspired the town of Rangeley, Maine, to write both their congressional representative William S. Cohen, a future secretary of defense, and the president with a proposal to solve a problem facing the small community. Recognizing the request was odd, if not downright ridiculous, they sought to transplant a beloved deer to the presidential mountain retreat, knowing she would be safe from the upcoming hunting season.

Frika, as the town came to know the deer, was one of five being fostered for eventual release into the wild. Four of the five, quickly adapted to the call of the wild. Frika, however, found a loving local family who took her in as their pet, allowing her "into the house for treats."[9] Seeking to protect Frika before hunting season and unable to find a petting zoo nearby, they sought sanctuary for the beloved deer. "Recalling your recent photo petting the fawn at Camp David, I took it upon myself to write and ask if you would like to include Frika in the Camp David wildlife. This may sound zany, but in 1955 we presented a fawn Bambi to the late President Eisenhower."[10] It was not the craziest request regarding Camp David within presidential files, and definitely not the last.

As expected, the request was ultimately rejected through a letter from counsel to the president in November 1974, for there were too many deer at Camp David. But there are layers to Frika's saga beyond the initial request and rejection. The request traveled through the office of Warren Rustand, the appointments secretary, where Mary Rawlins dutifully forwarded the request to the Camp commander, Lieutenant Commander Stephen Todd, whose witty reply matched the nature of the request. After lamenting deer overpopulation at camp, he explained even the photogenic fawn spawning this saga itself needed a new home as its adoptive military family approached their own transfer. He concluded the letter with a poem, apologizing to Ogden Nash:

---

9. Letter from Joanne Blythe to the president, dated September 6, 1974, located in Philip Buchen Files at Gerald R. Ford Presidential Library, Box 48, folder "President–Personal Camp David."

10. Within the "Camp David" folder of the Richard B. Cheney Files at the Ford Library is a chain of memos dealing with a visit request from Senator Ted Stevens to demonstrate the commonality of various requests regarding Camp David that attracted attention from the White House staff.

To add to my woe
you send the tale of Frika the doe.
Another little vamp
who wants to romp at the Camp.

Now besides pollution and erosion
we must face a deer explosion.
All these moosey mammals can play the devil
with national life on every level.

To suggest the Camp for use as a ranch
can only make me tremble and blanch.
I see it not with amusement and awe
only boggled mind and dangled jaw.

Forlorn they be, yet I speak not alone
when I say another fawn we cannot own.
What those sailors most want to get
is not another Bambi to love and pet.

Should with this beast I them saddle.
Camp would surely shake and rattle.
So, please heed what I have here pleaded
else my name there be expletive deleted.

Thus, Mary my dear, little Frika I fear
should not come to settle with us here.
I ask of you that this sweet little doe
to the nearest damn zoo should go.[11]

Wisely refraining from forwarding the Camp commander's creativity as the official response, Ms. Rawlins suggested the president's daughter, Susan Ford, accept the deer on behalf of the National Zoo, but lo "it

---

11. Memo from LCDR Stephen Todd to Mary Rawlins, October 4, 1974, located in Philip Buchen Files at Gerald R. Ford Presidential Library, Box 48, folder "President–Personal Camp David."

would be illegal to transport the deer across state lines."[12] The files never indicate where poor, innocent Frika lived out her days.

Amid interviews and requests for housing deer, the First Family enjoyed their time at Camp David, making their first visit on August 31, 1974. At that visit, Betty Ford noted in her diary, "Camp David is the best thing about the White House. Except you gain too much weight up there, because the staff is so glad to have you come that they prepare all these delicious meals. . . . The air, the trees, the sky—it's paradise, that place. If I get to return to this world, I'd like to come back to Camp David."[13]

First impressions matter, especially for First Families recuperating from medical crises. Diagnosed with breast cancer, Betty Ford underwent a mastectomy on September 28, 1974, and, not the norm to occupants of the White House, made her cancer journey public. This openness resulted in an outpouring of support and empathy for the First Lady, as well as creating a noticeable rise in women checking for signs of breast cancer. Noticing her impact on the nation, Betty reflected, "I'd come to recognize more clearly the power of the woman in the White House. Not *my* power, but the power of the position, a power which could be used to help."[14] Knowing the restorative power of Camp David, she visited soon after the surgery for recovery time where "the whole staff hugged and kissed me when I came in the door of Aspen. I walked the grounds with Liberty, ate food that was good for me (liver and onions, ugh) whether I liked it or not."[15] This visit wasn't totally relaxing as she also learned her son Steve had enrolled in a Wyoming school for aspiring rodeo riders. Not wanting to hear of her son injured by a tossing bull, she pondered telling Steve no, to which President Ford replied, "He's too old to stop. And you know how well he's taken our advice on everything else."[16]

12. Handwritten reply to memo from Mary Rawlins to Mr. Nicholson, October 4, 1974, located in Philip Buchen Files at Gerald R. Ford Presidential Library, Box 48, folder "President—Personal Camp David."
13. Betty Ford, *The Times of My Life*, 168.
14. Betty Ford, 194.
15. Betty Ford, 194.
16. Betty Ford, 194.

The Reasoner interview was not the only time the Ford Administration allowed the public glimpses behind the tight curtain of security afforded by Camp David. During the 1976 Republican National Convention in Kansas City, Ford's campaign created a short film hoping to highlight Gerald Ford as a family man. While there is debate on the effectiveness of the film bolstering the image of Ford as a relaxed everyman with whom to share a beer at the pub, the film sought to portray "a man who was 'open' and caring with his family [and] would be open and caring as president."[17] One scene recorded the First Family seated at the Aspen kitchen table discussing how they are ordinary citizens just like those casting votes in November.

While Ford struggled to show the voters he was a normal, everyday person, his time at Camp David shows that is exactly who he was. Humble and laid back at the retreat, he didn't visit to run from scandal or hide from the press. In fact, he is the only president to actively work with the Camp David press to improve the usually acrimonious relationship. As the accidental president, Ford provided the best glimpse behind the veil of secrecy surrounding the private retreat. Ford opened the gates in a way no other president had before or after him; it is interesting to consider how this transparency might have continued and how the retreat might have been viewed with a second term for Ford.

Unfortunately for the Fords, America felt another candidate would serve them better in the White House ending their opportunity to utilize the mountain top retreat. After awarding the Presidential Medal of Freedom to Henry Kissinger and Don Rumsfeld on January 13, 1977, the Fords took their last flight to Camp David, saying their final goodbyes to the place that could always brighten their mood.[18]

---

17. Gil Troy, *Mr. and Mrs. President*, 233.
18. Gerald Ford, *A Time to Heal*, 439.

CHAPTER 10

Peace

ON JANUARY 20, 1977, DURING THE RIDE FROM THE WHITE HOUSE TO the inauguration, Rosalynn Carter and Betty Ford engaged in small talk, eventually turning to the Fords' last weekend as the First Family at the mountain retreat. Betty mentioned the delectable food and how she would need to diet because of the Camp David chefs.[1] Despite a glowing review of the Camp David culinary scene, not long after taking office, Carter wanted to abandon Camp David to demonstrate his commitment toward cutting government costs.

Carter's aides consulted Stephen Hess, a former Nixon aide, regarding the usefulness of the retreat. Hess drafted a memo to Carter stating, "Herbert Hoover and John Kennedy were able to buy themselves rustic retreats, but should we have to count on a president being rich? . . . Do not dismantle it until you have determined that it does not serve a legitimate need."[2] Taking Hess's advice, Carter made his inaugural flight to the mountain on February 25, 1977. Immediately captivated by the Spirit of Camp David, the mountain retreat quickly became a relaxation staple of the Carters and, rather than an unceremonious closure, the recipient of upgrades. Carter appreciated the value of the retreat so much that when his director of Office of Management and Budget, Bert Lance, suggested Carter not seek the actual cost of the upgrades, he dutifully agreed and

---

1. Rosalynn Carter, *First Lady from Plains*, 3.
2. Kenneth T. Walsh, *From Mount Vernon to Crawford*, 295.

abandoned the line of questioning.[3] The president's initial plan to close the retreat was now a distant memory, and he said, "[I] had seen how much Camp David meant to me. It was just 35 minutes from the South Lawn. . . . Rosalynn and I both loved Camp David. . . . It's completely isolated. . . . We looked upon it as a prime attraction of our lives."[4]

Like presidents before, Carter enjoyed the seclusion and ability to escape Washington for a small slice of normalcy in the craziness of the presidency. While at Camp David the family would watch movies, read, fish, spend time in the woodworking and construction shop, and they appreciated quality time together. The family enjoyed the mountain so much that Carter visited at least once a month in forty-seven of his forty-eight months in office.

One source of enjoyment for Carter at Camp David centered on his ability to secret away to other locations. Helen Thomas recalled Carter saying to the press he wanted to be close to them only to slip away from an unknowing press corps to a favorite fishing spot in Pennsylvania.[5] Kenneth Walsh outlines the ruse: Carter took Marine One to Camp David on Friday afternoon so the press would see him land. Once they confirmed arrival, the press headed down the mountain to the Cozy Inn assuming he would remain at the retreat until his scheduled departure on Sunday. As the press departed, Carter and his guests changed clothes and flew to another location for a fly-fishing weekend. On Sunday, they returned to Camp David early enough to avoid the press arriving for his departure and then would reboard the helicopter in plain view of the press for the flight back to the South Lawn—the press none the wiser regarding the elaborate ruse.[6]

During one visit in September 1979, Carter participated in a local 10K running race, the Catoctin Mountain Run, whose course passed just outside the gates of Camp David. An avid runner, Carter couldn't participate in a small-town race unnoticed, so his adventure outside the gates occurred in full view of the public and the press. Near the mountain

---

3. Walsh, 295.
4. Walsh, 295.
5. Helen Thomas, *Front Row at the White House*, 329.
6. Walsh, 296.

summit and main gate, Carter nearly collapsed. Quick-thinking Secret Service agents running alongside grabbed the president to prevent his falling in full view of the crowd. They sat him in a golf cart where he received oxygen and fluids, eventually spending time in bed resting and recovering.[7] However, the press still managed to snap an unflattering photo, and the image of an exhausted president did not help the upcoming reelection campaign.

In July 1978, as President and Mrs. Carter walked the grounds of Camp David, a favorite activity of the couple when in residence, he pitched Rosalynn a daring idea which, if successful, would forever cement the name of Camp David in history and become the centerpiece of his presidency. "It's so beautiful here. I don't believe anyone could stay in this place, close to nature, peaceful and isolated from the world, and still carry a grudge. I believe if I could get Sadat and Begin both here together, we could work out some of the problems between them."[8] Enthusiastically encouraging the idea throughout the weekend, Rosalynn, the erstwhile voice of reason, voiced the shared concern of the couple, "Are you willing to be the scapegoat?" Knowing a bashing from the press came with the job, the president quipped, "What else is new?"[9] The Camp David Accords were born.

One month later, Carter sent Secretary of State Cyrus Vance to deliver Israel and Egypt presidential greetings and invitations for a trilateral meeting, to include their wives, at Camp David. The Carters hoped having the wives in attendance, alongside the serenity of Camp David, would foster the needed relaxed and congenial atmosphere. Sadat's enthusiastic acceptance surprised the Carters, seeing how his first visit to Camp David did not get off to the best start.

Sadat and his wife, Jehan, arrived on a bitter cold February 3, 1978, with snow covering the ground. Upon the Sadats' landing, as was the Carters' unique custom at Camp David, the president and First Lady suggested the Egyptian couple join them in walking the quarter mile

---

7. Walsh, 297.
8. Rosalynn Carter, 238.
9. Rosalynn Carter, 238.

from the helipad to their cabin. While the foursome all had on coats, President Sadat refused to wear a hat and arrived at his cabin shaking from the cold.[10] Saving face for the Carters, the forward-looking Camp crew had a blazing fire warming the cabin to melt the miserable cold. Due to the frigid weather, the foursome spent most of the visit inside getting to know each other, working to thaw the coolness of the personal relationship between the leaders.

The bitter cold didn't freeze every outdoor activity. One afternoon the foursome took to the trails and hills of the retreat on snowmobiles. Ensuring President Sadat was properly bundled against the icy breeze, the foursome made their way to the large field where not only helicopters land, but guests shoot skeet during hospitable weather. Anwar rode with Rosalynn and Jehan with the president, racing each other around the field. Enthralled with the endeavor, the Sadats pondered the feasibility of snowmobiles speeding along the sands of Egypt.[11]

Seven months later, September 5, 1978, the presidential moment arrived. The Carters sat in Aspen watching news coverage of each leader arriving at Andrews Air Force Base and boarding helicopters for the quick trip to Camp David. Sadat arrived first, without Jehan who remained in Paris caring for an ill grandson.[12] Two hours later, Prime Minister Begin arrived, also without his wife Aliza, delayed in travel and set to arrive the next day. Each arrival, surrounded in good will and warm embraces between the leaders and President Carter, did not reflect the temperature of the visiting delegations.

Shortly after arrival, the three leaders met in Aspen for a discouraging first exchange of ideas. A good night's sleep did little to improve the mood as, during Carter's morning meeting with Sadat, the Egyptian presented a rigid plan with extensive demands. Despite this acrimonious meeting, Carter scheduled a second round of discussions between the three men the afternoon of September 6 to present Sadat's proposal. Ini-

---

10. Rosalynn Carter, 241.
11. Rosalynn Carter, 241.
12. Rosalynn Carter, 243.

tially shell-shocked and speechless, in a separate meeting, the Begins and the Carters surmised Sadat was exerting maximum pressure for effect with a strong opening gambit.[13] September 7 witnessed two additional trilateral discussions with Sadat and Begin further digging into and fortifying their fighting holes. This day's events would prove the last formal negotiation for the next ten days.

Despite hostile negotiations, two events cracked tensions just enough for all sides to glimpse the humanity of each other and open space for Camp David to work its magic. As both Begin and Sadat arrived at Aspen on the seventh for their scheduled morning discussion, both men deferred first entry to the other creating a diplomatic impasse. Laughter ensued with Begin following protocol and insisting Sadat go first because Sadat was a president and Begin was a mere prime minister. That evening President Carter arranged for a performance by the Marine Corps Silent Drill Platoon on the landing zone field. From bleachers, the delegations breathlessly watched the Marines "perform intricate maneuvers, sometimes twirling the heavy firearms and sharp blades within a hairbreadth of one another. Then came the music, including medleys of patriotic tunes from all three nations."[14] Despite glimpses of humanity, a fog of despair descended as word spread of both sides showing unwillingness to budge—placing the talks in grave danger of collapse before the hard work began. "Carter's hope that he could encourage Sadat and Begin to trust each other and to work out their differences had fallen flat. Now Carter would have to inject himself more forcefully into the discussions."[15]

From this moment, the onus lay on President Carter to keep the two sides on the mountain. Never giving up and always looking for connections with each side to keep the delegations talking despite the leaders avoiding each other, Carter displayed keen diplomacy. On Friday, September 8, camp staff prepared a Sabbath dinner for the Israeli delegation, attended by curious members of the Egyptian delegation, converting the movie theater into a banquet hall for the evening. During the meal,

---

13. Rosalynn Carter, 245.
14. Jimmy Carter, *Keeping Faith*, 368.
15. William Quandt, *Camp David: Peacemaking and Politics*, 225.

tensions of the moment evaporated, as Begin related to Rosalynn, "They always put aside their concerns and observed the Sabbath with rejoicing and singing because the Bible says that you cannot serve God with sadness."[16] As the Israeli delegation observed Sabbath the next day, the American team drafted a moderate proposal for both sides to consider.

As exhaustion overcame all three delegations, the Americans scheduled a negotiating break on Sunday, September 10. President Carter invited the delegations to join him for a tour of the nearby town of Gettysburg. Along with Rosalynn Carter and Aliza Begin, Sadat and Begin rode in the same limousine with Carter between the two leaders. During the short, winding journey down the mountain, "Both Begin and Sadat, who had both been in prison for their political actions, talked about their experience as prisoners."[17] A powerful, human conversation, it revealed how both men coped with the loss of reading, the power of meditation, and the time spent teaching fellow prisoners from their vast wealth of knowledge.

According to Moshe Dayan, the Israeli minister of foreign affairs, those participating in the tour received a detailed six-hour tour of the battlefield with Carter injecting lively commentary to overcome dry narration by the official tour guide. "[Carter] seemed to know every hill and boulder which had served [General Lee's men] as cover. And when he told the story of how the tattered, bedraggled, and barefoot Southern fighters had an additional incentive to capture Gettysburg upon hearing that it had large stores of boots, he seemed to be talking about his own family."[18] A combat veteran himself, Dayan connected not so much with the retelling of the battle, but with how Americans feel "a personal identification with the men, their brothers, who fought in that bitter and bloody struggle with courage, dedication, and self-sacrifice."[19] President Carter observed that military veterans among the delegations studied the tactics of the battle while Begin showed little interest in the battle,

---

16. Rosalynn Carter, 251.
17. Rosalynn Carter, 253.
18. Moshe Dayan, *Breakthrough*, 171.
19. Dayan, 171.

instead focusing his attention and excitement toward the site of Lincoln's famous Gettysburg Address.[20]

The delegations returned to Camp David later in the afternoon continuing discussions while Begin and Sadat retreated to their own corners to not set eyes on each other until the final day, one week later. Over the next few days, progress occurred in fits and starts as Carter conducted shuttle diplomacy spending equal, individual time with each leader, using the rest of his energy conversing and negotiating with the delegations, sometimes with their leader present. Despite the beautiful surroundings and relaxed atmosphere, shared meals with the delegations, tension-breaking events, and every other thing Carter tried, the delegations sensed impending doom regarding achieving a mere joint statement, much less lasting peace. Camp David's magical power to bring people together appeared destined to failure.

Carter's unease and worry regarding the increasing tension, specifically Sadat, culminated on the night of September 13, the ninth day of the talks, as he spent most of the night wide awake due to an unsettling premonition Sadat's life was in danger. Carter noted, "I have little trouble sleeping well. I was worrying about President Sadat, and whether he was safe."[21] Recalling a heated discussion he observed on the porch of Sadat's cabin and the fact members of Sadat's own delegation were not committed to Sadat's goal of peace, instead preferring the goals of the Palestinian Liberation Organization, and upon hearing Sadat had "uncharacteristically retired early and could not be disturbed," his fear peaked.[22] Rosalynn said she "woke up suddenly at 4:00 a.m. and realized that Jimmy was awake too. He was worried about Sadat: 'I don't know exactly why, but I have an uneasy feeling about Sadat's safety.'"[23] Ignoring the hour, the president directed Secret Service to discreetly check on Sadat and increase security to his cabin. At eight o'clock the next morning Sadat appeared at Aspen cabin, "hale, hearty, ready for his daily walk. Relieved, Jimmy immediately joined him, and [the] fears of the night dissipated in

---

20. Jimmy Carter, 380–381.
21. Jimmy Carter, 397–398.
22. Jimmy Carter, 398.
23. Rosalynn Carter, 260.

the morning sun."[24] (That relief was short-lived as Carter's premonition materialized on October 6, 1981, when Sadat fell to an assassin while watching a parade in Cairo.)

After ten days with each other, isolated from the world, "claustrophobia was setting in. . . . The outside world was beginning to seem remote and exotic. Jokes were being made about 'prison' and the 'concentration camp' atmosphere. Psychologically and physically, time seemed to be running out."[25] This feeling, along with a formidable impasse, led Sadat to abandon all hope. On September 15, day eleven, the Egyptian delegation packed their bags and Sadat requested helicopters for transport to Andrews Air Force Base. Learning of the development through Secretary of State Vance, Carter donned business attire and headed to Sadat's cabin. Carter informed Sadat that leaving now would damage the relationship between Egypt and the United States, but, more importantly, Carter told him it would "damage one of my most precious possessions—his friendship and our mutual trust."[26] The gambit worked as Sadat agreed to remain for a few more days to see what would arise. Fearing the worst, the American delegation drew up plans for how to deal with failed talks.

Later that evening, Carter and Sadat watched the Muhammad Ali–Leon Spinks rematch. Like many around the world, Sadat admired Muhammad Ali and was eager to watch the fight despite the seclusion atop the mountain. Lasting all fifteen rounds, Ali conquered through a unanimous decision. Immediately following the bout, the president placed an unanswered congratulatory call to Ali, later receiving a return call at 1:30 a.m. well after Sadat had retired for the night.[27]

Sunday, September 17 arrived: the day Carter set as the final day of the talks, regardless of outcome. The president began the day with a worship service at Camp David led by an Army chaplain from nearby Camp Ritchie before cautiously continuing final negotiations. Hope hung in the air as major differences began disappearing, but just as previous days had

24. Rosalynn Carter, 260.
25. Quandt, 235.
26. Jimmy Carter, 401.
27. Jimmy Carter, 402–403.

shown, when on the brink of a breakthrough, someone would develop cold feet and derail progress.

Begin and Carter met after church agreeing "on formulae for those issues which until then had remained unresolved."[28] An unexpected agreement looked possible. However, "during lunch in the refectory, Vice President Mondale showed our [the Israeli] Ambassador to Washington the draft of a letter President Carter was about to deliver to Sadat. In it, Carter stated that the United States considered East Jerusalem to be conquered territory."[29] Israel would never agree to a mere hint of ceding territory. Carter walked to Aspen with a member of the Israeli delegation offering to reword the letter, a suggestion quickly forwarded to Begin.

As is customary on the final day of such talks, Begin asked Carter to sign photographs of the three men for Begin's grandchildren. Carter's secretary, Susan Clough, suggested personalizing the photos to help ease tensions with the Israelis, good advice the president took a step further by personally delivering the photos to Begin. Arriving at Begin's cabin, Carter noticed a nervous prime minister on the porch, concern visible across his face regarding the prospect of failure. Begin thanked the president for the photographs and, glancing down, noticed his granddaughter's name on the top photograph. Carter said Begin "then looked at each photograph individually, repeating the name of the grandchild I had written on it. His lips trembled, and tears welled up in his eyes. He told me a little about each child, and especially about the one who seemed to be his favorite. . . . Then he asked me to step into his cabin, requesting that everyone else in the room leave."[30] During this meeting, Carter informed Begin of the reworded letter, stating he would honor his agreement with Sadat and exchange formal letters. Carter returned to Aspen finding Sadat nervously awaiting his arrival, and he informed Sadat of the dim reality Begin was most likely walking away. Sadat reassured Carter, "I will accept the letter you have drafted on Jerusalem."[31] After more negotiating

---

28. Dayan, 177.
29. Dayan, 177–178.
30. Jimmy Carter, 408.
31. Jimmy Carter, 409.

regarding the wording of the letter, the Israeli delegation accepted. Perhaps Camp David's magic still worked, and peace stood a chance.

Having anticipated inevitable defeat, Rosalynn Carter had departed Camp David that somber Sunday morning returning to the White House to attend a concert the administration could not reschedule. That afternoon, Aliza Begin descended the mountain to join Rosalynn for the concert. Prior to the concert, Rosalynn phoned Carter and learned of a possible end to the stalemate. Without tipping her hand, she slyly stalled Aliza's return. Following the concert, Rosalynn sent Aliza to the Israeli Embassy under the guise no helicopters were available, a true statement as the entire presidential helicopter fleet stood ready to whisk the delegations off the mountain.[32] Shortly after the concert President Carter phoned exclaiming, "We're coming home! The agreements are initialed, and we'll sign them in the East Room tonight!"[33] The helicopters commenced ferrying the delegations to the White House around 8:00 p.m., and at 11:00 a.m. the three men signed the Framework for Peace in the Middle East on live television. Sadat and Begin would receive the 1978 Nobel Peace Prize, the Nobel Committee ignoring Carter's hard work and key role in the enduring peace agreement. Snubbed in 1978, Carter later received the Peace Prize in 2002 for decades of work seeking peace around the world.

Playing a pivotal role in the defining achievement of Carter's presidency, Camp David also intersected with low points of his administration. In early July 1979, during the OPEC oil crisis, Carter brought "leaders from every segment of American life to Camp David for a 'domestic summit' to talk about the bigger problem facing America, how to convince the public that the energy crisis was real, how it tied in to unemployment and inflation, and, most important, how our nation could rally to resolve the oil crisis and renew our confidence in the social, political, and economic future of the country."[34] The result of these ten days of meetings was a

---

32. Rosalynn Carter, 266.
33. Rosalynn Carter, 267.
34. Rosalynn Carter, 303.

televised speech on July 15, which would earn the moniker of the "malaise speech" despite Carter never uttering those words.

While Carter's presidency did not survive to see a second term, his legacy, like that of Camp David, will live on as a beacon of peace and hope. Carter and Camp David are forever linked. It's impossible to think of one without recalling the other. Carter harnessed everything the retreat could do and focused it on one goal: bringing two long-time enemies together as people with more in common than not and letting the seclusion and the protective cocoon of the mountain air and breathtaking beauty of a Maryland autumn work its magic. Camp David delivered in ways that surprised everyone, even Carter. The little-known retreat was thrust into the public gaze, yet retained its veil of secrecy, ever guarding the privacy of its guests. The world now knew of the Spirit of Camp David, but its superpower remained hidden from view, available only at the invitation of the president.

Eight months later, on March 22, 1980, while at Camp David, Carter "authorized the US military to send a small plane to a swath of desert about two hundred miles south of Tehran, to determine if the area could be used as a staging ground for a rescue mission."[35] Those in need of rescue? Fifty-two American hostages who were seized at the US Embassy in Tehran on November 4, 1979. On March 31, Major John Carney Jr. secretly flew into Iranian territory to survey and mark the landing site known as Desert One with infrared strobes. Three weeks later, the mission to rescue the hostages, Operation Eagle Claw, was launched using Desert One as the in-country staging area for the rescue attempt. Rapidly deteriorating into a debacle, the failed operation served as a symbol of futility for Carter's critics and dealt a mortal wound to his reelection campaign. Iran released the hostages on January 20, 1981, minutes after Ronald Reagan took the oath of office as the 40th president of the United States.

---

35. Walsh, 298.

CHAPTER 11

Seclusion

AFTER THE 1980 ELECTION, PAT NIXON SPOKE WITH NANCY REAGAN offering, "Without Camp David, you'll go stir crazy."[1] At first, the incoming First Family, like those before them, did not fully understand the accuracy of Pat Nixon's advice. The Reagans would soon treasure Camp David as a place of refuge from the day-to-day pace of the job and the attending 24/7 watch over every aspect of their lives.

Reflecting on Camp David's role in his peace and comfort, Regan wrote, "There were plenty of things to compensate for the freedom we lost, one of the greatest being Camp David—a slice of heaven a half hour's helicopter ride from the White House."[2] He routinely compared the freedom of Camp David to that of his California ranch. "Just as we did at Rancho del Cielo, Nancy and I experienced a sense of liberation at Camp David that we never found in Washington. Because the perimeter was guarded, we could just open a door and take a walk. That's a freedom, incidentally, that you don't fully appreciate until you've lost it."[3] Nancy's reflections echo those of her husband. "When you're president, there's no such thing as a vacation. No matter where you go there are always briefing books to study, papers to read, intelligence reports to review, speeches to work on, decisions to be made."[4] Because of the unrelenting pressures

---

1. Ronald Reagan, *An American Life*, 396.
2. Ronald Reagan, *An American Life*, 396.
3. Ronald Reagan, *An American Life*, 397.
4. Nancy Reagan, *My Turn*, 255.

of the office, it is no surprise the couple found solace on the mountain. The First Lady noted, "Thank God for Camp David! I never expected that we would use it practically every weekend, but it became a regular and welcome part of our routine."[5]

The Reagans would use the retreat more than any First Family. Frequenting Camp David during their eight years in office, the Reagans guarded the privacy of the retreat more than any administration since Roosevelt, but for different reasons. Roosevelt restricted the circle of trust regarding Camp David due to wartime security concerns. Reagan limited access to safeguard a private retreat away from the prying eyes of the media and Washington leaks. Even family visits were rare. Reagan's daughter Maureen, "who lived nearby in Washington, got to the camp only once, in 1985. Nor did Reagan let his staff use the camp when he wasn't there."[6]

Nancy described the couple's reasoning, "It was impressed on us from the beginning that Camp David was the president's most private retreat, and that every president who has used it has gone to great lengths to keep it that way. So did we. We really guarded the privacy of the place. Prime Minister Nakasone of Japan once joined us there for lunch, and Mrs. Thatcher came twice, and we had a visit from President Lopez Portillo of Mexico, but except for family—mostly Ron and Doria, when they lived in New York, and my brother Dick, and his family, from Philadelphia— that was about it. Even Ronnie's closest advisers were rarely there."[7] As the presidency never leaves the individual, the First Family can never establish a truly private retreat because a number of individuals, such as the White House doctor, personal aides, and a military aide are always nearby.

If not for the detailed descriptions of Camp David from President and Mrs. Reagan in their memoirs, there would be scant information on their use of the camp because of their dogged determination to guard the retreat's privacy. It seems ironic that the family who guarded the magic of

5. Nancy Reagan, *My Turn*, 253.
6. Walsh, 298.
7. Nancy Reagan, *My Turn*, 253.

the retreat more than any other First Family provided some of the most detailed insight into their use of Camp David in their writings.

President Reagan remarked, "The days I liked best were those Fridays when I could break away a little early, about three or three thirty, and take off for Camp David."[8] Nancy enjoyed the location, not the journey, "I was never crazy about the helicopter, although as helicopters go, ours was large, and the ride was fairly smooth."[9] President Reagan loaded up necessary papers for work and any preparation material for his weekly radio address, but made sure to bring nonwork items as well, "There was almost always time to relax in front of a fire with a book."[10]

Upon arrival, the First Family received the customary greeting from the Camp David commander followed by acknowledgment by the Marine posted at the flagpole. "And the moment the president arrives at Camp David, the presidential flag goes up. The moment he leaves, it comes down."[11] After disembarking Marine One, President and Mrs. Reagan traveled to Aspen for pre-dinner relaxation. "The president's home at Camp David, called Aspen, is a beautiful rustic house with beamed ceilings, wood-paneled walls, and big windows that look out at the forest."[12]

After dinner, the couple would invite a small group into Aspen for a movie with popcorn and peanut brittle for all. Nancy Reagan noted, "We had to stop serving popcorn after Ronnie's cancer operation, and instead of peanut brittle, Mark [Weinberg] started bringing chocolate."[13] Early in the administration, this close-knit group watched new or recent releases from Hollywood. "Then I began trying to sandwich in a few older movies from my generation,"[14] said the president. "Before long, even the younger members of the audience started asking for more golden oldies . . . especially when Ronnie would tell behind-the-scenes stories

---

8. Ronald Reagan, *An American Life*, 396–397.
9. Nancy Reagan, *My Turn*, 254.
10. Ronald Reagan, *An American Life*, 397.
11. Nancy Reagan, *My Turn*, 254.
12. Ronald Reagan, *An American Life*, 397.
13. Nancy Reagan, *My Turn*, 255.
14. Ronald Reagan, *An American Life*, 397.

about the actors and the studios,"[15] added Nancy. When asked, the Reagans would screen movies they had starred in, including *Bedtime for Bonzo*, the movie for which Reagan was lampooned throughout his political career.

Saturday morning included reading newspapers and making last-minute preparations for the weekly radio address Reagan would conduct for five minutes from Laurel either in the conference room or, on those glorious weather days on the mountain, outside from the back patio. Following the radio address they "walked over to the gym . . . then it was back to Aspen for lunch."[16] Once lunch was finished, and provided the weather cooperated, the couple journeyed out on horseback. On their first visit to Camp David, they were shocked to realize Nixon paved the riding trails to allow more room for golf carts. So, the Reagans had the trails around Camp David restored to accommodate their frequent sojourns on horseback.[17]

"I would ride behind Ronnie rather than beside him because our horses didn't like each other; if my horse got too close, Ronnie's horse would try to kick him. But even when we ride together at the ranch, we don't talk much. One thing I hate is riding with someone who keeps up a steady stream of conversation. You're there to relax, to look at the trees, and the sky, to think."[18] Sometimes the couple headed through "the back gate and rode through the lush green national forest surrounding it, following an old road,"[19] causing a good deal of anxiety for the Secret Service.

While on horseback, the couple often passed the ruins of a house looming large in local lore. On the heels of divorce around 1918, a woman named Bessie Darling purchased a property, built in 1907, set on the slope of

---

15. Nancy Reagan, *My Turn*, 256.
16. Nancy Reagan, *My Turn*, 256.
17. Nancy Reagan, *My Turn*, 257.
18. Nancy Reagan, *My Turn*, 257.
19. Ronald Reagan, *An American Life*, 399.

what would become part of the Catoctin National Park.[20] She opened the Valley View Manor for summer boarding in 1918, catering to elites living in Baltimore, her city of residence during the winter months.[21] In 1933, Darling's boyfriend, George F. Shultz, became convinced Bessie was seeing another man, suspicions heightened by Darling's refusing to return to Baltimore at the conclusion of the 1933 boarding season.[22] Shultz decided to find out for once and all the status of his relationship with Bessie, and he boarded a train from Baltimore on October 31, 1933.

Departing the train around 7 a.m. on that Halloween morning, Shultz made his way to Valley View Manor, storming toward the rear entrance where he encountered the young maid, Maizie Willard on her way to gather firewood. Shultz demanded Bessie's whereabouts.[23] Willard said Darling was in her bedroom, but noting his anger attempted to close the door on Shultz, who forced his way into the house. Willard rushed to Darling's bedroom to warn her, locking the door to keep Shultz away from Bessie. Forcing his way past the locked door and seeing Darling with her own weapon, Shultz fired one shot severing Bessie's artery and instantly killing her.[24] As the only witness, Shultz kept Willard hostage in the house for almost an hour before releasing her to get help and saying, "When you come back, you'll find two of us dead."[25] Willard notified the county sheriff who arrived with a deputy around 9:30 a.m. finding a dead Darling and Shultz critically injured from a self-inflicted gunshot to the chest.[26]

Shultz recovered and stood trial on March 12, 1934, entering a not guilty plea. The jury deliberated an hour returning a guilty verdict of murder in the second degree.[27] The judge delivered an eighteen-year sentence,

20. James Rada Jr, *Bessie Darling's Murder Haunts Us Still*, https://historyarchive.wordpress.com/2016/05/19/bessie-darlings-murder-haunts-us-still/ (retrieved November 10, 2020).
21. K. C. Clay, "Bessie Darling: A Brief Report on the Life of a Catoctin Mountain Proprietress," May 2018, National Park Service, 5.
22. Rada, *Bessie Darling's Murder Haunts Us Still*.
23. Rada.
24. Clay, 5.
25. Rada.
26. Rada.
27. Clay, 6.

with Shultz serving nine years before his release on parole.[28] Darling's son wanted no connection to the property, purchasing the property in foreclosure in 1934 and immediately signing it over to Bessie's parents.[29] The creation of the Catoctin Recreation Demonstration Area presented an opportunity for the family to rid themselves of the tragic property. The National Park Service made scant use of the property, so it stood empty until the park installed electricity in 1940 hoping to rent out rooms with a less rustic feel than the cabins at the three camps built by the Works Progress Administration.[30]

As World War II dawned, park usage was limited to military endeavors, placing summer rentals of the Darling house on the back burner. As part of the lend-lease agreement with the British, sailors from mine laying ships undergoing refit in Baltimore would stay out of the public eye in the Catoctin Recreational Demonstration Area, including the Bessie Darling House. British sailors from the mine layers HMS *Menestheus* and *Agamemnon* and the communications ship HMS *Bulolo* are the last recorded users of the legendary home.[31] Following the war, after years of neglect, nature reclaimed the house, covering the ruins of the once stately manor. At some point, a fire consumed the property. One local legend claims British sailors caused the fire during a raucous party. Because of her death on Halloween, its location in the middle of the woods, and its decrepit state, Bessie's legend played in the Reagans' ears. Reagan said, "Everyone joked that the ruins were haunted by the young woman who died there, and every time I passed on a horse, I'd say, 'Hi Bessie.'"[32]

After paying Bessie their respects, the couple would finish the ride returning to relax on the retreat property. During the afternoons, especially when they couldn't ride, the First Family would "curl up in front of the fire"[33] and read. Rarely utilizing the amenities such as the bowling alley, golf hole, or tennis courts, the president occasionally enjoyed the

---

28. Clay, 6.
29. Clay, 8.
30. Clay, 8.
31. Clay, 8.
32. Ronald Reagan, *An American Life*, 399.
33. Nancy Reagan, *My Turn*, 258.

skeet range on his own, as Nancy "tried skeet shooting once, but once was enough. Too loud!"[34] After dinner, they watched a movie in Aspen before retiring for the evening.

Sunday morning began with breakfast and watching "the television news and interview shows, especially *This Week with David Brinkley*."[35] Religious in their personal manner, the couple wished Camp David had a chapel to allow them to worship without causing a commotion. Nancy recalled, "After the shooting, the increased security measures made it virtually impossible for us to go to church without causing an enormous disruption. If it was known in advance that we were coming, everybody had to go through a metal detector, which just didn't seem right. But if we showed up unexpectedly, the congregants were so busy watching us that they didn't pay attention to the service. That didn't seem right either, so we rarely went to church during our years in Washington."[36] They did, however, begin the laborious process of planning a chapel at Camp David, departing office before construction began noting, "But it's good to know that just about the only thing Camp David lacked will be in place one day."[37]

Following the morning shows and wrapping up any pressing business, the couple boarded Marine One for the White House, usually arriving on the South Lawn around 3 p.m. Recalling those returns to the White House Nancy Reagan said, "But coming back was always a slight letdown, and even now, when Ronnie looks at pictures from Camp David, he feels a pang."[38]

President Reagan routinely brought letters from citizens to Camp David to personally address their concerns and suggestions. His staff would review them, "and each week chose thirty or so for me to look over. I tried to answer as many as I could during the weekends at Camp

34. Nancy Reagan, *My Turn*, 258.
35. Nancy Reagan, *My Turn*, 258.
36. Nancy Reagan, *My Turn*, 258.
37. Nancy Reagan, *My Turn*, 258.
38. Nancy Reagan, *My Turn*, 259.

David."[39] One such letter from Mrs. Bonnie M. Porter inquired about the feasibility and fiscal responsibility of his transportation to Camp David. Reagan's response: "We don't take Air Force One to Camp David. The camp is only 20 minutes from the White House by helicopter. The helicopters have to fly a required number of hours every week to keep crew and machine in shape."[40] One memorable exchange occurred between the president and a young Rudolph "Ruddy" Hines of Washington, DC. A frequent author of letters to the president, Reagan answered Ruddy's many questions, including about the time he spent at Camp David, signing letters, "Your Pen Pal." "I ride [horses] on weekends up at Camp David. I tried Rock Creek Park once but so many Secret Service agents had to go along and the concern about security was so great it didn't seem worth it. I'll just keep on doing it at Camp David and of course at our ranch when I can get to California. I'll be there this Thanksgiving for a few days and riding every day."[41]

As much as a president would prefer a time to get away from it all, even Camp David cannot seclude the individual from the ever-present office of the presidency. Just like those before and after, Reagan dealt with crises—foreign and domestic, personal and professional.

Early in Reagan's first term, trouble erupted with the air traffic controller union. In July 1981 while at Camp David, "Transportation Secretary Drew Lewis paid him a visit at Camp David with news that the union representing air traffic controllers was about to strike."[42] The union sought pay increases and a thirty-two-hour workweek. Reagan never wavered from his initial reaction upon hearing the news at Camp David: If the air traffic controllers went on strike, he would fire them as he felt deeply any strike by a federal employee was illegal—especially air traffic controllers whose oath of acceptance stated they would not strike.

In September 1983 as civil war raged in Lebanon, the president received calls at Camp David from both Secretary of Defense Caspar

---

39. Ronald Reagan, *An American Life*, 398.
40. Kiron K. Skinner, *Reagan A Life in Letters*, 302.
41. Skinner, 799.
42. Walsh, 299.

Weinberger and Deputy National Security Advisor Bud McFarlane informing him, "Syria had launched a ground-to-air missile at one of our unarmed reconnaissance planes during a routine sweep over Beirut."[43] Reagan ordered an airstrike against the offending missile sites, destroying a number of those sites, and resulting in the loss of one American serviceman and the capture of another. However, the attack led, in part, to a ceasefire in Lebanon two days later.

December 1984 brought Margaret Thatcher to Camp David for a debriefing of her meeting with Mikhail Gorbachev, then secretary of the Soviet Central Committee. Thatcher relayed how Gorbachev "expressed strong Soviet reservations over the SDI [Space Defense Initiative]"[44] Reagan sensed his good friend also harbored misgivings about SDI and the resulting removal of the American nuclear umbrella if either SDI or Reagan's hopes of eliminating nuclear weapons materialized. He assured Thatcher, "We were simply embarking on a long-term research effort, not making a commitment to deploy the SDI."[45]

On July 12, 1985, Reagan headed to Bethesda Naval Hospital to allow his doctors to remove a colon polyp discovered in March of that year. Expecting the procedure to be routine, the president and Mrs. Reagan made plans to head to Camp David after the anticipated one-night stay at Bethesda. The procedure had seemed to go according to plan, at least until the doctors spoke alone with Nancy while the president recovered. They had discovered a mass that was, at best, precancerous but most likely a malignant tumor needing removal. The doctors offered three choices. Mrs. Reagan recalled, "We could continue up to Camp David, as we had planned, and then return to Bethesda on Sunday for an operation on Monday morning. Or we could stay where we were and have it taken care of the following morning. Or, if absolutely necessary, we could wait ten days and schedule the operation after the state visit by President Li of China."[46] Knowing her husband's inclinations, Nancy preferred having

---

43. Ronald Reagan, *An American Life*, 464.
44. Ronald Reagan, *An American Life*, 609.
45. Ronald Reagan, *An American Life*, 609.
46. Nancy Reagan, *My Turn*, 272.

the issue taken care of while at Bethesda, so she decided "to play on his feelings about GoLytely, which he absolutely hates. Otherwise, he might have wanted to go right on up to Camp David."[47] (GoLytely is a prescription medicine used to clean the colon before procedures.) After the tumor was removed, Regan responded to those asking about his cancer diagnosis saying, "I didn't have cancer. I had something inside of me that had cancer in it, and it was removed."[48]

Nancy's own cancer diagnosis also played out inside the boundary of Camp David. Days after a mastectomy, Nancy and the president headed to the mountain for some private time to aid her recovery. Before departure Friday afternoon, Nancy learned her staff had received over thirty-six thousand notes and cards from around the world.[49] Saturday, less than a week after her surgery, Nancy began the arm exercises recommended by her doctors, specifically to swing her arms when walking. "I think the Secret Service men [behind] me must have thought I was crazy because I was swinging my arms back and forth so vigorously."[50] Three weeks later she noted she was back at the gym "with John Hutton [the White House physician] to do my exercises."[51] Her openness regarding her breast cancer and mastectomy helped destigmatize the illness and inspired women to seek early detection, thereby saving many lives.

Reagan's biggest scandal, the Iran-Contra Affair, invaded the quiet of Camp David. The weekend before Thanksgiving 1986, Reagan recalled, "Nancy and I spent the weekend at Camp David, where the weather was crisp and very cold. I spent a good part of Saturday and Sunday watching myself being pilloried on television because of the Iran initiative."[52] The following week, more news exploded regarding the White House and the National Security Council—specifically Oliver North, at ground zero of transferring funds to Nicaragua. As the scandal grew, the Tower

---

47. Nancy Reagan, *My Turn*, 272.
48. Nancy Reagan, *My Turn*, 273.
49. Nancy Reagan, *My Turn*, 299.
50. Nancy Reagan, *My Turn*, 299.
51. Nancy Reagan, *My Turn*, 310.
52. Ronald Reagan, *An American Life*, 530.

Commission convened hearings to determine the extent of the allegations. In February 1987, new evidence arose concerning Colonel North. Nancy Reagan remembered North claimed spending "several weekends with us at Camp David. But he was never at Camp David. He said he sometimes spent time alone with Ronnie in the Oval Office. But that never happened."[53]

Over two weekends at Camp David in the middle of February 1987, Nancy Reagan discussed her feelings with Ronnie regarding Don Regan, the president's chief of staff. In early February, the acrimony between the chief of staff and the First Lady boiled over during a phone call resulting in Regan hanging up on the First Lady, not the first such occurrence. During their visit to Camp David that weekend, Nancy informed Ronnie with vehemence "how disappointed [she] was in the whole situation, and how morale had sunk very low in the office."[54] The tension surfaced in the news, with reporters assuming Nancy as the source leaking information regarding the arguments on the telephone, a charge she vociferously denied. "I *didn't* make them public. I didn't speak to a single reporter about Don Regan. I spoke to Ronnie a number of times, but never to the press."[55] She even took a call from Mike Wallace at Camp David, and she told him "Please tell Chris [Wallace's son] that I did *not* leak the story to the press about Don's hanging up on me."[56] After a deluge of negative press over the furor, on February 27, Nancy's view prevailed as Don Regan resigned as chief of staff.

Camp David served as a quiet second home for the Reagans to escape the busy world of the presidency for a few days at a time. Its isolation allowed them to recharge and reconnect away from the draining pressure of the public eye. They let their guards down ever so slightly around the staff stationed on the mountain and showed glimpses of their true selves. In fact, Reagan's comfort level inspired him to wear his glasses at Camp

---

53. Nancy Reagan, *My Turn*, 326.
54. Nancy Reagan, *My Turn*, 327.
55. Nancy Reagan, *My Turn*, 330.
56. Nancy Reagan, *My Turn*, 328.

David instead of his contact lenses[57] and gather bags of acorns as treats for the squirrels outside the Oval Office.[58] Nancy would dress casually wearing jeans and redecorating as she saw fit, "because there wasn't a whisper of controversy about the renovations I made there. Because the entire place is off-limits to the press, nobody ever knew what I did. Not that I changed all that much. The furniture was drab, so I had some of it slipcovered and painted... And when I saw how narrow the windows were in the cabins, I had them enlarged so you could enjoy the magnificent view."[59]

Despite the new openness of Camp David for Presidents Ford and Carter, Reagan reversed course and slammed the gates shut, even to his staff. Returning access to that of the days of Roosevelt, Camp David once again became a personal retreat for the president and his family. This is understandable because Reagan's preferred getaway was on the other side of the country in California. Following Reagan's example, no subsequent president has attempted to reinstate the openness of Ford's administration regarding Camp David. Others have held summits, but none have opened the gates for the press to walk freely and conduct wide-ranging interviews. In fact, most presidents have followed Reagan's lead and closely guarded the privacy of Camp David, fueling the mysterious secrecy of the retreat and its role in the presidency.

Reagan's extensive use of the facility, and its restorative nature on his soul, did not escape the notice of his vice president. As the presidency passed to George H. W. Bush, the retreat's operational tempo would increase, despite the Bush compound's relative proximity in Maine.

57. Walsh, 298.
58. Nancy Reagan, *My Turn,* 259.
59. Nancy Reagan, *My Turn,* 258–259.

CHAPTER 12

Family

GEORGE H. W. BUSH FIRST JOURNEYED UP THE MOUNTAIN IN 1972
summoned by President Nixon to discuss serving as the chairman of
the Republican National Committee, a posting he accepted against the
advice of his wife, Barbara.[1] As Reagan's vice president, George H. W.
Bush found himself on the short list of those invited to Camp David,
even then visiting only three times as vice president, and only during
Reagan's second term in office. Upon his inauguration on January 20,
1989, the staff of the retreat saw a complete reversal in use of the camp.

The frequency of use would remain the same, with Bush averaging
over thirty visits a year, yet he frequently brought along friends and family using the retreat not for himself but for relaxing and working with
those close to him. Bush kept the guest list secret, "especially entertainers
and sports figures who didn't want their political associations known,"
because "the Bushes didn't want their visitors to think they were being
exploited politically by their hosts."[2]

His visits to Camp David comprised more than relaxation, as he
worked frequently from the mountain. Each morning, including weekends, he checked in with his staff receiving "his national security briefing
and domestic policy update starting at 7 a.m."[3] Completing his work for
the day, the president would then engage in relaxation including tennis,

1. Barbara Bush, *Barbara Bush: A Memoir*, 98.
2. Walsh, 302.
3. Walsh, 302.

skeet shooting, jogging, bowling tournaments, and walks with Barbara and the family, especially the grandchildren.[4]

Bush preferred the company of family so much that, just before Christmas 1989, he cancelled a scheduled trip to Camp David at the last minute because Barbara couldn't join him. Barbara Bush was scheduled to fly from Texas to Andrews Air Force Base and then drive up to join her husband, but bad weather closed in and threatened an icy drive up the mountain at night as Barbara wouldn't arrive until late. "George opted not to go on the chance that I couldn't make it. Thus, bad weather gave us one of the very nicest experiences we had in George's four years as president: watching the Christmas decorations go up."[5]

Following two hectic weeks of White House parties leading up to Christmas, the couple finally broke free of Washington on December 23, 1989, beginning a Bush family tradition: Christmas at Camp David. While in office Barbara and George spent all four Christmases at Camp David, with their son George W. Bush continuing the tradition during his own presidency spending eight Christmases on the mountain. Doing so alleviated the number of personnel needed to support the family and allowed more White House staff to spend time with their respective families than if the First Family stayed in the residence or traveled to Kennebunkport.

During that first Christmas Eve, Bush "flew down to the White House to have a press conference and back again."[6] Upon his return, he headed to the gym to engage in one of his favorite activities when at Camp: Wallyball, essentially a volleyball game played in a racquetball court ensuring constant activity and exciting scoring rallies. President Bush introduced the game to the staff at Camp David and frequently invited them to play alongside and against him.

Yet, during that first Christmas the president fully felt the weight of the office. Just four days earlier, Bush deployed troops to Panama to oust Manuel Noriega. The operation would continue through the end of the

4. Walsh, 302.
5. Barbara Bush, 317.
6. Barbara Bush, 321.

year with Noriega surrendering on January 3, 1990. Driving home the cost of combat on service members and their families, during a Christmas caroling session, a Navy chaplain approached the president recounting a recent trip to Wilford Hall in San Antonio, "I told the boys that if they had a message for the president, I'd be seeing you tonight. They said, please tell the president we're proud to serve a great country, and we're proud to serve a great man like George Bush."[7]

As part of Mikhail Gorbachev's visit to Washington in May of 1990, the Bushes hosted the Soviet leader and his wife, Raisa, at Camp David on the weekend of June 2–3. As the two couples flew above the Maryland countryside, Barbara noticed awe on the faces of the Soviet personnel as they sped over homes on the short flight. "One Soviet security man couldn't believe it when a Secret Service agent told him that he lived down below in one of the lovely subdivisions."[8] The mountain visits lowered barriers allowing leaders and staff to see the other side in a more human light.

After arriving, Barbara and Raisa went to their cabins to change for a walk around the grounds of the retreat. As they reconvened for their walk, Barbara noticed very high heels on Raisa's feet. Always compassionate, Barbara suggested Raisa change into more suitable footwear, but Raisa claimed these were her walking shoes, so Barbara wisely "decided we should tour the camp in a golf cart instead."[9] At lunch, Barbara noticed that despite her attempts to save Raisa's feet by choosing the golf cart, her feet looked as if the pair had walked the entire time. Talking over a wide range of subjects, Barbara confessed that Raisa "suddenly became a person to me and not just this woman who had done all her homework (although, as always, she had)."[10] It was yet another example of Camp David working its magic and bringing stated enemies together through their shared humanity.

---

7. George W. Bush, *Decision Points*, 184–185.
8. Barbara Bush, 342.
9. Barbara Bush, 342.
10. Barbara Bush, 343.

After lunch with their husbands, the women continued talking while the leaders discussed things outside. Following the afternoon session, the couples made their way to the horseshoe pit Bush installed shortly after taking office. Having never seen horseshoes, Gorbachev seemed perplexed at the odd setup, which surprised Bush. Not wanting to offend his gracious host, after hearing the basics of the game, the Soviet leader "gamely participated in the president's pastime and threw a ringer on his first toss."[11] Following the meeting, commenting on this stroke of beginner's luck to reporters, President Bush quipped, "I pride myself as a horseshoe player, and President Gorbachev picked up a horseshoe, never having played the game to my knowledge, and literally, literally—all you horseshoe players out there—threw a ringer on the first time. Really. And I like to think—there's not much more to say."[12] Retreat staff promptly retrieved the magical horseshoe and mounted it on a plaque for presentation to Gorbachev prior to his departure.

On August 4, 1990, Bush gathered his senior advisors on the mountain to determine a plan to confront Saddam Hussein who had invaded Kuwait just two days earlier. As tensions with Iraq rose, Bush summoned the Joint Chiefs to Camp David on December 1, 1990, to discuss "the details of what the war might be like."[13] While at Camp David over the Christmas holidays, on New Year's Eve Bush wrote a letter to all five of his children discussing his "thoughts and emotions on the eve of war."[14] Making the decision to send ground troops into Kuwait to drive out Hussein, Bush flew to Camp David on February 22, 1991, as "a ruse to suggest that nothing special was about to happen. The next day, he flew back to Washington to announce that the ground war designed to push Iraq out of Kuwait had begun."[15]

---

11. Walsh, 302.

12. "George H. W. Bush, Exchange with Reporters Following Meetings at Camp David, Maryland, with President Mikhail Gorbachev of the Soviet Union," June 2, 1990. https://bush41library.tamu .edu/archives/public-papers/1943 (retrieved May 21, 2020).

13. Walsh, 301.

14. Walsh, 301.

15. Walsh, 301.

During the run-up to the war, the Bushes continued visiting Camp David, frequently bringing friends, "people with no agenda and with whom George could relax."[16] In mid-January 1991, the family arrived with Arnold Schwarzenegger in tow during a substantial snowstorm that brought out their inner children, as guests scrounged around for anything that would allow them to slide down the snow-covered hills after church services. However, a slight thaw on Saturday followed by a solid freeze overnight, provided an icy surface upon which to ride. As Barbara Bush hurtled down the hill, she recalled "spinning around and around so fast that I can still feel the fear that I felt. I knew that I should fall off, but I just could not seem to let go."[17] Those watching, sensing impending disaster, implored Barbara to bail out and sled another day, to no avail. "Luckily, I hit a tree with both my legs and not my head, which might easily have happened. I was shaky . . . but not hurt . . . I felt."[18]

Ever cautious, her doctor insisted on properly evaluating the injury at a hospital, so off to Hagerstown, Maryland, Barbara Bush went in an ambulance. As she exited, she saw "George, Arnold, Spike and Maria and all the grandchildren sleighing."[19] Diagnosed with a thin fracture of the fibula, she endured a walking boot for several weeks. The incident played well in speeches over the next few weeks. "Poor Arnold [Schwarzenegger]. For weeks afterwards I claimed in my speeches that the last thing I heard before crashing was Arnold yelling, 'Break a leg!' and therefore I was never going to invite an actor for the weekend again."[20] The incident remained a joke between the First Family and the governor, with President Bush remarking before Schwarzenegger received an award in June 1991, "Arnold spent a day with us up at Camp David, and competing with Barbara in tobogganing, she broke her leg. Then Arnold spent a day with us at the White House promoting fitness, and I ended up in the

16. Barbara Bush, 387.
17. Barbara Bush, 388.
18. Barbara Bush, 388.
19. Barbara Bush, 388.
20. Barbara Bush, 388.

hospital with arterial fibrillation, or something like that . . . Talk about 'The Terminator.'"[21]

During a visit in May 1991, President Bush experienced shortness of breath jogging inside the boundary of Camp David. Barbara was swimming when she was informed of the news. She put on a robe and headed to the medical facility to check on her husband and found him "hooked up to a cardiac monitor and with an IV in his arm."[22] Despite the doctors' concern over a fibrillating heart, the president broke the tension of the moment through humor. Looking at Barbara entering the room, he joked, "'Remembering how sympathetic I was when you broke your leg, I know you'll be caring.' That was a family joke, as I had kidded him about continuing to sled while I went off in the ambulance to be X-rayed."[23] Just as Barbara had been, Bush was sent off to the hospital, this time in Marine One with a machine monitoring his heart and a needle in his arm "in case he went into cardiac arrest."[24] After more tests, a few days later the Bushes received the formal diagnosis: Graves' disease. The same disease affecting Barbara's eyes affected George's heart.

The emergency trip to the hospital from Camp David drove the final nail in the coffin for reporters traveling to Thurmont on standby during presidential visits to Camp David. Unaware of the developing health scare six miles away, and with the president's staff keeping a tight lip, the journalists continued their normal weekend activities in Thurmont, congregating at the Cozy Inn. Long gone were the days of the duck blind and the press trailer. And it was only after the Bushes arrived at Bethesda Naval Hospital that the reporters in Thurmont learned of the president's condition. The episode highlighted the lack of sense in financing a team of reporters standing by for news that was routinely released through other channels.

21. George H. W. Bush, "Remarks at the Simon Wiesenthal Center Dinner in Los Angeles, California," June 16, 1991, https://bush41library.tamu.edu/archives/public-papers/3103 (retrieved May 21, 2020).
22. Barbara Bush, 410.
23. Barbara Bush, 410.
24. Barbara Bush, 410.

The fall of 1991 brought much joy to the president and those around him. The Bushes' dog Millie gave birth to a single male pup, who later found a home with the Bushes' son Marvin and his family. As autumn touched off the fire of color in the mountains, George invited Ranger, Millie's pup, to Camp David for the weekend, and, according to Barbara, suggested "that [Marvin's wife] Margaret bring Ranger over to the White House on Thursday nights so he would be sure to be there in time to leave for Camp the next day. Then he suggested that we return him on Monday morning instead of Sunday."[25] Ranger, everything the president desired in a dog, found a new home at the White House.

Ranger charged "around Camp David in the snow and the rain" endearing himself to everyone. Bush eventually installed a device in his Laurel office that "looked like an old-fashioned gumball machine, but the contraption actually dispensed multicolored dog biscuits to the family canines. A handle in the shape of a bone would release the treats into a slot. Bush later said the dogs never got the knack of pushing it, so they would stand forlornly near the contraption until the President of the United States took pity on them and pushed the handle himself."[26]

Ranger finagled treats from everyone he met. On February 6, 1992, Bush sent an important memo to the entire staff concerning Ranger's expanding waistline. Claiming a choice between a diet or entering Ranger "in the Houston Fat Stock show as a Prime Hereford," he demanded a pledge of all offices to refrain from enabling Ranger's treat habit.[27] Specifically discussing Camp David, "Although Ranger will still be permitted to roam at Camp David, the Camp David staff including the Marines, Naval personnel, All Civilians and Kids are specifically instructed to 'rat' on anyone seen feeding Ranger. Ranger has been asked to wear a '*Do not feed me*' badge in addition to his ID."[28]

June 27, 1992, brought a joyous occasion of another kind to Camp David and the newly constructed chapel, which had become an important spiritual refuge for the entire family, and that was a wedding. It was

25. Barbara Bush, 361–362.
26. Walsh, 303.
27. Barbara Bush, 362.
28. Barbara Bush, 362.

the first and only wedding inside the retreat's perimeter. George and Barbara's daughter, Doro, married Robert "Bobby" Koch. After a rehearsal dinner at the White House the previous evening, the joyful crowd gathered on the mountain preparing for the momentous event. "All the off-duty White House butlers volunteered to serve as a present for Doro. . . . White House chefs Pierre Chambrin, Franette McCulloch, and Roland Mesnier made a beautiful cake and cooked a lovely buffet supper."[29]

The "chapel looked so beautiful with peach roses, and there was music in the balcony. . . . All four boys had on blue suits and the ties Bobby had given them,"[30] but the president wasn't prepared for the service. Barbara recounted, "At 4:30 the father of the bride showed up to change into his clothes and asked what people were wearing to the wedding. I told him his navy-blue suit would be just fine. I couldn't believe it when he confessed that he hadn't brought a suit. He said that he thought it would be informal!"[31] The president cobbled together acceptable attire, and the wedding went off without a hitch as the Camp David chaplain led the service. Like many other weddings, the groom served as the object of a practical joke, revealed during the service. "When Doro and Bobby knelt to be blessed there was a BUSH/QUAYLE reelection sticker on Bobby's soles. His brothers put it there. Neither George nor I noticed. I suspect we were praying."[32]

Losing reelection in November 1992 deflated spirits and spurred the First Family to reminisce about Camp David during a series of visits marking "one last time" for their friends. The first weekend after the loss, Colin Powell, then chairman of the Joint Chiefs of Staff, joined the president and discussed possible changes with the new administration. Later that month, the president planned a big weekend at Camp David just before Thanksgiving, inviting five Republican governors along with Amy Grant, Bruce Willis, Demi Moore, and their respective families. During that visit, Amy and her husband, Gary Chapman, performed with the

29. Barbara Bush, 468–469.
30. Barbara Bush, 469.
31. Barbara Bush, 469.
32. Barbara Bush, 469.

chapel choir during a vespers service that also included John Ashcroft singing gospel favorites.[33]

December brought the annual Camp David Christmas where the large Bush clan gathered to enjoy mountain festivities one last time. The grandchildren dressed up, held secret play rehearsals, made costumes, and enjoyed the magic of the mountain. This visit contained "the well-known snowball fight where George got a black eye from a snowball that had a tiny piece of ice in it. The guilty party was so upset that George swore her to secrecy, and he, in turn, never told on her."[34]

The weekend of January 15–17, 1993, marked President Bush's last visit to Camp David while in office. Arriving at Camp David for the last time proved emotional for the family. Guests, including the prime minister of Canada, Brian Mulroney, and his wife; George and Norma Strait; the Joint Chiefs of Staff; the Supreme Court justices and spouses; as well as the heads of the transition teams, including Vernon Jordan and Warren Christopher for President-elect Clinton, filled all the available beds.[35] President Bush scheduled one final Saturday night vespers service at the chapel with George Strait singing "All My Ex's Live in Texas" to joyous laughter and ending the evening with "The Cowboy Rides Away," prompting tears from the Bushes.[36] Following the final chapel service the next morning, as most guests departed, the Straits remained so the Georges could watch the Dallas Cowboys play that afternoon.

After the game, the camp staff gathered in the helicopter hangar surprising the Bushes with a farewell ceremony. After a short, emotional speech the Camp commander turned to the president, who, overcome with emotion, couldn't speak. Over four short years, Camp David had become a second home and place of respite for the Bushes, and they couldn't hide their disappointment over possibly never returning to see the special family who adopted them as one of their own.

---

33. Barbara Bush, 503. This would not be the last time John Ashcroft sang gospel songs while at Camp. He would make a repeat appearance during George W. Bush's first year in office.
34. Barbara Bush, 508.
35. Barbara Bush, 514.
36. Barbara Bush, 514.

Any look into the life of George H. W. Bush reveals the importance of family and his love for each member of his family. More than any other president, H. W. Bush transformed Camp David into a retreat not just for the president, but for the president's entire family. He placed a horseshoe pit next to a playground, so he could spend time doing an activity he loved with the grandchildren he adored and spoiled as only a grandparent can. This family legacy remains today as those presidents following Bush routinely bring family on most visits, but also extend the invitations to friends, even famous ones, with a request to keep the visits discreet in an effort to maintain the privacy of the family as well as the veil of secrecy that permeates the humble retreat. Camp David is perfectly suited for the entire First Family and their friends because it is the only place the First Family can be themselves and escape the ever-present prying eyes following their every move. Behind the steel gates of the mountain retreat the First Family can maintain relationships forged before they were thrust into the presidential world. At some point the magic ends and the First Family must return to their previous lives. Camp David provides space to strengthen those relationships and eases the transition from First Family to everyday citizens.

CHAPTER 13

Evergreen Chapel

ON NOVEMBER 22, 1963, A CONTRACTOR NAMED KENNETH PLUMMER was working on Camp when news broke of President Kennedy's assassination.[1] Like the rest of the country, Plummer followed the day's events on the news, watching replays on television. From his perspective at the mountain retreat, he noticed two things: the depth of care the staff of Camp David had for "their president" and that neither Jackie and her children, nor the staff, had a dedicated space to grieve the loss of the president away from the public eye. During an interview for his local paper in 1988, Plummer reminisced, "We were all just sitting there. I thought it would have been better if we had had somewhere to go, a chapel of some kind."[2] In a moment of national mourning, he vowed to ensure the construction of a chapel on the grounds of Camp David.[3]

Fast-forward to October 30, 1987. Ken Plummer received authorization from Secretary of the Navy James Webb to form a nonprofit with one purpose: raising funds for construction of a Camp David chapel. The next step occurred on July 2, 1988, when President Reagan and Nancy Reagan broke ground to begin construction on Plummer's twenty-five-year-old goal. More than figureheads breaking ground at their retreat, the Reagans provided the first donation toward the chapel's construction, a

---

1. Ken Plummer's connection to camp wasn't just as a contractor, he spent several weekends at the retreat before it's conversion to presidential use during his time as a Boy Scout utilizing Camp #3.
2. Ted Haas, "Chapel Called Gift from 'People of Faith,'" *Chambersburg Public Opinion*, December 7, 1997.
3. Giorgione, *Inside Camp David*, 192.

gift of $1,000. A ceremonial groundbreaking because construction was not ready to proceed. Plummer purposely held off construction until the project was fully funded. Later realizing physical progress would spur more donations, Plummer relented, and construction commenced mid-1990, once $650,000 of the $1,000,000 budget was on hand.

While frustrating for all involved, such a delay revealed an unexpected benefit by providing time for the Navy to identify a chaplain for Camp David. As the search progressed, President George H. W. Bush expressed a desire to worship with camp staff and families during visits. In the interim before the first chaplain arrived, chaplains from local bases rotated to Camp David providing services when the president was in residence. Apparently, preaching on the Prodigal Son was a popular theme in 1989 as three consecutive chaplains used the famous parable as the basis for their sermons. Noticing the same Scripture on repeat, Barbara Bush commented to the commanding officer, "Well, I think we've covered that one pretty well."[4] The commanding officer, already providing the guest chaplains a list of dos and don'ts when preaching to the president, added a prohibition on preaching the parable of the Prodigal Son.

As fundraising continued, Ken Plummer ensured the chapel represented a diverse group of Americans. When soliciting funds, he envisioned most monetary gifts in the $1,000 to $50,000 range and set a limit for any individual cash gift at $100,000. He further set a limit of $300,000 from any single religious tradition. Desiring a chapel representing the rich, religious diversity of the country given on behalf of the American people, the donation limits helped ensure this could happen. His strategy worked as most donations were $1,000 or less with only two individuals donating the maximum gifts of $100,000.

In the late 1980s, a Maryland manufacturer breathed its final gasps amid declining demand: W. P. Moller Pipe Organ Company. Founded by a Danish immigrant, it was once the largest pipe organ manufacturer in the world, producing thousands of organs during its century of operation, including organs at the Fox Theater in Atlanta, Georgia, and the Basilica

---

4. Giorgione, *Inside Camp David*, 194.

of the National Shrine of the Immaculate Conception in Washington, DC. Moller Organs anchored the business district of Hagerstown, fifteen miles west of the presidential retreat. A thriving small business since 1881 after moving from Greencastle, Pennsylvania, their future had faded as demand for pipe organs declined rapidly in the 1980s. Seeking to keep the chapel's construction as local as possible, selecting this world-renowned company—which also supplied organs to all three military service academies—for the presidential chapel was inevitable.

Keeping to the committee's goal of limiting individual contributions to $100,000 resulted in the selection of an 827-pipe organ, seemingly too large for the space, which immediately draws your eyes to the center sixteen-foot pipe (the smallest pipe, at six inches, hides in the rafters out of sight). Paid for through a contribution from the Knights of Columbus, the organ design began in November 1989 with an eventual cost of $107,000. Due to the security concerns of constructing a massive organ for Camp David, Moller built and tested the organ at the factory prior to complete disassembly and reassembly at the chapel in early 1991.[5] Because the chapel had not yet hired a musician, the president of Moller Organs, Ronald Ellis, by no means a professional organist, played the inaugural notes of his company's creation during the dedication in April 1991.

One personal donation, valued at the maximum individual amount of $100,000—yet priceless as a one-of-a-kind piece of art—has an intriguing backstory.

The story revolves around Dr. Rudolph Sandon, a renowned stained-glass artist who designed and constructed the stained-glass windows, and the protagonist of a larger-than-life story. Rudy grew up in Italy, and at eighteen years of age, while studying art at the University of Padua, most likely to hone his skill before taking up his family's traditional craft, he received notice to join the Italian Army. After his enlistment, before the winds of the Second World War blew, Rudy served in distant campaigns

5. Terry Headlee, "Moller Organ Debuts Before President."

such as the Ethiopian War.[6] During World War II he was assigned to the Alpine Corps serving throughout France, Greece, and Russia as he rose to the rank of lieutenant colonel with rumors he spent time as a bodyguard for Mussolini. An accomplished skier, Rudy competed on Italy's military patrol (the precursor to modern biathlon) team in the 1936 Winter Olympics in Garmish, Germany, and planned to compete again in Helsinki in 1940 until war interrupted the Olympics. According to a secondary account recalled by Patrick Cullen, Rudy's Italian team won the gold medal in 1936 when military patrol debuted as a demonstration sport.[7]

A legend exists that while serving on Mussolini's personal detail, Rudy secretly provided information to the French Resistance saving at least one French village during the War and earning him the Croix de Guerre.[8] Continuing this legend, the Croix attracted the attention of Billy "Wild Bill" Donovan, himself a recipient of the Croix and founder of the Office of Strategic Services. Wild Bill realized Rudy's precarious situation in Italy and secured his passage to the United States, ensuring his safety and ability to embark on a new life in America where the two larger-than-life personalities remained lifelong friends, possibly living in the same neighborhood at one time.

Regardless of the circumstances surrounding his arrival in America, Rudy thrived in his new home. Eventually earning doctoral degrees in theology, art, and architecture, Rudy's story reflects those stories of many immigrants to America. Arriving with nothing much to his name and no friends or family in the United States, he set about making his mark, settling near the banks of Lake Erie in Painesville, Ohio. A sixth-generation stained-glass maker, Rudy introduced his family's tradition to the United States, craftsmanship begun in 1736 by Galeazzo Sandon. From a distinguished family line of artisans, Rudy's father, Arturo,

6. "Museum Window Reflects Masonry and America," April 1975, The Northern Light, Ancient Accepted Scottish Rite of Freemasonry, Northern Masonic Jurisdiction, United States of America, 14.

7. Patrick J. Cullen, "Stained Glass Artist's Leaded Glass Came Knife."

8. Cullen, "Stained Glass Artist's Leaded Glass Came Knife."

crafted the only stained-glass Rose window within St. Peter's Cathedral in Rome.[9]

As chapel fundraising began, Joe Bartlett, a brigadier general in the US Marine Corps Reserve and clerk at the US House of Representatives, connected the nonprofit overseeing construction with Rudy. Rudy eagerly donated his time and material crafting a stunning pair of windows for the chapel. Originally envisioned as two full walls of stained glass, at the request of President and Mrs. Bush, who preferred a view of the natural surroundings of Camp David from inside the chapel, Rudy revised the design to two stained glass trees each set within a larger clear window.

Walking into the chapel, the stunning stained glass trees direct the viewer away from the Moeller organ and the rich oak color of the altar area. The left tree represents the Tree of Life, with the right tree representing the Tree of Knowledge. Each tree has four "fruits" hanging from its branches with a larger emblem embedded in the trunk's center. Scanning the Tree of Life branches from the rear of the chapel, the observer first notices the sea as the waters of life with an anchor of hope amid the raging water. The next glance takes in a mountain representing the faith of humanity and the quest to overcome the mountains in life. Gazing forward, there is an abstract vision of God in vibrant red, orange, and yellow glass. These three colors were purposely chosen to symbolize love, goodness, and beauty. Now the viewer sees a globe with the word "Oikumene" over the top hemisphere depicting ecumenism, as people of all or no faith are welcome in the chapel. Finally, at the front of the chapel, the last emblem on the Tree of Life is a book representing the teaching of life.[10]

On sunny days, glancing to the rafters on the right, the keen observer notices small red apples in the upper reaches of the Tree of Knowledge, an homage to the original tree in the Garden of Eden. As with the Tree of Life, there are five emblems within or hanging from branches of this tree. In the front, right above the piano where President Clinton would sing with the choir, there is a simple sheaf of wheat signifying the bounty

9. Mary Elizabeth Dunbar, "Sandon Studios R.D. Little Valley, New York."

10. Rudolph Sandon, "Descriptive Summary of Medallions for the Camp David Chapel," Sandon Studios, June 12, 1989.

of God. Next, tracing the tree to the back of the chapel, there are seven small flames, reminders of the seven gifts of wisdom: Honor, Intellect, Council, Divinity, Wisdom and Understanding, Virtue, and Fear of God. At the center of the Tree of Knowledge is an unmissable interpretation of the presidential seal with the words "We the People" prominently below the seal, acknowledging the strength of the United States. Just to the right of the trunk is a white dove flying with a sprig in its beak, signifying the universal desire for peace. Continuing to the rear of the chapel, the final medallion highlights the lamp of knowledge lit by a flame, depicting the enlightenment of humanity.[11]

Rudy created this ecumenical design, without religious symbols, to create a space for everyone to encounter their divine. In keeping with the ecumenical nature of the chapel, Muslim, Jewish, and Christian faith communities donated various relics and faith-specific items and truly made Evergreen Chapel a gift from all of the United States.

Not all the material donations were as grand as stained-glass windows or the Moeller organ. One such gift is so subtle it is easily overlooked as it blends into the chapel's design. Outside the main entrance to the chapel is a patio made of the same local flagstone as the chapel's interior flooring. Because of the patio's elevation from the ground, a wall is necessary to keep young, rambunctious children safe from falling a few feet to the ground. This stone wall first resided at Scenic View Orchards in Sabillasville, Maryland, one of the many local orchards dotting the hills and roadsides in the surrounding area. Donated by Betty Calimer, the matriarch of the family-owned orchard business, the wall was removed from her property stone by stone and repurposed as the patio wall for the chapel.

Built onto a section of the patio wall is the ship's bell from the USS *Endicott* (DD 495). Commissioned in 1943 and named after Samuel Endicott, a gunner onboard the USS *Enterprise* during the Barbary Wars, the *Endicott* conducted numerous convoy operations in the Atlantic Ocean during WWII. One such convoy connects her legacy with Camp David. In January 1945, the *Endicott* received top-secret orders

11. Sandon, 2.

directing a rendezvous with the cruiser *Quincy* (CA 71) off the coast of Bermuda on January 26, 1945, to form an escort convoy to Gibraltar. Once at Gibraltar, the *Endicott* loitered awaiting the return escort voyage. It wasn't until completing the escort mission that the crew learned their group escorted President Roosevelt to the Yalta conference. Soon after this escort mission, the *Endicott* underwent conversion to a high-speed minesweeper and in May 1945 transferred to the Pacific Theater, arriving in San Diego three days after the surrender of Japan.[12] The end of the war only highlighted the importance of minesweepers with *Endicott* arriving in Okinawa on September 23, 1945, to clear the Yellow Sea of mines.[13] The *Endicott* continued serving through the Korean War, eventually decommissioning in August 1954.

On April 21, 1991, after decades of planning and years of construction and fundraising, Evergreen Chapel[14] at Camp David was formally dedicated. President George H. W. Bush received the chapel as a gift from the American people. Various faith leaders, including the archbishop of Washington, DC, Cardinal Hickey, and the Navy chief of chaplains, attended the dedication. First Lady Barbara Bush read from Revelation 21 as President Bush formally opened the interfaith worship space between prayers and readings offered from multiple faith groups. The president exerted some personal prerogatives inviting friends to attend the ceremony, including best-selling Christian singer Sandi Patti, who wrote and performed an original song for the occasion.[15]

In its thirty years of service to the presidents and their guests, every president has attended faith services in Evergreen Chapel.

---

12. https://www.history.navy.mil/research/histories/ship-histories/danfs/e/endicott.html.

13. https://www.history.navy.mil/research/histories/ship-histories/danfs/e/endicott.html.

14. The name comes from submissions from personnel stationed at Camp David at the time. The list was comprehensive enough that other names generated during this solicitation were matched with future buildings.

15. Program for dedication of Evergreen Chapel, April 21, 1991.

CHAPTER 14

White House Annex

SOON AFTER HIS ELECTION, DURING A TRIP TO LOS ANGELES, BILL Clinton carved time in his schedule to visit Ronald Reagan. While not their first meeting, it was the most important. For over an hour, the two men chatted about the presidency with Reagan offering advice to the incoming commander in chief. One familiar piece of advice echoed that was frequently given upon election to the highest office in the land: use the retreat in the mountains of Maryland. Reagan offered sage advice to "get out of Washington every weekend you can and make thorough use of Camp David. The fresh air, the chance to freely roam the complex . . . even the brief time away from Washington were all good for body and soul."[1] As the meeting concluded, the jovial, charismatic former president presented the president-elect with a jar of red, white, and blue jellybeans (the favorite candy of the former White House resident), which President Clinton kept throughout his term of office.[2]

Having lived in the Arkansas governor's mansion for nearly ten years, Clinton arrived in Washington, DC, without a personal residence, and, not a man of wealth unlike many of his predecessors, Clinton did not own a private retreat to which he could escape. First Lady Hillary Clinton met with one predecessor who did have her own retreat, Jackie Kennedy. Hillary said, Jackie, knowing the need to escape from the chaos of the White House, "urged me to use Camp David and to stay with friends

---

1. Gibbs and Duffy, *The Presidents Club: Inside the World's Most Exclusive Fraernity,* 414.
2. Gibbs and Duffy, 415.

who had homes in secluded places so we could avoid the curiosity seekers and paparazzi."[3] Never viewing Camp David as a second home, breaking from their two immediate predecessors, the Clintons made sparing use of the camp, averaging only seven visits a year. As his presidency (and view of Camp David) progressed, the pace of visits grew from a drip to a thin stream of trips to the mountain.

Like his predecessors, Clinton wasted no time in looking over the retreat. First visiting the second weekend after the inauguration, his view of the facility was less as a personal retreat and more as a conference center to gather his advisors and work away from the public. For this first visit he summoned his cabinet and senior staff to the mountain for "a corporate-style retreat, helped along by a professional facilitator recommended by Vice President Al Gore."[4] Serving to crystallize their agenda over the next few years, this visit followed the advice of Hillary Clinton because as President Clinton said, "We'd failed in Arkansas in my first term by doing too many things at once, without a clear story line and an effort to prepare people for a long, sustained struggle."[5] Following the retreat, the communications team shaped a messaging strategy focused on themes outlined atop the mountain.

The facilitator spent the second half of the weekend bonding the new team, though not everyone showed enthusiasm toward the team-building exercises. President Clinton "enjoyed it, and managed to confess that, as a child, [he] was overweight and often ridiculed."[6] Lloyd Bentsen, secretary of the treasury, was having none of it leaving the meeting for the comfort of his cabin. Then ambassador to the United Nations, Madeline Albright recalled, "This was a bizarre event, with barely acquainted people crowded into cabins and force-fed a dose of New Age relationship building."[7] Secretary of State Warren Christopher participated "because he was the most disciplined man on the planet and thought this baby-boomer

3. Hillary Clinton, *Living History*, 137.
4. Walsh, 304.
5. Bill Clinton, *My Life*, 489.
6. Bill Clinton, 489.
7. Madeline Albright, *Madam Secretary*, 194.

version of Chinese water torture would somehow strengthen his already considerable character."[8]

Less than three months in office, grief struck the First Family as Hillary's father, Hugh Rodham died in early April 1993, just before Easter. The Clintons invited immediate family and close friends from Scranton, Pennsylvania, Hugh's hometown, to Camp David for Easter. Providing a place to alleviate the stress and worry from the funeral, they realized the uniqueness of Camp David as "the only haven where we would have the peace and privacy we craved."[9] Far from a picture-perfect weekend as cold rain enveloped the mountain, Hillary said, "It fit my mood perfectly. I went for a long walk in the drizzle with my mother, and I asked her if she wanted to live with us in the White House."[10] On Easter Sunday, the family attended services in Evergreen Chapel where Hillary recalled, "I sat in my pew and thought of how my father used to embarrass my brothers and me with his loud, off-key hymn singing. I share his tone deafness, but that morning I sang out, hoping the discordant notes might reach the heavens."[11]

Despite their early visits, the president and First Lady kept their distance during their first term. At the end of his first year, 1993, a senior official commented on the low use saying, "It doesn't surprise me that he probably feels like Camp David may be a little boring."[12] Kenneth Walsh surmised the lack of use to the likings of their daughter, Chelsea, who "preferred to entertain her friends at glamourous 1600 Pennsylvania Avenue."[13] It was a reasonable assumption as their use of Camp David rose once Chelsea departed for Stanford University during their second term.

During their visits, the First Lady indulged a passion for bowling "where she easily outshined her husband in late-night excursions to the

8. Bill Clinton, 489.
9. Hillary Clinton, 165.
10. Hillary Clinton, 165.
11. Hillary Clinton, 165.
12. Walsh, 304.
13. Walsh, 304.

Camp David lanes with friends."[14] Ever personable and extroverted, Bill Clinton routinely brought family and friends up the mountain to keep him company. Visits included watching sports, shooting skeet, horseback riding, and golfing. However, he didn't appreciate the lack of challenge presented by the chip and putt behind Aspen, preferring instead to golf at a local course with friends. At night, the crowd gathered for dinner followed by hours of movie watching and cards—once playing a game until sunrise at 6:30 the next morning.[15] Then on Sunday mornings, the president would attend church at the chapel, singing with the choir after having the music delivered to his cabin the previous day so he could practice before arriving for the service.[16]

As their first Thanksgiving in office arrived, the Clintons chose Camp David as their location to celebrate, starting a family tradition during their two terms in office. President Clinton deemed the first Thanksgiving trip special because it would be the last Thanksgiving for his mother as "cancer had spread and contaminated her blood stream."[17] His mother thoroughly enjoyed the time at the retreat, living her days to the fullest. "She enjoyed the football games on television, the meals, and visiting with the young servicemen and -women at the Camp David bar."[18]

That Thanksgiving set the stage for future holiday visits to Camp David. Year after year, the Clintons invited their families and select friends to the mountain for a holiday weekend set apart from the rigors of life in DC, where everyone gathered in Laurel lodge for a big Thanksgiving meal with all the trimmings. Hillary remembered, "Melding the traditions of my family and Bill's meant we had both bread and cornbread stuffing, pumpkin and mincemeat pies. The buffet tables were straining under the weight of all the food while everyone observed one tradition that transcends all regions: overindulging."[19] The First Family

14. Walsh, 304.
15. Walsh, 304–305.
16. Bill Clinton, 948.
17. Bill Clinton, 562.
18. Bill Clinton, 562.
19. Hillary Clinton, 202.

routinely took time during the weekend visiting the "dining hall to greet the navy and marine personnel and their families."[20] To work off the calories consumed at the dinner, the family would bowl, and, once the tryptophan kicked in, they settled into the oversized recliners in the theater to watch movies, falling asleep as needed. Although not a president known for frequent golfing, Bill said, "At least once over the weekend, no matter how cold and rainy it was, Hillary's brothers, Roger, and I would play golf with whoever else was brave enough to go."[21]

After the disastrous 1994 mid-term elections where Democrats lost control of the House for the first time in forty years with a fifty-four-seat swing and a Republican gain of eight seats in the Senate, the president convened a gathering at Camp David around New Years. Marianne Williamson, a presidential candidate herself in 2020, suggested the Clintons "get together with a group of people outside the political world to discuss Bill's goals for the remaining two years of his term."[22] Marianne invited a number of guests including Tony Robbins, Stephen Covey, Mary Katherine Bateson, and Jean Houston. Bateson and Houston impressed Hillary, spending hours in conversation with the two pondering the role of First Lady and Hillary's upcoming trip to South Asia. The two women helped Hillary as she said, " . . . understand that the role of First Lady is deeply symbolic and that I had better figure out how to make the best of it at home and on the world stage."[23] Bateson stressed the importance of symbolic actions and encouraged Hillary to include Chelsea on the upcoming South Asia trip because "by traveling to South Asia as First Lady with Chelsea [it] would send a message about the importance of daughters. Visiting poor rural women would underscore their significance."[24] Following these conversations, Hillary began to "advance the Clinton agenda through symbolic action."[25]

---

20. Bill Clinton, 562.
21. Bill Clinton, 562.
22. Hillary Clinton, 263.
23. Hillary Clinton, 265.
24. Hillary Clinton, 265.
25. Hillary Clinton, 265.

Even the presidency does not give a pass on parental duties. When your children live in the White House, important milestones occur that require attention and acknowledgment. February 1996 brought Chelsea's sixteenth birthday and a party befitting the importance of that specific age. The Clintons treated Chelsea to a performance of *Les Misérables* before "hosting a busload of her friends for a weekend at Camp David."[26] Chelsea and her friends took full advantage of the amenities and space afforded by the mountain retreat playing paintball, bowling, watching movies, "and generally being kids as their high school years were coming to a close."[27] Only the president's daughter can enjoy a paintball game organized by Marines with the president shouting battle strategies from the side.

In the United States during the 1990s, a sixteenth birthday generally coincides with driving lessons for the prospective, young driver, challenging in the best circumstances, even more so for the First Family. As part of the birthday weekend, President Clinton engaged in a parenting rite of passage: driving lessons for Chelsea. According to President Clinton, "The best part of the weekend for me was giving Chelsea a driving lesson around the Camp David compound. I missed driving and wanted Chelsea to enjoy it, and to do it safely."[28] As someone not prone to praising Bill's driving, Hillary recalled the lesson differently. "Outside of golf carts, the Secret Service never let Bill drive himself around, which is a good thing . . . he doesn't always notice where he's going."[29] Borrowing a Secret Service vehicle, the president commenced teaching backing up and parallel parking. When Chelsea returned to Aspen, Hillary inquired how the lesson went. Chelsea's reply: "Well, I think Dad learned a lot."[30] February 1998 highlighted the special relationship between the United States and the United Kingdom as the president and First Lady invited Prime Minister Tony Blair and his wife Cherie for a state visit. For that visit, the Clintons flew them up to Camp David for a private dinner with

26. Bill Clinton, 701.
27. Bill Clinton, 701.
28. Bill Clinton, 701.
29. Hillary Clinton, 339.
30. Hillary Clinton, 339.

Al and Tipper Gore. The two leaders and their wives developed a close relationship, offering laughter as friends and public support as fellow leaders.

July 15, 1999, brought Israeli prime minister Ehud Barak and his wife Neva to Camp David for the night. After dinner, the president and the prime minister conversed well into the night, departing for their cabins around 3 a.m. Those discussions revolved around completing the peace talks between Israel and the Palestinian Authority. The negotiations had spanned years, most notably with conferences in Oslo and in Wye River, Maryland. Barak's renewed interest in finalizing the long process stemmed from obtaining a mandate in his recent election and President Clinton showing him, "the building where most of the negotiations President Carter mediated between Anwar Sadat and Menachem Begin had taken place in 1978."[31] Barak understood the Spirit of Camp David and suggested talks between Israel and Syria in late 1999, a proposal rejected by the Syrians because "other high-profile Middle East negotiations had occurred there."[32] Talks eventually did take place in nearby Shepherdstown, West Virginia.

After nearly a year of planning and negotiations on where to hold the peace talks, the Israeli and Palestinian delegations arrived at Camp David July 11, 2000, for a two-week summit. Doomed for failure from the outset, the weather failed to uplift spirits as, "night and day the lovely countryside was shrouded in a suffocating fog like a Biblical plague."[33] According to both the president and First Lady, Barak arrived prepared to finalize a peace deal while Arafat was not fully ready for peace in the region. For this reason, Clinton tempered his expectations to "at least narrow their differences so that we could finish before I left office."[34] Despite strong instincts of the process skidding off course to failure,

---

31. Bill Clinton, 867.
32. Bill Clinton, 885.
33. Albright, 482.
34. Bill Clinton, 911.

Clinton forged ahead "because I believed that the collapse of the peace process would be a near certainty if I didn't."[35]

Narrowly surviving a no-confidence vote in the Knesset by a mere two votes, Barak "pushed hard for the summit because the piecemeal approach of the 1993 [Oslo] settlement and the Wye River accord didn't work for him."[36] Feeling pressure from a threatened September deadline from Arafat to announce a Palestinian state, Barak showed eagerness for a deal and was confident Israelis would back him. He sought a peace plan that protected Israel's core interests: "security, the protection of its religious and cultural sites on the Temple Mount, an end to the Palestinian claim to an unlimited right of return to Israel, and a declaration that the conflict was over."[37]

President Clinton appeared to have studied well the Camp David Accords from 1978, as the major themes and planned activities closely mirrored the talks from twenty-two years prior. Echoing Carter's initial impressions from decades past, Clinton surmised "each leader saw his own position more clearly than he saw the other side," and he added, "I was immensely impressed with the quality of both delegations. They were all patriotic, intelligent, and hardworking, and they genuinely seemed to want an agreement."[38] Just as Carter had found, the individual delegation members appeared more willing to work together than their leaders.

Same as they had in 1978, the two leaders stayed in Dogwood and Birch because of the proximity to Aspen, and the equality of cabin floorplans ensured neither leader could complain of favoritism in their lodging. Unlike in 1978, both leaders ate dinner with the president in Laurel most nights. While they would not confer separately, they did appear in the same room for the duration of the summit, including a Friday night Shabbat service where "Arafat was in a gracious mood, blessed everyone, and even spoke a few words of Hebrew."[39] Echoing Carter's desire to seek informality among the leaders through family participation, the presi-

---

35. Bill Clinton, 912.
36. Bill Clinton, 911.
37. Bill Clinton, 911.
38. Bill Clinton, 912.
39. Albright, 488.

dent invited Chelsea to attend the summit "entertaining our guests and helping me deal with the endless hours of tension."[40] Secretary of State Albright, providing the bulk of heavy lifting in negotiations recalled how Chelsea "stayed in the background, absorbed what she was seeing, and kept us all, including her father, in good humor."[41]

History repeated itself in the 2000 Peace Summit negotiation cycle. The two sides spent the first few days feeling out the other's intentions and awaiting a proposal. Members of the delegations shared meals together and enjoyed the various amenities Camp David offered. They engaged in friendly competition getting to know each other and genuinely enjoyed the company of the other side. Further, the president cleared most of his schedule for the duration of the talks, however, keeping the G8 summit in Osaka, Japan, on the schedule, a meeting he attended and then immediately returned for the conclusion of talks. While in residence at Camp David, President Clinton frequently dropped in on negotiations between the delegations, as well as meeting privately with each leader to discuss matters and use his powerful charm to sway the pair toward a historic resolution.

Ehud Barak's negotiating stance essentially froze talks the first few days. Having survived a close no-confidence vote, a quick resolution would appear he caved too soon giving up more than Israel desired. Additionally, "Barak wanted others to wait until he decided the time was right, then, when he made his best offer, he expected it to be accepted as self-evidently a good deal."[42] It's not an optimal strategy when the opposing negotiator lacks trusts and assumes a good deal will never be offered.

Attempting to salvage a process she deemed doomed from the beginning, Secretary Albright pulled out all the stops to nudge negotiations in the right direction. She encouraged the sharing of meals and recreation activities together, even suggesting discussing the peace deal during those times and blending work and play. Once, she locked two negotiators inside the president's office in Laurel from midnight to 10

---

40. Bill Clinton, 913.
41. Albright, 358.
42. Bill Clinton, 913.

a.m.[43] Taking a page from Carter's playbook, Albright acted on Arafat's suggestion of travel off the mountain to visit a group of Palestinians staying in nearby Emmitsburg during the summit. During the visit, the Palestinian citizens suggested they were amenable to a deal, provided Israel make concessions.[44]

With no substantial progress after eight days, the president met with Barak to recommend they end the talks or, at a minimum, scale back negotiations to seek a limited settlement. During that conversation, Barak moved significantly toward peace, offering 91 percent of the West Bank and a partial land swap for the settlements. "Most dramatically, he had agreed to an arrangement that would allow Arafat to establish a capital for Palestine within Jerusalem."[45] Such a breakthrough could change everything in the Middle East—so much so, President Clinton delayed his trip to Japan by a day in hopes of making the agreement work. However, later that evening Arafat rejected the offer sending Clinton to Japan without a deal, while Albright continued informal talks with the delegations until the president's return.

Knowing the only way to a settlement was through personal connection and understanding, something Camp David is uniquely designed to bring about, Albright arranged separate trips off the mountain for each leader during the president's absence. On Saturday, she offered Arafat a trip to either Harper's Ferry or her family farm. Arafat chose the farm and thoroughly enjoyed the much-needed break. Albright had difficulty believing the cranky, intractable man she witnessed over the last week "was the same person who cheered my grandson, Jack, as he dove off the diving board, kissed my baby granddaughter Maddie, and happily posed for pictures with people in bathing suits."[46] On the return drive, she learned more of his life and dedication to the Palestinian cause.

The next day, Albright hosted Barak at Gettysburg, discussing the battle and leadership lessons learned. He too enjoyed himself, providing Albright more insight into his life and bargaining position. Regardless of

43. Albright, 488.
44. Albright, 489.
45. Albright, 489.
46. Albright, 492.

the outcome of negotiations, as often occurs, Camp David's magic broke through allowing people to be themselves and highlighting the personal side of statecraft.

When the president returned, the US delegation attempted a last-minute Hail Mary for a deal. "As the president sat down with the two sides at 11:30 p.m. on July 24, yellow pad in hand, I was reminded of the all-night session that climaxed in Wye. Maybe there was hope: breakthroughs in the Middle East always seemed to occur under cover of dark."[47] This particular session went through the night, finally ending at 5:30 in the morning. Another set of meetings occurred mid-morning on July 25, to no avail. Disappointed, knowing peace was an illusion, Clinton drafted a press statement in which he "tried to praise Barak without burying Arafat."[48] Hope sprung on September 25, when Barak invited Arafat to his home for dinner, resulting in both sides sending negotiators to Washington the next day.

Unfortunately, on September 28, Ariel Sharon walked on the Temple Mount, shattering any lingering hope of peace before the end of the Clinton administration. Despite all of its allure, the magic of Camp David could not overcome the animosity between Israel and Palestine—nor has anyone else succeeded.

While Clinton's use of the retreat did not equal the frequency of his predecessor or successor, his usage was above average for Camp David's history. His retreats with senior staff to make sweeping plans for his administrations demonstrates he understood the power of seclusion and relaxation to inspire great ideas. Despite a personal affinity for more popular locales for vacations, the Clintons appreciated the mountain's ability to allow them to grieve together away from the world in their times of need. A student of history, President Clinton knew there was only one place in the world that had a chance of helping broker peace between Israel and Palestine. He took his shot at an immortal legacy, and while the effort failed it was not due to location. In fact, there's a good chance

---

47. Albright, 493.
48. Albright, 493.

no other location could have held the two sides together for as long as Camp David did. Some ideas are just too far ahead of their time.

As 2000 closed, so did the Clinton presidency. During the last month in office, the Clintons spent time savoring the "lasts" of their time in the White House, including Camp David. Regulars at Renaissance Weekend, an off-the-record gathering of leaders in many fields, the family decided to forgo that event, spending their last New Year at Camp David. Then, during January 11–15, 2001, the family made one last visit to Camp David consisting of parties for White House staff, cabinet members, as well as family friends. Bill Clinton recounted that headlining the visit, "Don Henley gave us a wonderful solo concert after dinner in the Camp David chapel."[49] The following morning, they participated in their final worship service "in the beautiful chapel, where we had shared many services with the fine young sailors and Marines who staffed the Camp, and their families. They had even let me sing with the choir."[50] Later that Sunday afternoon, the family boarded Marine One for their final trip down the mountain to the South Lawn, and they finished packing for New York.

---

49. Bill Clinton, 947.
50. Bill Clinton, 947–948.

CHAPTER 15

9/11

As THE SON OF A PRESIDENT, GEORGE W. BUSH KNEW CAMP DAVID offered both relaxation and a workspace. It was no surprise when Bush, like President Clinton, first visited after less than two weeks in office. If the similarity in the timing of their first visits led some to think Bush would utilize the retreat the way Clinton did—Bush had his own retreat property in Crawford, Texas, after all—their idea was quickly proven wrong. Bush utilized this particular perk of the presidency more than twice as much as Clinton.

Not just a family gathering site during the George W. Bush administration, Camp David served as a status symbol for presidential guests. The bottom rung of the invitation ladder were those guests enjoying time at the White House. Next were the ones receiving extended time in the Oval Office or dining at the White House. On the second highest rung stood an invitation to Camp David, with time at Bush's Prairie Chapel Ranch in Crawford, Texas, atop the summit of invitations.[1] By the end of his administration, Bush held the record for the number of visits by individual heads of state as he typically invited one foreign leader at a time rather than hold summits or group meetings with foreign leaders at Camp David.

It didn't take long for President Bush to extend a Camp David invitation to the prime minister of the United Kingdom. On February 23, 2001, Prime Minister Tony Blair and his wife Cherie returned atop

---

1. Walsh, 266.

the mountain to a "low-key welcoming ceremony at the helipad . . . no national anthems, just the marine and navy honor guard displaying the national flags."[2] The visit provided space for the two leaders to get acquainted and see if their relationship would continue in a similar vein to that of Prime Minister Blair and President Clinton. Besides working to forge a personal special connection mirroring that of the two nations, the two leaders discussed matters of state including the development of a European Security and Defense Policy, where Blair saw a benefit in "independent European forces."[3] Additionally, the leaders discussed strengthening sanctions on Saddam Hussein and a possible US withdrawal from the Anti-Ballistic Missile Treaty.

On the evening of this first foreign visit, National Security Advisor Dr. Condoleezza Rice inadvertently provided a humorous interlude for the two leaders. Spending a great deal of time preparing for the visit had taken its toll on the national security advisor. After dinner, the entire entourage ventured to the movie theater to view *Meet the Parents*, during which, while she enjoyed the movie, Dr. Rice did not remain awake. "As the president tells it, I was laughing robustly through the first half of the movie and then fell silent. I awoke to the prime minister of the United Kingdom and the president of the United States standing over me, saying, 'Wake up Dr. Rice.'"[4]

Early in Bush's presidency, Camp David provided a space for relaxation and getting away from the policy and other debates that hound any president in the White House. Bush's White House director of communications, Dan Bartlett, remarked, "He can stretch his legs a little" while at Camp David and reflect on big plans, ideas, and decisions.[5] His typical schedule began with departing the South Lawn onboard Marine One on Friday afternoon and spending the weekend "watching sports on TV, working on jigsaw puzzles, jogging or riding a bicycle in the countryside, tooling around in a motorized vehicle called Golf Cart One, and taking

---

2. Condoleezza Rice, *No Higher Honor*, 38.
3. Rice, 39.
4. Rice, 40.
5. Walsh, 307.

strolls with Laura."[6] The president shared that he sat in Aspen with its "sunlit living room where I watched football with my brother Marvin and friends; and a stone fireplace beside which Laura and I liked to read at night."[7] Bush continued his father's traditional wallyball games with his staff, occasionally inviting service members stationed at Camp David to participate. The relaxed atmosphere allowed Bush to make "conclusions, decisions about big steps at Camp David" because "Camp David provide[s] a different kind of opportunity for thought and decision."[8]

While in office, Bush renovated the bowling alley and installed a rock-climbing wall and indoor batting cage.[9] Bowling games involved everyone with Bush assigning two teams of six bowlers for a fun, competitive game resulting in bonding and relaxation among his senior staff and advisors. Aides described Bush as a "vigorous, flamboyant bowler, throwing the ball halfway down the alley, with a huge amount of spin" and who would liberally dispense high fives to fellow teammates followed by an X with his arms anytime his team bowled a strike.[10]

Enhancing the relaxed atmosphere, Bush requested comfort food while staying at the retreat. The Navy chefs stationed at Camp David "became experts at comfort food, like fried chicken and chicken-fried steak, which we seldom had at the White House."[11] Served family-style, meals consisted of "platters of chicken-fried steak, big bowls of mashed potatoes and vegetables, and a side table offering cakes and Blue Bell ice cream in vanilla, chocolate, and strawberry."[12]

Based on the first few months of visits, Camp David emerged as Bush's close retreat for relaxation, focusing on use with friends and family. However, the events of September 11, 2001, changed not just the tone of the Bush presidency, it profoundly impacted the United States.

---

6. Walsh, 307.
7. George W. Bush, *Decision Points*, 185.
8. Walsh, 309.
9. Walsh, 307.
10. Walsh, 307.
11. Laura Bush, *Spoken from the Heart*, 263.
12. Walsh, 307.

The first few hours of that crisp, clear, autumn morning revealed nary a hint of the chaos that would soon envelop both New York City and Washington, DC, with the fog of war. At one point, there were reports of up to six hijacked planes serving as flying bombs with rumors of numerous targets including Camp David. Upon hearing word that Camp David endured an attack, Laura Bush recalls, "I began thinking of all the people who would have been there, like Bob Williams, the chaplain."[13] While Camp David avoided catastrophe on September 11, the retreat played a role in responding to the attacks of that day.

The president conducted many stops while onboard Air Force One in the immediate aftermath of the attacks, eventually spending the night in the White House as a show of strength and demonstrating a functioning government. To keep the line of succession intact during a possible further attack, the vice president recounted he "flew toward the Catoctin Mountains and Camp David, the presidential retreat that would be our undisclosed location on the night of September 11."[14] After spending the night, he and the Second Lady returned to the White House for a meeting of the National Security Council.

In the immediate aftermath of 9/11, the vice president spent a great deal of time traveling, many times to undisclosed locations, enhancing his own security by keeping himself and the president separate. During this shell game of keeping the vice president on the move, his most frequent "undisclosed location" was Camp David.[15] In fact, due to the increased worry of an attack in late October 2001, the Second Family spent Halloween at Camp David. The Cheneys' granddaughters were there, so the vice president's staff, along with Secret Service agents, ensured the grandchildren didn't miss out on trick-or-treating. Their Halloween costumes were delivered to the retreat, and between the security posts and guest cabins in which staff stayed, the children enjoyed the time-honored tradition.[16]

---

13. Laura Bush, 202.
14. Dick Cheney, *In My Time: A Personal and Political Memoir*, 10.
15. Cheney, 338.
16. Cheney, 338.

A true dog lover, Cheney often brought his golden Labrador, Dave. President Bush frequently traveled to Camp David with his Scottish Terrier, Barney. Most of the dog stories on Camp arise from the exploits and antics of the First Dogs. However, thanks to the public recollections of Vice President Cheney, we get a window into the trouble Second Dogs can cause when visiting the mountain retreat. Cheney describes one Camp David visit during this period of traveling to "undisclosed locations." Once, the two men were at Camp David together with their dogs for a National Security Council meeting. Cheney brought Dave with him to Laurel to grab breakfast one morning, walking into the lodge with arms full of briefing papers and newspapers from that morning. Once in the door, Dave spotted Barney and the chase was on.

The vice president frantically dropped the papers in his arms to corral Dave before the chase damaged dogs or furniture. As Cheney trailed the dogs into the dining room, he saw "Joyce Rumsfeld, Alma Powell, and Stephanie Tenet . . . seated for breakfast . . . watching aghast as Dave bounded around the dining table after a furiously scurrying Barney."[17] Adding to the chaos, Bush appeared moments later loudly inquiring about the racket. In an effort to quickly retrieve Dave, Cheney offered treats from the buffet and escorted the miscreant back to his cabin. Soon after returning to the cabin, he answered a knock at the door where the Camp commander personally delivered the news: Dave was forever banned from Laurel.[18]

On Thursday, September 13, fearing a second attack on Washington, DC, the Secret Service recommended the vice president and Second Lady return to Camp David. This caused the couple to miss the prayer service the following day at Washington National Cathedral and "the president's eloquent words about grief and justice."[19] In place of that memorial service, the couple attended a memorial service alongside the military members stationed at Camp David in Evergreen Chapel.

---

17. Cheney, 338.
18. Cheney, 338.
19. Cheney, 331.

The afternoon of Friday, September 14, the National Security Council joined Cheney at Camp David for planning meetings. The president was scheduled to arrive in the evening following his visit to Ground Zero where he addressed first responders through a bullhorn atop a rubble pile.

The vice president ate dinner that evening in Holly Lodge with Secretary of Defense Donald Rumsfeld, Secretary of State Colin Powell, and National Security Advisor Rice. They met to form a strategy of how to prosecute those behind the attack and, hopefully, ensure there would be no repeat of the events from earlier in the week. Over buffalo steak, Rice said the quartet "discussed how we would organize the next morning's session with the president. We all knew that the outcome would be a declaration of war against the Taliban and an invasion of Afghanistan."[20]

Saturday, September 15, the full National Security Council convened in Laurel Lodge, the same conference room in which George H. W. Bush received briefings on the invasion of Kuwait eleven years earlier. During the morning session, with a large map laid out on the middle of the conference table, the president received briefings from the director of the CIA, George Tenet, and the outgoing chairman of the Joint Chiefs, General Hugh Shelton, who laid out "a military plan that was not yet fully formed. It gave the president three options: a series of cruise missile strikes; cruise missile strikes plus a bombing campaign; or cruise missile strikes, a bombing campaign, and American forces on the ground in Afghanistan."[21] During the break for lunch, Vice President Cheney phoned Lyzbeth Glick, wife of Johnny Glick, "one of the heroes of United Flight 93," to let her know "her husband's last act had been one of tremendous bravery and heroism, for which the nation was deeply grateful."[22]

Following lunch, the National Security Council reconvened in Laurel with the president looking around the table, "asking each of us for our thoughts on the road ahead."[23] After considering the input of his advisors, including the vice president affirming "the war option and the need for

---

20. Rice, 83.
21. Cheney, 332.
22. Cheney, 333.
23. Cheney, 333.

an ultimatum,"[24] the president stated his need to "mull over what he just heard."[25] There would be no final decision during the weekend.

Before Saturday evening's dinner, the team gathered in Laurel where Attorney General John Ashcroft "played spirituals and we all sang."[26] An accomplished pianist herself, Dr. Rice sang to his accompaniment because, as she said, "Contrary to type, John plays wonderful gospel piano, while I play Brahms and Mozart."[27]

The next morning, Sunday, September 16, those of the team who chose to, gathered at Evergreen Chapel where "the president and his aides worship side by side with the officers and enlisted personnel and their families. That day, the commander in chief worshipped with those whom he would soon order to defend our wounded country in a most distant land."[28] During the service as the "late summer light streamed through the serene woods and into the chapel,"[29] the chaplain provided a sermon asking the question most on the minds of the nation: "Why? . . . How could this happen, God?"[30] The chaplain proclaimed there were no good answers but asked the congregation to take comfort through a passage attributed to St. Ignatius of Loyola, "Pray as if it all depends upon God, for it does. But work as if it all depends upon us, for it does."[31] Following the service, the president departed for the White House to chart the nation's course as it entered the turbulent waters of war.

While the events of 9/11 and the resulting war on terror dominated the remaining years of Bush's presidency, he utilized Camp David for more than wartime planning. In fact, over the years, most foreign policy decisions occurred off the mountain, leaving the retreat as a place for the First Family to get away and be themselves. This was especially true during

24. Rice, 87.
25. Rice, 87.
26. Rice, 87.
27. Rice, 87.
28. Rice, 88.
29. George W. Bush, *Decision Points*, 190.
30. George W. Bush, 190.
31. George W. Bush, 190.

Christmas each year. Camp David provided the extended Bush family a secure, private place to come together without the press while facilitating the machinations of government with minimal disruption to family traditions. As an added bonus, spending the holiday at Camp David allowed more of the president's staff and Secret Service agents time off to spend the holidays with their own families.

Christmas holidays spent at Camp David always included the president engaging in his annual Christmas Eve tradition of placing calls to troops stationed and deployed overseas and thanking them for their service and sacrifice. Then, after sunset, the First Family headed to Evergreen Chapel with the families of those stationed at Camp David to watch the annual Nativity story as "performed by the children of the sailors and Marines."[32] It was a highlight of their annual Christmas visit to the mountain bringing beaming joy "as a few pint-size angels, shepherds, and sheep scrunched up their faces in fear, overcome by sheer excitement and exhaustion."[33]

November 2001 arrived with the twentieth birthday of the Bushes' twin daughters Jenna and Barbara. Because of the uncertainty of the times and increased security for the First Family, the Bushes hosted a party for the twins and twenty of their friends at Camp David. The party was a distraction from the stress of the White House as "George devised contests for the guests, including tennis, basketball, and bowling for the boys, and we put a karaoke machine in the main lodge so the kids would have fun activities all weekend."[34]

Already close with the Bushes, her time working for the president on wartime footing brought Condoleezza Rice into the circle as family. During frequent trips to Camp David, she joined the First Lady and the wife of the chief of staff, Kathleen Card, to "walk the perimeter trail with the steep hill at the end that we nicknamed Big Bertha."[35] Never seeming to relax, Dr. Rice caught up on sleep in more places than the movie theater. Happening at least once in the presence of Laura Bush, "Condi

32. Laura Bush, 275.
33. Laura Bush, 275.
34. Laura Bush, 262.
35. Laura Bush, 263.

and I used to joke about her inadvertent nap, the one she took when she was sitting on the couch to work and, from sheer exhaustion, fell asleep."[36]

While Bush spent Christmas Day 2004 at Camp David savoring a recent reelection and planning the next four years of his administration, "deep under the Indian Ocean floor, the tectonic plates shuddered and the seabed cracked in the second largest earthquake in recorded history."[37] The prelude to one of the largest natural disasters in human history as the earthquake spawned a series of devastating tsunamis, killing over 200,000 people in fourteen countries throughout the Indian Ocean. Watching the early footage in horror with the rest of the world, Bush activated the country's initial response from Camp David and "immediately asked his father and Bill Clinton to spearhead a fundraising and relief effort in the United States."[38] All told, this effort resulted in nearly $1 billion in direct aid from the United States and nearly $2 billion from donations from American citizens.

In June 2006, Josh Bolten, White House chief of staff, and Joe Hagin, deputy chief of staff, devised a closely held plan to get the president to Iraq for a meeting with the newly assembled Iraqi government. Maintaining secrecy until arriving in Iraq, the duo suggested the trip originate from Camp David, as it was an ideal place from which the president could disappear due to the lack of press and secluded nature of the retreat. Scheduling a video conference between the US and Iraqi cabinets, the president assembled a selection of his cabinet at Camp David to unwittingly participate in the ruse. While the US contingent enjoyed dessert in Laurel, the president, Bolten, and a tight circle snuck off to a waiting helicopter, leaving Vice President Cheney to keep the conversation going and deflect inquiries into presidential whereabouts.[39]

The waiting helicopter, lights extinguished to lower the chance of prying eyes discovering the plan, whisked Bush from Camp David to Andrews Air Force Base, taxiing directly into the hangar housing Air

---

36. Laura Bush, 263.
37. Laura Bush, 307.
38. Laura Bush, 307.
39. The 1600 Sessions Podcast, Episode 30, "Life at Camp David," hosted by Stewart McLaurin July 29, 2019.

Force One where, donning a ball cap, the president unceremoniously boarded the aircraft from the rear to an awaiting preselected press gaggle sworn to secrecy.[40] Hours later, only after the president arrived at the US Embassy in Baghdad with his cabinet, was Prime Minister Maliki informed of Bush's arrival.

On January 10, 2007, President Bush announced a surge in the number of troops deployed to Iraq, increasing the troop levels by 20,000 to help stabilize and secure the country in an attempt to create space for political and social progress. Camp David played a part in the announcement as debates over the Iraq strategy occurred among the National Security Council in Laurel. Vice President Cheney recalls flying from his home in St. Michaels, Maryland, in June 2006 to Camp David to address the issues in Iraq: "Is there more we could be doing to defeat the insurgency? Do we need more troops? Are the Iraqis convinced that we'll see this through? What does it take to win?"[41] After months of meetings with the generals in the field through both face-to-face and video conferences—some at Camp David—the president decided on the troop level increase for Iraq, and not without serious pushback from many sides.

As with many First Ladies, Laura Bush put her stamp on Camp David "redecorating the cabins with privately raised funds; many of the buildings were now more than a half a century old. Foreign leaders had been staying in a cabin where the front hall looked directly into the bathroom."[42] Making the cabins more comfortable both modernized the rustic elegance of the accommodations while creating five-star living quarters that matched the superb service provided by Camp David personnel. Additionally, Laura Bush undertook a historical project and "gathered a historical archive of photos capturing famous visits to Camp David so that every president from Roosevelt forward and numerous foreign leaders are remembered and recognized."[43]

---

40. James Sturcke, "Bush Flies into Baghdad for Surprise Visit," June 13, 2006, www.theguardian.com/world/2006/jun/13/usa.iraq (retrieved on February 13, 2021).
41. Cheney, 435.
42. Laura Bush, 422.
43. Laura Bush, 422.

9/11

Like his father, George W. Bush leaned on Camp David's ability to bring people together in a private, secure, safe space and where, by being themselves, confidants could offer the president solid, unfiltered advice without the temptation of playing for television sound bites. Camp David's tranquil atmosphere provides an ideal setting to contemplate topics fraught with danger and subject to press leaks such as waging war. Because the Bush administration was dominated by the War on Terror, it follows that his staff would escape to the mountain to discuss sensitive war plans with minimal personnel. It would be interesting to see how using Camp David to plan for peace rather than battle during his time as president could have changed things regarding the length of the country's involvement in the War on Terror.

Alas, after eight years in office, and leaving their indelible mark on Camp's legacy, it was time for the second Bush family to step aside as a younger family took the baton to continue running the presidential relay.

Chapter 16

Summits

Continuing the tradition of his immediate predecessors, President Obama made his first trip to Camp David soon after the inauguration. Following that visit in February 2009, both he and the First Lady bestowed praise on the retreat. A few days later, speaking at the Interior Department, President Obama deemed it "a beautiful place" and added, "the beauty of those grounds . . . it was just wonderful to get a bit of a break and to spend some quality time as a family in nature."[1] Despite their pleasure with the secluded retreat, the pace of his visits slowed significantly compared to that of President Bush. While disappointing for the Camp David staff who looked forward to serving the president, it provided time for significant maintenance and upgrades of the facilities.

While the president visited less frequently, there were still many visits with which to keep the staff busy and the First Family relaxed. After settling into the role of First Lady and realizing she needed to reconnect with those close friends who provided necessary community, especially as she lived under the constant glare of the public spotlight, Michelle invited her friends to the mountain retreat on a routine basis for a "Boot Camp." The "woodsy, summer-camp-like presidential retreat"[2] set the perfect stage for a weekend of working out and attempts by attendees to refrain from wine and snacks.

---

1. Mark Knoller, "Obamas Return to Camp David after 8 month absence," June 10, 2011, retrieved from https://www.cbsnews.com/news/obamas-return-to-camp-david-after-8-month-absence/ on October 7, 2020.
2. Michelle Obama, *Becoming*, 361.

These weekends provided an opportunity to escape the rigors of work and family and allowed the group to focus on themselves and strengthen the bonds of friendship they worked so hard to forge. Lodging in "cozy, wood-paneled cabins surrounded by forest, [they] buzzed around in golf carts and rode bikes."[3] Activities included dodgeball and yoga as well as healthy, delicious meals prepared by the talented White House chefs. The exercises were overseen by Michelle's trainer and the Camp staff. And Michelle said they shared "thoughts and experiences, offering advice or funny stories or sometimes just the assurance that whoever was spilling her guts in a given moment wasn't the only one ever to have a teenager who was acting out or a boss she couldn't stand. Often, we steadied one another just by listening."[4]

While other presidents developed traditions of spending certain holidays at the mountain retreat, President Obama spent a yearly birthday weekend within Camp David's perimeter. Dubbed "Campathlon" by the staff, the celebration began at the military's Joint Base Andrews with a leisurely round of competitive golf, where the invited guests not only drove, chipped, and putted for bragging rights, but also the winning team scored the right to fly to Camp David aboard Marine One, and the losers were relegated to a long van ride up the mountain. Once at camp, the entourage enjoyed a variety of games of skill and strength facilitated by the staff, resulting in an eventual winner of the weekend. As competitive as his friends, the president won a few, but not all, of the annual competitions.

The president's fiftieth birthday would be the most interesting of his camp celebrations. A fan of SportsCenter on ESPN, Obama no doubt saw Dos Equis commercials featuring Jonathan Goldsmith, who portrayed "the most interesting man in the world." According to a *Vanity Fair* article from 2017 recollecting this connection, Goldsmith described their first meeting during the Obama reelection campaign in Vermont, where the president quoted back all the classic commercial taglines.[5] Leading up to the fiftieth celebration, Goldsmith received a surprise call

3. Michelle Obama, 362.
4. Michelle Obama, 362.
5. Kenzie Bryant, *Vanity Fair,* June 2, 2017, "The Most Interesting Man in the World Was Once Barak Obama's Birthday Present" (retrieved February 13, 2021).

from an Obama aide asking him to participate in the upcoming festivities. Goldsmith agreed and after landing at Reagan National Airport secretly drove to Camp David to surprise the president. After a quick tour of the grounds and meeting Bo, the family dog, Goldsmith awaited the president at the archery range. Staying in character "wanting to make a strong first impression, I thought of what my father had done in those woods at our camp so many years ago. I picked up five or six shafts and went over to the target and stuck them together in a tight cluster near the bull's-eye."[6] The humor scored a bull's-eye as the two hit it off, and Goldsmith participated in the weekend's events including bowling and skeet with the two of them meeting a few more times outside Camp David during Obama's presidency.

In a March 2009 effort to protect precious family time, President Obama arranged his schedule around his daughters' spring break, sending Vice President Biden to attend the Gridiron dinner in his stead while the First Family was at Camp David. Apparently, this upset the Washington, DC, press corps, who expected the new president to attend, just as his successors traditionally had early in their administrations to endure roasting by journalists. The disappointment was short-lived as Vice President Biden took the stage full of wit and wisecracks. Taking aim at the press he quipped, "I hate it when people say newspapers are obsolete. That's totally untrue. I know from firsthand experience. I recently got a puppy, and you can't housebreak a puppy on the Internet."[7] Perhaps to ease disappointment over the lack of presidential entertainment, not even President Obama was immune from vice presidential jokes, "President Obama does send his greeting, though. He can't be here tonight because he's busy getting ready for Easter. He thinks it's about him."[8]

Following the lead of those before him, President Obama utilized the retreat for more than just personal, family relaxation and fun. He

---

6. Jonathan Goldsmith, *Stay Interesting*, 298–299.
7. Jules Witcover, *Joe Biden: A Life of Trial and Redemption*, 448.
8. Witcover, 448.

hosted foreign leaders at Camp David in a low-key, relaxed atmosphere where important decisions were discussed over "informal, unscripted, unplanned, spontaneous meetings"[9] allowing more human and honest diplomacy. During his administration, President Obama would set the record for the number of foreign leaders visiting Camp David, as well as the most foreign leaders to visit at one time.

Citing anticipated severe disruptions from the now-routine protests surrounding any grouping of world leaders, in March 2012, just two months before the scheduled date, President Obama shifted the location of the 2012 Group of Eight (G8) summit from Chicago, Illinois, to Camp David. A stressful change for the staff to plan such a massive undertaking in a short time frame and despite doubts of local residents that "we could be prepared in such a small period of time,"[10] those stationed at the retreat welcomed the challenge and, as normal, excelled. The G8 summit remains the largest single event in the history of Camp David with fourteen world leaders and hundreds of staff and press visiting over a mere forty-eight hours.

Despite a snub from Vladimir Putin, sending his prime minister Dmitry Medvedev in his stead, the summit accomplished many of its goals due to the relaxed atmosphere. Before attending, Prime Minister of the United Kingdom David Cameron, anticipated the retreat's success, "I will get things done at the G8 . . . I am convinced that a focused, results-oriented G8 can be a powerful tool for good."[11] According to President Obama, "I think the surroundings gave us an opportunity to hold some intimate discussions and make some genuine progress."[12] The

---

9. Mike Froman quoted during press conference from Camp David on May 19, 2012. Retrieved from https://obamawhitehouse.archives.gov/the-press-office/2012/05/19/press-briefing-press-sec retary-jay-carney-mike-froman-deputy-national-se (retrieved December 30, 2020).

10. Ben Eisler quoting Katrina Bigelow, 2012 "G8 Summit moves to Camp David as Thurmont Prepares," March 7, 2012, retrieved on December 30, 2020, at https://wjla.com/news/local/2012 -g8-summit-moves-to-camp-david-as-thurmont-prepares-73502.

11. Joanna Rea, "2012 G8 Summit—Private Sector to the Rescue of the World's Poorest," May 25, 2012, retrieved on December 30, 2020, at https://www.theguardian.com/global-development/ poverty-matters/2012/may/25/2012-g8-summit-private-sector.

12. Barak Obama quoted in closing statement. Retrieved on December 30, 2020, at https:// obamawhitehouse.archives.gov/the-press-office/2012/05/19/statement-president-obama-clos ing-g8-summit.

Spirit of Camp David was alive and well during the summit. World leaders freely walked and talked with their peers away from press and gaggles of staff, exercised at the gym together as did President Obama and Prime Minister Cameron, watched the World Cup together, and even celebrated the fifty-fifth birthday of Japanese prime minister Yoshihiko Noda with a chocolate cake.

After forty-eight hours of discussion, the G8 put forth the Camp David Declaration focused on three main areas: the global economy, energy and climate change, and food security and nutrition, as well as statements on Afghanistan and political and security issues across the globe. Economically, the leaders recognized the slow recovery of the global commons focusing their efforts on promoting growth and jobs as the primary driver of confidence in economic systems as well as promoting investment in small businesses and exploring public-private partnerships. Regarding energy and climate change, the summit recommitted to the principles adopted previously in St. Petersburg, Russia, as well as increasing the use of renewable energy and carbon mitigation efforts as outlined in the Durban Platform.

Perhaps the most notable result stemmed from the food security portion of the talks. Focusing on a new initiative regarding food security in Africa, the collected countries outlined "agreement by 45 local and multilateral companies to invest $3bn in African agriculture."[13] The G8 also noted the interplay of food security and nutrition with poverty and maternal and child health. Demonstrating the importance of Africa in the global commons, the leaders of Ethiopia, Ghana, Tanzania, and Benin received invitations to participate in discussions the second day of the summit. Of note, Yayi Boni, the president of Benin, also served as chairman of the African Union, representing the interests of fifty-five countries.

Inviting leaders from smaller countries to sit with global power players became a trend at Camp David during Obama's administration. In 2015, President Obama's secretary of state John Kerry hosted the President of Afghanistan, Ashraf Ghani, and Chief Executive Abdullah

---

13. Joanna Rea, 2012 "G8 Summit—Private Sector to the Rescue of the World's Poorest."

Abdullah to Camp David for discussions. Dwight Eisenhower was the first US president to visit Afghanistan in 1959, so having a high-level visit between the two countries at the presidential retreat named after his grandson was a fitting tribute to the connections between the two nations. The Afghan leaders held discussions with Secretary Kerry, Secretary of Defense Ash Carter, Treasury Secretary Jack Lew, Director of National Intelligence James Clapper, and Director of the Central Intelligence Agency John Brennan. The delegations met over three sessions "beginning with security, then moving on to the issues of reconciliation and regional cooperation and concluding with economic matters."[14]

Just two months later, the president invited the Gulf Cooperation Council (Saudi Arabia, Kuwait, Bahrain, Qatar, Oman, and the United Arab Emirates) for a summit amid tension regarding US nuclear talks with Iran. However, only two heads of state attended—the emir of Kuwait, Sabah al-Ahmad al-Jaber al-Sabah, and the emir of Qatar, Tamim bin Hamad Al Thani—with the remaining four countries sending high-level emissaries. During the one-day summit, leaders discussed the possibility of a strategic partnership to improve security cooperation, especially in combatting terrorism, as well as Iran's growing influence in the region.

While nothing groundbreaking occurred during the day, the talks served to enhance the American relationship with the Gulf states, particularly the relationship between the United States and Saudi Arabia. A friendship formally began between Roosevelt and King Ibn Saud on February 14, 1945, aboard USS *Quincy* in the Great Bitter Lake "to exchange greetings and cement what by then was already a growing American-Saudi Arabian embrace."[15] The United States made clear that it would not normalize relations with Iran and came close to a security commitment with the Gulf states similar to Article 5 of the North

---

14. John Kerry in Press availability on March 23, 2015, at Camp David. Retrieved on January 17, 2021, at https://2009-2017.state.gov/secretary/remarks/2015/03/239713.htm.

15. John Duke Anthony, "The GCC-US Summit: An Opportunity for Strategic Reassurance?" May 12, 2015, National Council on US-Arab Relations, 9.

Atlantic Treaty Organization.[16] Further, there was a statement to rid Syria of Bashar al-Assad as well as affirming the pursuit of a peace agreement between Israel and Palestine with an independent Palestinian state. Diplomacy prevailed as the talks assuaged fears that the United States would abandon its partners in the aftermath of an Iranian nuclear deal eventually named the Joint Comprehensive Plan of Action (JCPOA) and finalized on July 14, 2015.

Over Labor Day weekend 2016, the Obamas hosted arguably the biggest celebrity to ever pass through the gates of Camp David: Beyoncé. She flew into Maryland on a private jet that Friday, September 2, and took a motorcade through the gates to spend her thirty-fifth birthday with the First Lady at the secluded retreat.[17] Wealthy celebrities like Beyoncé typically flew into either Frederick or Hagerstown, because those small airports offer a degree of privacy that larger airports cannot guarantee. From there it was a short drive to Thurmont and up the mountain to the gates of the fabled retreat for private relaxation with the First Family.

Because the press likes to cover visits to Camp David as leisure with little work done, Obama's legacy at Camp David is undervalued. The Obamas preferred to vacation in Hawaii, where the president was born, but they utilized Camp David for significant foreign policy events and accomplishments. Visitors walking the grounds of Camp David, will notice how little open space there is because the majority of the area is forest, which protects the privacy of guests not only from the public but from each other. Each cabin is separated from the others with dense vegetation, so it seemed audacious to cram so many people into limited space for one of the largest gatherings of foreign leaders every year. Yet, despite the influx of people and press, Camp David kept its veil of

---

16. CSIS, "More than keeping up the façade: The US-GCC Summit at Camp David" retrieved on December 30, 2020, at https://www.csis.org/analysis/more-keeping-facade-us-gcc-summit-camp-david.

17. Sarah Lindig, "Beyoncé and Blue Ivey Are Spending Labor Day with the Obamas," *Elle*, September 3, 2016, https://www.elle.com/culture/celebrites/news/a38991/beyonce-labor-day-obamas/ (retrieved April 20, 2023).

secrecy because of the greenery and layout. Hosting the G8 proved Camp David's ability to protect the privacy of its guests even with a press invasion. As the press tried to get photos and sound bites, the staff and nature kept the leaders isolated and protected so they could relax and get things done without unwanted distractions. Ironically, by opening up the retreat to other leaders, it proved Camp David's importance in the health of the presidency and ensured its operations for decades.

While not making the short trip up the mountain as often as his immediate predecessors, Obama's time at Camp David set records for the total number of foreign leaders visiting as well as hosting the largest single event in Camp David's storied history. After eight years utilizing the retreat to host world leaders and for his annual birthday extravaganza, mixed with personal escapes from Washington, President Obama prepared to leave office having put his mark on Camp David. Turning over the presidency to someone who in many ways is Obama's antithesis, Camp staff pondered what the future held for their special, beloved slice of presidential privacy.

CHAPTER 17

Pandemic

As President Trump assumed office, the staff predicted usage of the presidential retreat would decline over the next four to eight years. Multiple news reports cited the president's desire to spend the majority of his time away from Washington, DC, at properties he owned—not an unusual expectation as most people would appreciate escaping the chaos of the office to comfortable, familiar surroundings. After his inauguration, the staff expected President Trump's first look at the retreat to occur within a few weeks. However, the staff was disappointed as their new commander in chief delayed his much-anticipated first visit until June 2017, coinciding with Father's Day.

Despite his public comments to the contrary before and after that first visit, many news outlets repeated the idea President Trump disliked the retreat because it was not as palatial or opulent as Mar-a-Lago. These ideas were based on a comment President Trump made to the German press that Camp David was "rustic," and one would only enjoy the retreat for approximately thirty minutes. After his first visit, accompanied by the First Lady and his youngest son, Trump offered praise through Twitter, his favorite communication method while in office: "Camp David is a very special place. An honor to have spent the weekend there. Military runs it so well and are so proud of what they do!"[1] During this visit, he continued the tradition of every president since George H. W. Bush in attending church services in Evergreen Chapel when staying at Camp

---

1. Tweet from President Donald J. Trump at 2:51 p.m. on June 18, 2017.

David. While the retreat does portray a rustic feel, the five-star service and understated elegance of the furnishings impress all visitors, including the seemingly reluctant ones.

During this first visit, the president recognized the value of the retreat not just for relaxing with the family, but also in getting things done with his staff and Congress. In early January 2018, President Trump gathered Vice President Pence as well as a large number of his Cabinet, alongside Republican congressional leadership, on the mountain to discuss their plans for 2018.[2] At the conclusion of this leadership summit, the president held a rare Camp David press conference. Bringing reporters inside the gates of the storied retreat is indeed a rare occurrence and this would mark the only Camp David press conference of the Trump presidency. The president answered questions on a range of topics from domestic issues to that of North Korea. Believed to be the coldest weather for a presidential visit, temperatures hovered around five degrees Fahrenheit with wind chills below zero. Even the helicopter hanger could not escape the record cold of that weekend. The cold inside the hangar even prompted a comment about the temperature from the president during the press conference.[3]

While not using the retreat nearly as often as any of his predecessors, President Trump recognized the value of this unique retreat and the power of the Spirit of Camp David. In September 2019, after years of negotiations, the administration neared a peace agreement with the Taliban. Recognizing the importance of such an achievement toward ending nearly twenty years of Americans in combat, as well as the tenuous nature of such an agreement, Trump offered the secluded mountain retreat, one of the crown jewels of American prestige, as the signing location. Without any leaks to the press, a plan developed to bring all interested parties across the Atlantic Ocean to the lush, green Catoctin Mountains under strict secrecy. Only a select few within the inner circle were made aware.

2. Jacob Pramuk, "Here's Who Will Join Trump at Camp David This Weekend to Plan the 2018 GOP Agenda," CNBC, January 5, 2018, https://www.cnbc.com/2018/01/05/trump-heads-to-camp-david-this-weekend-to-talk-2018-gop-agenda.html (retrieved June 12, 2022).
3. CSPAN video, https://www.c-span.org/video/?439420-1/president-trump-calls-michael-wolff-book-work-fiction, comment regarding temperature around the 13:00 minute mark.

Unfortunately, attacks in the week leading up to the event prompted an abrupt cancellation, followed by a presidential announcement of the secret plans and reason for abandoning the talks.[4]

Once news of the attempted peace talks leaked the evening of Saturday September 7, all hell broke loose with chatter about the failed negotiations. All three sides, the United States, the Taliban, and Afghanistan, left the ordeal with bitterness for completely different reasons. The Taliban wanted to ink a deal with the United States first, before they sat down with the Afghan government, something the United States partially agreed to as the "idea was for Mr. Trump to hold separate meetings at Camp David with the Taliban and with Mr. Ghani, leading to a more global resolution."[5] The Afghan government felt betrayed by the talks occurring behind their back, only finding out about the meetings with the rest of the world. The hosts were angry because the Taliban couldn't even make it to the talks before resuming attacks against US forces.

Meanwhile, the most peculiar antics were from those on Twitter stating that Camp David is reserved only for "nice" countries and their leaders, terrorists need not apply, wholly forgetting President Clinton sat down with Yasser Arafat, head of the Palestinian Liberation Organization, in 2000, or that a number of presidents invited leaders of the Soviet Union, often considered public enemy number one for the United States, for talks at the storied retreat.[6] This idea was reinforced by Secretary of State Mike Pompeo the following day, "Some pretty bad actors have travelled through that place throughout recorded history."[7] Because of the seclusion and relaxed atmosphere, absence of press and prying eyes, and

---

4. Ron Elving, "At Camp David, Trump Sought the Mantle of History. But Afghanistan is Different," NPR, September 10, 2019, https://www.npr.org/2019/09/10/759268550/at-camp-david -trump-sought-the-mantle-of-history-but-afghanistan-is-different (retrieved June 12, 2022).

5. Peter Baker, Mujib Mashal, and Michael Crowley, "How Trump's Plan to Secretly Meet with the Taliban Came Together, and Fell Apart," *The New York Times*, September 8, 2019, https://www .nytimes.com/2019/09/08/world/asia/aghanistan-trump-camp-david-taliban.html (retrieved June 12, 2022).

6. A glance at the replies to President Trump's tweet at 3:51 p.m. EDT on September 7, 2019, shows the overall negative reaction to inviting the Taliban to Camp David.

7. Robin Wright, "Trump's Stunt with the Taliban Was Not About Negotiating Peace," *The New Yorker*, September 9, 2019, https://www.newyorker.com/news/our-columnists/trumps-stunt-with -the-taliban-was-not-about-negotiating-peace (retrieved June 12, 2022).

the power of the Spirit of Camp David, it is the ideal location to talk with adversaries and to conduct discussions with those who disagree.

September 2019 brought a unique group of visitors to Camp David. The president's daughter Ivanka Trump and Vice President Pence hosted members of the American Workforce Policy Advisory Board for a dinner meeting at Camp David. Over the years, several individual CEOs and other titans of industry made the trip up the mountain at the invitation of the president as personal guests, but this groundbreaking visit extended the exclusive presidential invitation to a group of influential businesspersons of all political leanings. This was meant as a thank-you for their commitment to serve the government on a voluntary basis. The visit's rarity even prompted a report by CNBC and research by their journalists to reveal the event was a first of its kind at the storied retreat.[8]

President Trump realized the Spirit of Camp David worked on more than foreign leaders. Throughout its eighty-year history, presidents from both parties utilized the power of the retreat to woo politicians and legislators to their thinking, and Trump was no different. Knowing an invitation to Camp David could serve as a carrot to bring others along to his thinking, President Trump allowed Chief of Staff Mick Mulvaney to bring members of congress to the retreat over the weekend to present the White House's agenda in a relaxed atmosphere in hopes of solidifying legislative support. Invitations up the mountain, even without the president on site, gave those visiting a leg up as to how other Republican members of congress viewed their ties to the leader of the party.

While at the retreat, the congressmen and congresswomen went hiking, shot skeet, and made s'mores at an outdoor fire pit to "make House Republicans feel like they're part of Trump's family."[9] The president personally called the lawmakers during dinner to ensure they knew he was involved in the details of their excursion to Camp David. Representative

8. Video report by CNBC from September 16, 2019, https://www.cnbc.com/video/2019/09/16/pence-and-ivanka-to-meet-with-ceos-at-camp-david-javers.html (retrieved June 12, 2022).

9. Ben Geldon, "How Donald Trump Is Using Camp David to Woo Republicans," CNN, November 24, 2019, https://www.cnn.com/2019/11/24/politics/camp-david-republicans-trump-ip-forecast-cnntv/index.html (retrieved June 12, 2022).

Ann Wagner, a long-term congresswoman from Missouri recalled, "I've worked with a number of Republican presidents over various administrations . . . and I've never, ever been invited to Camp David. It was amazing to go for the short weekend. So historic."[10] Ever the master negotiator, the tactic worked as inter-party loyalty reached record highs during Trump's administration.

As COVID-19 rampaged the world, the United States continued planning to host the 2020 G7 Summit (Russia lost its membership after invading Ukraine in 2014). As with each time hosting the event, numerous places received consideration and site visits from administration staffers and Secret Service to determine a safe, reliable location offering a level of service and comfort leaders of the world's greatest economies expect. After careful evaluation, Camp David once again received the nod to host the annual summit. Camp staff feverishly set about to ensure another successful gathering of world leaders atop the president's mountain, especially in light of the tight six-month timeline. To the disappointment of the staff, the continuing pandemic caused a cancellation of the gathering soon after the announcement of Camp David as the host venue.

While not hosting the 2020 G7 Summit deflated the staff, Camp David did not fully shutter its doors to the president during the height of the COVID-19 pandemic in the United States. After most of the country was issued stay-at-home orders in March 2020, even the president stayed mostly within the confines of the White House. In only his second trip outside the White House since the beginning of the pandemic, the president and a small group of aides made the short trip to Camp David the first weekend of May 2020.[11] The retreat's isolation offered a perfect

10. Seung Min Kim, Rachael Bade, and Josh Dawsey, "Trump Opens Up Camp David as an 'Adult Playground' to Woo GOP Lawmakers During Impeachment," *Washington Post*, November 22, 2019, https://www.washingtonpost.com/politics/trump-opens-up-camp-david-as-an-adult -playground-to-woo-gop-lawmakers-during-impeachment/2019/11/22/ec6e7810-0c6f-11ea -8397-a955cd542d00_story.html (retrieved June 12, 2022).

11. Betsy Klein and Kaitlan Collins, "Trump Escapes Washington Isolation for Camp David," CNN, May 1, 2020. https://www.cnn.com/2020/05/01/politics/trump-camp-david-coronavirus/index.html (retrieved June 12, 2022).

location to get away from the White House for relaxation with relative safety from the raging virus. So successful was this first pandemic escape, the president returned two weeks later with members of Congress to discuss the pandemic response and to continue to court legislators on upcoming votes.[12]

After losing reelection in November 2020, President Trump and his family quickly began their own set of last visits and saying goodbye to the perquisites of the presidency. As with many First Families before them, the Trump family packed in a number of visits to Camp David to soothe the election loss and say farewell to the private retreat they came to love. One notable post-election visit was the pilgrimage of the family to Camp David for Thanksgiving 2020. Gathering most of the family on the mountain to enjoy the crisp mountain air, time around the firepit, and, of course, a spectacular Thanksgiving meal prepared by the talented Camp David Navy chefs served as a last hurrah for the family's time at the center of the United States government. During the visit, family members and close staff provided a behind-the-scenes glimpse of the rejuvenating power of Camp David through their social media accounts.

The press made a larger issue of President Trump's initial impression of Camp David than was warranted. Many presidents toyed with the idea of closing the retreat because they wanted to look fiscally responsible upon taking the reins of the government. However, Camp David always works its magic in getting them to change their minds, and they eventually come to appreciate, if not love, visiting the mountain. Trump was no different. Camp David afforded a quick escape to do work away from the White House in a serene atmosphere where much can be accomplished, even with breaks for relaxation. While the chip and putt encompassing a large portion of the Aspen lawn couldn't compare to Trump's own golf courses, it did provide ample opportunity to practice his swing efficiently as it was just a few steps from his cabin to hit golf balls. As with those before him, Trump left a lasting legacy at Camp David by overseeing the

12. Anna Palmer, Jake Sherman, Eli Okun, and Garrett Ross, "POLITICO Playbook PM: Camp David Guest List," https://www.politico.com/newsletters/playbook-pm/2020/05/15/new-camp-david-guest-list-489239 (retrieved June 12, 2022).

renovation of Aspen Lodge, the president's cabin. The tasteful design touches that modernized Aspen while honoring its history and legacy will stand for decades and provide a peaceful home away from the White House for whomever has the privilege of calling Camp David theirs.

The 2020 election loss forced the Trump presidency to make way for the Biden administration in January 2021, setting up a quick turn of administrations on the camp staff. Comfortable with one way of doing things, another set of expectations and requirements arrived in the blink of an eye. Continuing the tradition set among most administrations, President Biden and his wife, Dr. Jill Biden, first visited the retreat soon after inauguration, in their case over Valentine's Day weekend in February of 2021, and they continued to use the retreat on a somewhat regular basis, in addition to trips to Wilmington and Rehoboth Beach, Delaware.

During his four years in office, President Biden visited Camp David a total of thirty-nine times, ironically matching the total number of visits from President Obama's eight years in office. Biden's usage looks low when compared to other one-term presidents such as Presidents Carter and George H. W. Bush. However, with Biden's personal home and beach house closer to the White House than the homes of those recent presidents, it was surprising he spent that much time at Camp David. His visits did not typically make the news because President Biden took a page from President Reagan's use of the retreat with routine visits during Easter and Christmas but primarily utilizing it to gather with close friends and family—rarely inviting guests beyond his inner circle. The couple enjoyed time with family at the retreat, as evidenced by an Instagram photo of the president playing Mario Kart with his grandchildren.

Knowing the significance of Camp David and its role in history, in August of 2023 President Biden hosted President Yoon of South Korea and Prime Minister Kishida of Japan at Camp David for the first ever trilateral summit between the three countries. Overcoming decades of tensions between South Korea and Japan, the leaders of those countries arrived at the peaceful retreat and let the Spirit of Camp David work its magic.

Over the course of just a few hours, the three leaders finalized an agreement strengthening the partnership between their nations on a wide range of issues—notably their role in the Indo-Pacific area in countering the cyber threat from North Korea and cooperating on Ballistic Missile Defense.[13] The agreement called for future annual meetings between not just the three leaders, but also their defense ministers, foreign ministers, and national security advisors, strengthening international ties as Camp David has fostered for more than eighty years. In fact, following the summit, the trio of leaders named their joint statement, "The Spirit of Camp David."[14]

Both President Yoon and Prime Minister Kishida paid homage to the legacy of the secluded retreat in world affairs during the joint press conference concluding the day's meetings. Acknowledging Camp David's place in world history, President Yoon remarked, "Camp David is a site that bears historical significance where important diplomatic decisions were made at critical junctures of modern history."[15] While Prime Minister Kishida stated, "Here at Camp David, numerous historical meetings have taken place. And it is a huge honor to have printed a fresh page in its history with this meeting."[16]

Perhaps the most consequential visit of President Biden's four years in office occurred in late June 2024. With his reelection campaign in full swing, President Biden headed to Camp David to prepare for his first presidential election debate with former President Trump, scheduled

---

13.˜White House. "FACT SHEET: The Trilateral Leaders' Summit at Camp David, August 18, 2023, https://bidenwhitehouse.archives.gov/briefing-room/statements-releases/2023/08/18/fact -sheet-the-trilateral-leaders-summit-at-camp-david/ (retrieved April 20, 2025).

14.˜Khalid, Asma and Franco Ordonez. "How Biden used Camp David to elevate a summit with Japan and South Korea," NPR, August 18, 2023, https://www.npr.org/2023/08/18/1194220556/ camp-david-biden-japan-korea (retrieved April 20, 2025).

15.˜White House. "Remarks by President Biden, President Yoon Suk Yeol of the Republic of Korea, and Prime Minister Kishida Fumio of Japan in Joint Press Conference, Camp David, MD," August 18, 2023, https://bidenwhitehouse.archives.gov/briefing-room/speeches-remarks/2023/08/ 18/remarks-by-president-biden-president-yoon-suk-yeol-of-the-republic-of-korea-and-prime -minister-kishida-fumio-of-japan-in-joint-press-conference-camp-david-md/ (retrieved April 20, 2025).

16.˜Ibid.

for June 27. The privacy and seclusion of the retreat provided an ideal location to prepare for the high-stakes debate. Presidential aides could come and go as needed without prying eyes tracking their every move. If the president needed outside experts to provide debate coaching and preparation, they could also arrive in secrecy. After spending grueling hours memorizing facts and rebuttals, President Biden and his family could relax and let the peaceful setting revitalize them before the next day's work.

Following his preparation, President Biden left the serenity of Camp David for the debate stage in Atlanta, Georgia, on June 27. Ultimately, the preparation did not provide the results his team hoped for. He was roundly criticized for his performance in the debate, sparking near-immediate calls for him to bow out of the election.[17] Following a post-debate appearance in Raleigh, North Carolina, the next day, President Biden returned to Camp David with his family for a previously scheduled photo shoot with celebrity photographer Annie Leibovitz.[18]

Reminiscent of Nixon's final visit to Camp David, President Biden huddled with his family to discuss his political future. Like Nixon's family, the Biden family urged the president to stay in the race and keep fighting toward victory. According to the *New York Times*, his son Hunter was "one of the strongest voices imploring Mr. Biden to resist pressure to drop out. . . . Hunter Biden wants Americans to see the version of his father that he knows—scrappy and in command of the facts—rather than the stumbling aging, president Americans saw."[19]

Less than a month later, on July 21, President Biden withdrew from the presidential race. History will reveal details of what occurred that fateful week for President Biden's aspirations for a second term. After deciding not to seek reelection, the First Family began the process of saying goodbye to one of the most special places connected with the

17. Sharma, Shweta. "Biden meets family at Camp David as calls mount for him to quit US presidential race," *The Independent*, July 1, 2024, https://www.independent.co.uk/news/world/americas/us-politics/biden-camp-david-debate-stepping-down-b2571607.html (retrieved April 20, 2025).

18. Rogers, Katie and Peter Baker. "Biden's Family Tells Him to Keep Fighting as They Huddle at Camp David," *New York Times*, June 30, 2024, https://www.nytimes.com/2024/06/30/us/politics/biden-debate-anxious-democrats.html (retrieved on April 20, 2025).

19. Ibid.

presidency. Like those before him and those who will follow, President Biden will always be part of Camp David's history, and the Spirit of Camp David will forever be part of his presidency.

CHAPTER 18

Continuing Legacy

REGARDLESS OF ADMINISTRATION, OR POLITICAL PARTY, CAMP DAVID remains a trusted place of seclusion and rejuvenation for presidents and their families. Its relaxed setting, combined with an infrastructure allowing a fully functioning office away from the White House, makes it an ideal location to accomplish the wide-ranging duties of the office with minimal outside interference or stressors. This is the resiliency of Camp David and why it always overcomes any individual or administration's initial desire to close the facility.

It is an awe-filled first impression for those afforded the opportunity to traverse the mountain and enter through the gates. The place has meaning beyond the secrecy conjured by its original name. Overwhelming at first, many people recall their first, and at times only, visit as one of meeting someone of great admiration, with either a vivid recollection or brief snapshots held together inside a thin web of memories. A danger for those who work there for years is to let the sense of awe fade, ignoring the Spirit of Camp David and losing its sense of place in history.

Camp David is a national treasure that has played a major role in world-changing events: wars, financial crises, peace negotiations, global summits. However, its greatest gift is its unique ability to provide the First Family with a place of refuge from the pressure and rigors of living in the White House. At Camp David, the security bubble doesn't feel as intrusive, and the fresh mountain air breathes in new life and energy. Strolling through the woods renewing friendships or sitting on the Aspen patio soaking in the breathtaking view of the Maryland countryside provides a welcome escape. Without Camp David, the presidency would be exponentially more difficult than it already is. Each president develops a relationship with Camp David and leaves a bit of himself on top of the mountain. Everyone who has passed through the gates becomes part of the history, and those who walk the grounds years from now will also add to it.

Future presidents will love and appreciate the retreat and use it to accomplish big, world-changing things. Some may hold it at arm's length like Truman, but even then, Camp David will be part of their presidency and be a valued support for them. The White House is known as the people's house, so Camp David really is the one place the First Family can go where everything and everyone is focused on them. That reason alone should ensure its continued use.

If anyone reading this book aspires to the presidency, I wish you the best of luck and hope you remember one thing: Keep Camp David around for the sanity of you and your family. As someone who lived and breathed the Spirit of Camp David for over three years, immersed myself in its history, and loved seeing the effect it had on everyone who crossed the gates, regardless of their fame or fortune, I'm biased. I think it's the best perk of the presidency. It lets you be yourself and literally walk in the footsteps of history. It's worth the cost, so I hope it's always there for the president and First Family. I don't think words alone can do it justice, so I hope you've gotten a small glimpse of its power and importance through these pages.

There may come a time when a president doesn't think Camp David is needed or not worth the cost. If that happens, like it almost did a few years after its construction when Truman debated getting rid of Roosevelt's retreat, I hope it will be preserved. If needed, revert it back to the National Park Service, but keep all the buildings and let it stand not as just another historical site. Or, use it as a center working toward world peace and advancing cooperation between opposing viewpoints. Camp David brings people together, and the idyllic setting will provide the ideal space to do that.

This book is for those whose one visit wasn't long enough—to relive a vaguely familiar story and to reawaken the dormant memory of a special place. It is also for those who will never visit—most readers—to provide a small glimpse into a central character of presidential history for eighty years. It's a place with a mind and soul of its own that touched fifteen First Families and counting. With the passing of time, it has an expanding personality as records unseal and others recount their interactions with this larger-than-life historic place.

This is also a book for those who worked there, sacrificing time with their own families to support the president and guests, some so often they forgot the unique nature of their duty. For those alumni of Camp David or the White House to whom Camp David may have become just another place, hopefully, these pages rekindle the passion and awe of their first trip through the gate (or initial approach for those lucky enough to arrive by air) and remind them of their small, yet important, part of not just presidential but also world history.

Roosevelt didn't expect the retreat to last eighty years, he desired a place to get away from the daily grind of the White House without the long journey to Hyde Park or Warm Springs that would also offer seclusion. His vision quickly assumed its own character becoming a private, presidential home rather than the people's White House in which all presidents live. No matter the individual, all come away from Camp David awed by the power of its spirit, for it leaves an indelible mark.

Those who experience the Spirit of Camp David feel history surround them as Camp David's secrets come alive. James Hilton named his idyllic, fictional retreat Shangri-La to conjure a far-away locale without worry about the pressures of life. Roosevelt realized Shangri-La wasn't as far away as a mythical place of fiction, it was just fifty miles north of the pressures of the presidency. Secluded, available to a select few, rarely discussed, difficult to find, Shangri-La is real—it's on the president's mountain and answers to the name of Camp David.

BIBLIOGRAPHY

BOOKS

Adams, Sherman. *Firsthand Report: The Story of the Eisenhower Administration*. 1st ed. New York: Harper & Brothers, 1961.

Albright, Madeleine Korbel, and Bill Woodward. *Madam Secretary: A Memoir*. New York: Miramax Books, 2003.

Ambrose, Stephen E. *Eisenhower: Soldier and President*. New York: Simon and Schuster, 1990.

Ambrose, Stephen E. *Nixon: Ruin and Recovery, 1973–1990*. A Touchstone Book. New York: Simon and Schuster, 1991.

Ambrose, Stephen E. *Nixon: Volume 2: The Triumph of a Politician, 1962–1972*. New York: Simon and Schuster, 1989.

Baier, Bret, Catherine Whitney, and Cloud Library. *Three Days in January: Dwight Eisenhower's Final Mission*. New York: HarperCollins, 2017.

Behrens, Jack. *Camp David Presidents: Their Families and the World*. Bloomington, IN: Author House LLC, 2014.

Benze, James G. *Nancy Reagan: On the White House Stage*. Modern First Ladies. Lawrence, KS: University Press of Kansas, 2005.

Brower, Kate Andersen. *The Residence: Inside the Private World of the White House*. 1st ed. New York: Harper, 2015.

Bryant, Traphes, and Frances Spatz Leighton. *Dog Days at the White House: The Outrageous Memoirs of the Presidential Kennel Keeper*. New York: Macmillan Publishing Co, 1975.

Bush, Barbara. *Barbara Bush: A Memoir*. New York: Scribner's Sons, 1994.

Bush, George. *All the Best, George Bush: My Life in Letters and Other Writings*. Hardcover ed. New York: Scribner, 2013.

Bush, George W. *Decision Points*. 1st ed. New York: Crown, 2010.

Bush, Laura Welch. Spoken from the Heart. New York: Scribner, 2010.

Califano, Joseph A. *The Triumph & Tragedy of Lyndon Johnson: The White House Years*. New York: Simon & Schuster, 1991.

Carter, Jimmy. *Keeping Faith: Memoirs of a President*. Toronto: Bantam Books, 1982.

Carter, Rosalynn. *First Lady from Plains*. Boston: Houghton Mifflin, 1984.

Cheney, Richard B, and Liz Cheney. *In My Time: A Personal and Political Memoir*. New York: Threshold Editions, 2011.

Churchill, Winston, and Franklin D Roosevelt. Edited by Warren F. Kimball. *Churchill & Roosevelt: The Complete Correspondence*. Princeton, NJ: Princeton University Press, 1984.

Churchill, Winston S. *The Hinge of Fate*. Boston: Houghton Mifflin Company, 1950.

Clinton, Bill. *My Life*. New York: Knopf, 2004.

Clinton, Hillary Rodham. *Living History*. New York: Simon & Schuster, 2003.

Cook, Blanche Wiesen. *Eleanor Roosevelt*. New York: Viking, 1992.

Cross, Robert F. *Sailor in the White House: The Seafaring Life of FDR*. Annapolis, MD: Naval Institute Press, 2003.

Dallek, Robert. *Flawed Giant: Lyndon Johnson and His Times, 1961–1973*. New York: Oxford University Press, 1998.

Dallek, Robert. *An Unfinished Life: John F. Kennedy, 1917–1963*. 1st ed. Boston: Little, Brown, 2003.

Dayan, Moshe. *Breakthrough: A Personal Account of the Egypt-Israel Peace Negotiations*. 1st American ed. New York: Knopf, 1981.

Dean, John W. *Blind Ambition: The White House Years*. New York: Simon and Schuster, 1976.

Deaver, Michael K. and Mickey Herskowitz. *Behind the Scenes: In Which the Author Talks About Ronald and Nancy Reagan . . . and Himself*. 1st ed. New York: Morrow, 1987.

Eisenhower, Susan. *Mrs. Ike: Memories and Reflections on the Life of Mamie Eisenhower*. 1st ed. New York: Farrar, Straus and Giroux, 1996.

Ford, Betty, and Chris Chase. *Betty: A Glad Awakening*. 1st ed. Garden City, NY: Doubleday & Company, 1987.

Ford, Betty, and Chris Chase. *The Times of My Life*. 1st ed. New York: Harper & Row, 1978.

Ford, Gerald R. *A Time to Heal: The Autobiography of Gerald R. Ford*. 1st ed. New York: Harper & Row, 1979.

Gibbs, Nancy, and Michael Duffy. *The Presidents Club: Inside the World's Most Exclusive Fraternity*. 1st ed. New York: Simon and Schuster, 2012.

Giorgione, Michael. *Inside Camp David: The Private World of the Presidential Retreat*. 1st ed. New York: Little, Brown and Company, 2017.

Goldsmith, Jonathan. *Stay Interesting*. New York: Dutton, 2017.

Goodwin, Doris Kearns. *No Ordinary Time: Franklin and Eleanor Roosevelt: The Home Front in World War II*. New York: Simon and Schuster, 1994.

Gould, Lewis L. *Lady Bird Johnson: Our Environmental First Lady*. Modern First Ladies. Lawrence, KS: University Press of Kansas, 1999.

Greene, John Robert. *Betty Ford: Candor and Courage in the White House*. Modern First Ladies. Lawrence, KS: University Press of Kansas, 2004.

Greene, John Robert. *The Presidency of Gerald R. Ford*. American Presidency Series. Lawrence, KS: University Press of Kansas, 1995.

Gulley, Bill with Mary Ellen Reese. *Breaking Cover*. New York: Simon and Schuster, 1980.

Haldeman, H. R. *The Haldeman Diaries: Inside the Nixon White House*. New York: G.P. Putnam's, 1994.

Hill, Clint and Lisa McCubbin. *Five Presidents: My Extraordinary Journey with Eisenhower, Kennedy, Johnson, Nixon, and Ford.* New York: Gallery Books, 2016.

Hilton, James. *Lost Horizon,* New York: Open Road Integrated Media, 2011.

Holt, Marilyn Irvin. *Mamie Doud Eisenhower: The General's First Lady.* Modern First Ladies. Lawrence, KS: University Press of Kansas, 2007.

Johnson, Lady Bird. *A White House Diary.* 1st ed. New York: Holt, Rinehart and Winston, 1970.

Johnson, Lyndon B. *The Vantage Point: Perspectives of the Presidency, 1963–1969.* 1st ed. New York: Holt, Rinehart and Winston, 1971.

Kearns, Doris. *Lyndon Johnson and the American Dream.* New York: St. Martin's Press, 1991.

Leuchtenburg, William E. *In the Shadow of FDR: From Harry Truman to Barack Obama.* 4th ed., rev. and updated ed. Ithaca, NY: Cornell University Press, 2009.

Levingston, Steven. *Barack and Joe: The Making of an Extraordinary Partnership.* 1st ed. New York: Hachette Books, 2019.

L'Heureux, Ray. *Inside Marine One: Four Presidents, One Proud Marine, and the World's Most Amazing Helicopter.* New York: St. Martin's Press, 2014.

Mason, James. *Memoirs of a Marine: From Boot Camp to Camp David.* Self-published, 2013.

McCarthy, Dennis V. N. and Philip W. Smith. *Protecting the President: The Inside Story of a Secret Service Agent.* 1st ed. New York: Morrow, 1985.

McLaughlin, Patrick. *No Atheists in Foxholes.* Nashville, TN: Thomas Nelson, 2010.

McNally, George J. *A Million Miles of Presidents,* 2nd ed. Washington, DC, 1600 Communications Association, Inc., 2009.

Meacham, Jon. *Destiny and Power: The American Odyssey of George Herbert Walker Bush.* 1st ed. New York: Random House, 2015.

Meacham, Jon. *Franklin and Winston: An Intimate Portrait of an Epic Friendship.* 1st ed. New York: Random House, 2003.

Mondale, Walter F. and Dave Hage. *The Good Fight: A Life in Liberal Politics.* 1st ed. New York: Scribner, 2010.

Nelson, W. Dale. *The President Is at Camp David.* 1st ed. Syracuse, NY: Syracuse University Press, 1995.

Nixon, Richard M. *RN: The Memoirs of Richard Nixon.* Norwalk, CT: Easton Press, 2012.

Obama, Barack. *A Promised Land.* 1st ed. New York: Crown, 2020.

Obama, Michelle. *Becoming.* 1st ed. New York: Crown, an imprint of the Crown Publishing Group, 2018.

Perry, Barbara A. *Jacqueline Kennedy: First Lady of the New Frontier.* Modern First Ladies. Lawrence, KS: University Press of Kansas, 2004.

Quandt, William B. *Camp David: Peacemaking and Politics.* Washington, DC: Brookings Institution Press, 1986.

Quayle, Dan. *Standing Firm: A Vice-Presidential Memoir.* 1st ed. New York: HarperCollins, 1994.

Reagan, Nancy and Ronald Reagan. *I Love You, Ronnie: The Letters of Ronald Reagan to Nancy Reagan.* 1st ed. New York: Random House, 2000.

Reagan, Nancy and William Novak. *My Turn: The Memoirs of Nancy Reagan*. 1st ed. New York: Random House, 1989.

Reagan, Ronald. *An American Life*. New York: Simon and Schuster, 1990.

Reeves, Richard. *President Nixon: Alone in the White House*. 1st ed. New York: Simon & Schuster, 2001.

Rice, Condoleezza. *No Higher Honor: A Memoir of My Years in Washington*. New York: Crown, 2011.

Rigdon, William M. and James Derieux *Sailor in the White House*. Pathfinder Books, 2015. Originally published as *White House Sailor*. Garden City, NY: Doubleday & Company, Inc, 1962.

Roosevelt, Eleanor. *The Autobiography of Eleanor Roosevelt*. 1st ed. New York: Da Capo Press, 1992.

Schlesinger, Arthur M. *A Thousand Days: John F. Kennedy in the White House*. Boston: Houghton Mifflin Company, 1965.

Skinner, Kiron K, Annelise Anderson, and Martin Anderson. *Reagan: A Life in Letters*. New York: Free Press, 2003.

Smith, A. Merriman. *Thank You, Mr. President: A White House Notebook*. New York: Harper & Brothers, 1946.

Smith, Gary Scott. *Religion in the Oval Office: The Religious Lives of American Presidents*. New York: Oxford University Press, 2015.

Sorensen, Theodore C. *Kennedy*. 1st ed. New York: Harper & Row, 1965.

Stafford, David. *Roosevelt and Churchill: Men of Secrets*. 1st ed. Woodstock, NY: Overlook Press, 1999.

Tehabi Books. *Ronald Reagan: An American Hero: His Voice, His Values, His Vision*. 1st American ed. London: DK, 2001.

Thomas, Helen. *Dateline: White House*. New York: Macmillan, 1975.

Thomas, Helen. *Front Row at the White House: My Life and Times*. New York: Scribner, 1999.

Thomas, Helen. *Thanks for the Memories, Mr. President: Wit and Wisdom from the Front Row at the White House*. New York: Scribner, 2002.

Troy, Gil. *Hillary Rodham Clinton: Polarizing First Lady*. Modern First Ladies. Lawrence, KS: University Press of Kansas, 2006.

Troy, Gil. *Mr. and Mrs. President: From the Trumans to the Clintons*. 2nd ed., rev ed. Lawrence, KS: University Press of Kansas, 2000.

Truman, Harry S, Bess Wallace Truman, and Robert H. Ferrell. *Dear Bess: The Letters from Harry to Bess Truman, 1910–1959*. 1st ed. New York: Norton, 1983.

Truman, Harry S. *Memoirs*. 1st ed. Garden City, NY: Doubleday & Company, 1955.

Truman, Harry S. *Mr. Citizen*. New York: Geis Associates; distributed by Random House, 1960.

Truman, Margaret. *Bess W. Truman*. New York: Macmillan, 1986.

Tully, Grace. *F.D.R. My Boss*. New York: Charles Scribner's Sons, 1949.

Walsh, Kenneth T. *From Mount Vernon to Crawford: A History of the Presidents and Their Retreats*. 1st ed. New York: Hyperion, 2005.

Wapshott, Nicholas. *Ronald Reagan and Margaret Thatcher: A Political Marriage.* New York: Penguin Group, 2007.

West, J. B. and Mary Lynn Kotz. *Upstairs at the White House: My Life with the First Ladies.* New York: Coward, McCann & Geoghegan, 1973.

Wireman, George S. *Gateway to the Mountains.* Hagerstown, MD: Hagerstown Bookbinding and Printing Co, 1969.

Witcover, Jules. *Joe Biden: A Life of Trial and Redemption.* William Morrow paperback 1st edition, Updated and revised ed. New York: William Morrow, an imprint of Harper Collins Publishers, 2019.

Woodward, Bob and Carl Bernstein. *The Final Days.* New York: Simon and Schuster, 1976.

ARTICLES, PAPERS, AND SPEECHES

Anderson, Erik. "The Mystique of Camp David," *Frederick News Post,* June 4, 2017.

Anthony, John Duke. "The GCC-U.S. Summit: An Opportunity for Strategic Reassurance?" National Council on US-Arab Relations, May 12, 2015, https://ncusar .org/blog/2015/05/upcoming-gcc-us-summit/#gsc.tab=0 (retrieved December 30, 2020).

Baker, Peter, Mujib Mashal, and Michael Crowley. "How Trump's Plan to Secretly Meet with the Taliban Came Together, and Fell Apart," *The New York Times,* September 8, 2019, https://www.nytimes.com/2019/09/08/world/asia/aghanistan -trump-camp-david-taliban.html (retrieved June 12, 2022).

Barlow, Bill. "The History of Submarine Warfare Off the Jersey Coast," October 4, 2018, https://whyy.org/articles/the-history-of-submairne-warfare-off-the-jersey-coast/ (retrieved on June 25, 2020).

Borzogmehr, Najmeh and Roula Khalaf. "Gulf Summit Accused of 'Iranophobia,'" *Financial Times,* May 13, 2015.

Brimley, Shawn, Ilan Goldenberg, and Nicholas Heras. "Can Obama Save the GCC Summit?" *Foreign Policy,* May 11, 2015, https://foreignpolicy.com/2015/05/11/ gulf-cooperation-council-summit-camp-david-iran-saudi-arabia-king-salman/ (retrieved on December 30, 2020).

British Broadcasting Corporation. "Russia President Putin Will Miss G8 Camp David Summit," BBC, May 10, 2012, www.bbc.com/news/world-europe-18016106 (retrieved on December 30, 2020).

Brockell, Gillian, and Avi Selk. "Trump Finally Went to Camp David. It's no Mar-a-Lago," *Washington Post,* June 18, 2017, https://www.washingtonpost.com/news/ retropolis/wp/2017/05/15/trump-camp-david-and-the-history-of-presidential -retreats/ (retrieved on June 12, 2022).

Brown, Les. "ABC Delays Ford Film, Cites Election," *New York Times,* October 31, 1974. https://www.nytimes.com/1974/10/31/archives/abc-delays-ford-film-cites -election-800000-for-realidades.html (retrieved on April 3, 2021).

Bryant, Kenzie. "The Most Interesting Man in the World Was Once Barack Obama's Birthday Present," *Vanity Fair,* June 2, 2017, www.vanityfair.com/style/2017/06/

barack-obama-dos-equis-most-interesting-man-jonathan-goldsmith (retrieved February 13, 2021).

Buck, Tara E. "Catoctin Home to Presidents," *Frederick News Post*, July 20, 2003, 22–23, 26–27, 32, 34, 37.

Burton, R. R. "Ceremonial Adventures: Marine Barracks, Washington, DC, 1955–1959," http://www.8thandi.com/cdburton.pdf (retrieved August 7, 2020).

Bush, George H. W. "Remarks at the Simon Wiesenthal Center Dinner in Los Angeles, California," June 16, 1991, https://bush41library.tamu.edu/archives/public -papers/3103 (retrieved May 21, 2020).

Bush, George H. W. "Exchange with Reporters Following Meetings at Camp David, Maryland, with President Mikhail Gorbachev of the Soviet Union," June 2, 1999. https://bush41library.tamu.edu/archives/public-papers/1943 (retrieved May 21, 2020).

Capeci, Bob. "Reflections on serving at Camp David," http://www.8thandi.com/mem50 -01capeci.pdf (retrieved August 7, 2020).

Chambers, John Whiteclay. "OSS Training in the National Parks and Service Abroad in World War II," National Park Service, Chapter 4, https://www.nps.gov/park history/online_books/oss/ (retrieved April 23, 2019).

Clay, K. C. "Bessie Darling: A Brief Report on the Life of a Catoctin Mountain Propri-etress," National Park Service, May 2018.

Clay, K. C. "Rest Camp: A Report on the WWII Use of Catoctin Recreational Demon-stration Area by the Royal Navy," National Park Service, July 2018.

Clinton, Bill. "Remarks at the Full Gospel A.M.E. Zion Church in Temple Hills, Mary-land," August 14, 1994, www.presidency.ucsb.edu/documents/remarks-the-full -gospel-ame-zion-church-temple-hills-maryland (retrieved on October 7, 2020).

Connor, Roger. "Ike and the First Presidential Helicopters," July 12, 2010, Smithsonian https://airandspace.si.edu/stories/editorial/ike-and-first-presidential-helicopters (retrieved on August 7, 2020).

Cordesman, Anthony H. "More Than Keeping Up the Façade: The U.S.-GCC Summit at Camp David," CSIS, May 15, 2015, https://www.csis.org/analysis/more-keeping -facade-us-gcc-summit-camp-david (retrieved on December 30, 2020).

Crogan, Ed. Reflections on serving at Camp David, http://www.8thandi.com/skunk PDF (retrieved August 7, 2020).

Cullen, Patrick J. "Stained Glass Artist's Leaded Glass Came Knife," American Museum of Cutlery, November 8, 2015, http://www.amcut.com/stories/2015/11/8/dr -rudolph-r-sandons-contribution-to-cattaraugus-history (retrieved on December 30, 2020).

Devroy, Ann. "A Bonding Experience at Camp David: Clinton Used Professional 'Facili-tators' to Guide Weekend Retreat," *The Washington Post*, February 5, 1993.

Dunbar, Mary Elizabeth. "Sandon Studios R.D. Little Valley, New York," Cooperative Extension Association of Cattaragus County, https://historicpath.com/article/san don-studios-rd-little-valley-new-york-626 (retrieved December 30, 2020).

Eisler, Ben. "2012 G8 Summit Moves to Camp David as Thurmont Prepares," *WJLA,* March 7, 2012, https://wjla.com/news/local/2012-g8-summit-moves-to-camp-david-as-thurmont-prepares-73502 (retrieved on December 30, 2020).

Eilperin, Juliet. "Camp David is Obama's Retreat of Last Resort," *The Washington Post,* March 20, 2015.

Elving, Ron. "At Camp David, Trump Sought the Mantle of History. But Afghanistan is Different," NPR, September 10, 2019, https://www.npr.org/2019/09/10/759268550/at-camp-david-trump-sought-the-mantle-of-history-but-afghanistan-is-different (retrieved June 12, 2022).

Evans, Lacey. "Obama Heads to Camp David for 54th Birthday," *KOIN,* August 1, 2015, www.koin.com/news/obama-heads-to-camp-david-for-54th-birthday (retrieved February 13, 2021).

Geldon, Ben. "How Donald Trump Is Using Camp David to Woo Republicans," CNN, November 24, 2019, https://www.cnn.com/2019/11/24/politics/camp-david-republicans-trump-ip-forecast-cnntv/index.html (retrieved June 12, 2022).

Gleiter, Sue. "Landmark Fitzgerald's Shamrock Restaurant Closes After 57 Years," *Penn Live Patriot News* January 8, 2020, https://www.pennlive.com/life/2020/01/landmark-fitzgeralds-shamrock-restaurant-closes-after-57-years.html (retrieved April 7, 2021).

Glenn, Vicki. "Camp David Presidential Shangri-La in the Catoctins," *Frederick Magazine,* February 1992, 20–23, 42–43.

Greene, David L. "Camp David's Neighbors Wary," *Baltimore Sun,* September 17, 2001, https://www.baltimoresun.com/maryland/bal-te.david17sep17-story.html (retrieved April 20, 2023).

Haas, Ted. "Chapel Called Gift from 'People of Faith,'" Chambersburg Public Opinion, December 7, 1997.

Hanieh, Akram. "The Camp David Papers," *Journal of Palestine Studies,* Vol. 30, No 2 (Winter 2001), pp. 75–97, University of California Press on behalf of the Institute for Palestine Studies.

Headlee, Terry. "Moller Organ Debuts Before President," *The Daily Mail,* Hagerstown, MD, April 25, 1991.

Hilleary, Cecily. "Gulf States Coming to Washington with Big Wish List," *Voice of America News,* May 13, 2015, www.voanews.com/world-news/middle-east-dont-use/gulf-states-coming-washington-big-wish-list (retrieved on December 30, 2020).

Hillinger, Charles. "Shenandoah: Gift from Virginia Series: Charles Hillinger's America," *Los Angeles Times,* December 1987, 6.

Hunter, Robert E. "Was the US-GCC Summit Worth It?" *LobeLog,* May 21, 2015, https://lobelog.com/was-the-us-gcc-summit-worth-it/ (retrieved December 30, 2020.

Jackman, Tom. "Northern Virginia's Slice of Camelot: The Kennedys in Fauquier County, 1961–1963," *Washington Post,* November 21, 2013, https://www.washingtonpost.com/blogs/local/wp/2013/11/21/northern-virginias-slice-of-camelot-the-kennedys-in-fauquier-county-1961-63/ (retrieved July 28, 2020).

Jones, David L. and Joshua M. Koselak. "Camp David History," Naval Support Facility Thurmont, July 1999.
Keelan, Donald. "The Camp David Story," *Novascope*, September 1993, Vol. 8, no. 3, republished in *Vermont Magazine*, May/June 2017, 47–53.
Khalid, Asma and Franco Ordonez. "How Biden used Camp David to elevate a summit with Japan and South Korea," NPR, August 18, 2023, https://www.npr.org/2023/08/18/1194220556/camp-david-biden-japan-korea (retrieved April 20, 2025).
Kidd, David. "How Thurmont Coexists with Presidents and Camp David," Governing.com, October 8, 2021, https://www.governing.com/context/how-thurmont-co exists-with-presidents-and-camp-david (retrieved December 28, 2021).
Kim, Seung Min, Rachael Bade, and Josh Dawsey. "Trump Opens Up Camp David as an 'Adult Playground' to Woo GOP Lawmakers During Impeachment," *Washington Post*, November 22, 2019, https://www.washingtonpost.com/politics/trump-opens -up-camp-david-as-an-adult-playground-to-woo-gop-lawmakers-during-im peachment/2019/11/22/ec6e7810-0c6f-11ea-8397-a955cd542d00_story.html (retrieved June 12, 2022).
Kirkconnell, Barbara M., "Catoctin Mountain: An Administrative History" (MA thesis, University of Maryland at College Park, 1988).
Klein, Betsy, and Kaitlan Collins. "Trump Escapes Washington Isolation for Camp David," CNN, May 1, 2020, https://www.cnn.com/2020/05/01/politics/trump-camp -david-coronavirus/index.html (retrieved June 12, 2022).
Knoller, Mark. "Obamas Return to Camp David After 8 Month Absence," June 10, 2011, www.cbsnews.com/news/obamas-return-to-camp-david-after-8-month-absence/ (retrieved on October 7, 2020).
Kormann, Katie, and Nick Miller. "G8 Summit: Eight Things to Know About the G8," Redline Project, May 1, 2012, www.redlineproject.org/g8things.php (retrieved on December 30, 2020).
Kroenig, Matthew. "More Give, Less Take Needed at the GCC Camp David Summit," Atlantic Council, May 7, 2015, https://www.atlanticcouncil.org/blogs/menasource/ more-give-less-take-needed-at-the-gcc-camp-david-summit/ (retrieved December 30, 2020).
Lindig, Sarah, "Beyoncé and Blue Ivey Are Spending Labor Day with the Obamas," *Elle*, September 3, 2016, https://www.elle.com/culture/celebrites/news/a38991/ beyonce-labor-day-obamas/ (retrieved April 20, 2023).
MacInnis, Laura. "Obama Opens Up Camp David for Rustic VIP Sleepover," *Reuters*, May 19, 2012, www.reuters.com/article/us-g8-summit-campdavid/obama-opens -up-camp-david-for-rustic-vip-sleepover-idUSBRE84I0EN20120519 (retrieved on December 30, 2020).
Martin, Judith. "All the President's Yachts," *The Washington Post*, April 2, 1977.
Matson, Jennifer. "President Obama Celebrates 51st Birthday at Camp David," *Global Post*, August 4, 2012, www.pri.org/stories/2012-08-04/president-obama-celebrates -51st-birthday-camp-david (retrieved February 13, 2021).

McGowen, Deane. "CBS Bars Ford Interview Calls Proposed Date Too Near Election," *New York Times*, October 25, 1974, https://www.nytimes.com/1974/10/25/archives/cbs-bars-ford-interview-calls-proposed-date-too-near-election.html (retrieved on April 3, 2021).

McLaughlin, Tom. "Camp David, Part II Frederick County's Presidential Retreat," *Frederick Magazine*, December 2005, 77–85.

McLaughlin, Tom. "Camp David, Part III Frederick County's Presidential Retreat," *Frederick Magazine*, February 2006, 78–87.

McLaughlin, Tom. "Camp David: The History and Lord Behind Frederick County's Mountaintop Retreat," *Frederick Magazine*, October 2005, 99–104.

McNally, George J. "The White House Signal Team," *Army Information Digest*, August 1947, 24–32.

Melvin, John, Gene Smallwood, and Lee Miles. Reflections on Serving at Camp David, http://www.8thandi.com/CDseastories.pdf (retrieved on August 7, 2020).

Meredith, Mark. "Glen Ora," February 15, 2019, https://househistree.com/houses/glen-ora (retrieved July 28, 2020).

"Museum Window Reflects Masonry and America," April 1975, The Northern Light, Ancient Accepted Scottish Rite of Freemasonry, Northern Masonic Jurisdiction, United States of America, 11–14.

Nazer, Fahad. "Main Obstacle to New US-GCC Partnership May Be GCC Itself," Atlantic Council, June 3, 2015, https://www.atlanticcouncil.org/blogs/menasource/main-obstacle-to-new-us-gcc-partnership-may-be-gcc-itself/ (retrieved on December 30, 2020).

Nealand, David. "Camp David," Prologue, National Archives and Records Administration, Winter 2008 Vol. 40, no. 4, 28–33.

Offley, Ed. "U Boat Attacks of World War II: 6 Months of Secret Terror in the Atlantic," www.newenglandhistoricalsociety.com/u-boat-attacks-of-world-war-ii-6-months-of-secret-terror-in-the-atlantic/ (retrieved on June 25, 2020).

Palmer, Anna, Jake Sherman, Eli Okun, and Garrett Ross. "POLITICO Playbook PM: Camp David Guest List," https://www.politico.com/newsletters/playbook-pm/2020/05/15/new-camp-david-guest-list-489239 (retrieved June 12, 2022).

Pincus, Walter, and Bob Woodward. "Presidential Posts and Dashed Hopes; Appointive Jobs Were Turning Point," *Washington Post*, August 9, 1988.

Pramuk, Jacob. "Here's Who Will Join Trump at Camp David This Weekend to Plan the 2018 GOP Agenda," CNBC, January 5, 2018, https://www.cnbc.com/2018/01/05/trump-heads-to-camp-david-this-weekend-to-talk-2018-gop-agenda.html (retrieved June 12, 2022).

"Press at Camp David Gets 50-Foot Trailer," *Washington Post*, November 18, 1972.

Py, Ray. "Camp David: Plush Digs for Presidents in Our Backyard," *Gazette Regional News*, January 9, 1997, A-18, A-19.

Rada, Jim. "Bessie Darling's Murder Haunts Us Still," https://historyarchive.wordpress.com/2016/05/19/bessie-darlings-murder-haunts-us-still/ (retrieved November 11, 2020).

Radcliffe, Donnie. "The Bells of Camp David: Going to the Chapel," *Washington Post*, January 26, 1988.

Rea, Joanna. "2012 G8 Summit—Private Sector to the Rescue of the World's Poorest?" *The Guardian*, May 25, 2012, www.theguardian.com/global-development/poverty-matters/2012/may/25/2012-g8-summit-private-sector (retrieved on December 30, 2020).

The Reliable Source, "Obama's Birthday Weekend: Golf with the Boys, Party at Camp David," The Washington Post, August 4, 2013, www.washingtonpost.com/news/reliable-source/wp/2013/08/04/obamas-birthday-weekend-golf-with-the-boys-party-at-camp-david/ (retrieved on February 13, 2021).

Ridgley, Jaime. "Camp David and the Cozy," *Frederick Magazine*, October 2005, 106.

Riley, Erika, "Shamrock to Close After 57 Years in Business," *Frederick News Post*, November 26, 2019, https://www.fredericknewspost.com/news/economy_and_business/retail/shamrock-to-close-after-57-years-in-business/article_2a78fde4-25f9-51ca-8558-958c3c78bc9b.html (retrieved April 7, 2021).

Ritchie, Charles. "The Day the President of the United States Struck Fear and Trembling into the Heart of Our PM," *MacLean's*, January 1, 1974, https://archive.macleans.ca/article/1974/1/1/the-day-the-president-of-the-united-states-struck-fear-and-trembling-into-the-heart-of-our-pm (retrieved on March 19, 2021).

Roberts, Dan. "Obama Summit with Arab Allies Begins Despite Saudi King's Absence," *The Guardian*, May 14, 2015, https://www.theguardian.com/us-news/2015/may14/barack-obama-arab-gulf-leaders-camp-david-summit (retrieved on December 30, 2020).

Rogers, Katie and Peter Baker. "Biden's Family Tells Him to Keep Fighting as They Huddle at Camp David," *New York Times*, June 30, 2024, https://www.nytimes.com/2024/06/30/us/politics/biden-debate-anxious-democrats.html (retrieved April 20, 2025).

Rubin, A. James. "Camp David Chapel Affirms Religious Diversity," *The United Methodist Reporter*, July 19, 1991.

Sandon, Rudolph, "Descriptive Summary of Medallions for the Camp David Chapel," Sandon Studios, June 12, 1989.

Sayler, Zoe, "The Presidential Portrait That Was the 'Ugliest Thing' L.B.J. Ever Saw," Smithsonianmag.com, February 16, 2018, https://www.smithsonianmag.com/history/presidential-portrait-was-ugliest-thing-lbj-ever-saw-180968190/ (retrieved August 27, 2020.

Shane, Brian. "The Cozy: Longtime Restaurant Near Camp David Closes," *USA Today*, August 8, 2014, https://www.usatoday.com/story/news/nation/2014/08/08/camp-david-restaurant-cleses/13760815/ (retrieved April 20, 2023).

Sharma, Shweta. "Biden meets family at Camp David as calls mount for him to quit US presidential race," *The Independent*, July 1, 2024, https://www.independent.co.uk/news/world/americas/us-politics/biden-camp-david-debate-stepping-down-b2571607.html (retrieved April 20, 2025).

Snyder, David, "Bush Disappears into Presidential Retreat," *Washington Post*, January 20, 2002.

Sturcke, James and agencies. "Bush Flies into Baghdad for Surprise Visit," June 13, 2006, www.theguardian.com/world/2006/jun/13/usa.iraq (retrieved February 13, 2021).

Thomas, Helen. "Bush Attends Dedication for new Camp David Chapel," *Washington Post*, April 21, 1991, https://www.upi.com/Archives/1991/04/21/Bush-attends -dedication-for-new-Camp-David-chapel/5667672206400/ (retrieved March 25, 2021).

Thomas, Helen. "Camp David Starting to Look Like Armed Camp," *Hagerstown Daily Mail*, October 17, 1983.

Thomas, Helen, "Camp David and its Stately Residents," UPI Archives, May 26, 1990, https://www.upi.com/Archives/1990/05/26/Camp-David-and-its-stately-resi dents/8137643694400/ (retrieved September 15, 2020).

Tooker, Megan Weaver and Adam Smith. "Camp David Historic Resources Survey," US Army Corps of Engineers Engineer Research and Development Center, January 2011.

U.S. Department of State. "Joint Press Availability with Secretary of Defense Ash- ton Carter, Afghan President Ashraf Ghani, and Afghan Chief Executive Abdullah Abdullah," March 23, 2015, https://2009-2017.state.gov/secretary/ remarks/2015/03/239713.htm (retrieved January 17, 2021).

Voice of America News. "Obama Invites African Leaders to G8 Summit," May 3, 2012 www.voanews.com/archive/obama-invites-african-leaders-g8-summit (retrieved December 30, 2020).

Wehrle, Edmund F. *Catoctin Mountain Park: A Historic Resource Study*. Washington, DC: National Park Service, March 2000 (accessible at https://www.nps.gov/park history/online_books/cato/hrst.htm).

Weiler, Sara, and Vermont Magazine staff. "Straight Talking Marine," *Vermont Magazine*, May/June 2017, 41–46.

Westner, Joe. "Reflections on serving at Camp David," http://www.8thandi.com/Camp DavidWestner.pdf (retrieved August 7, 2020).

White House. "Camp David Declaration," May 19, 2012, https://obamawhitehouse .archives.gov/the-press-office/2012/05/19/camp-david-declaration (retrieved December 30, 2020).

White House. "FACT SHEET: The Trilateral Leaders' Summit at Camp David, August 18, 2023, https://bidenwhitehouse.archives.gov/briefing-room/statements -releases/2023/08/18/fact-sheet-the-trilateral-leaders-summit-at-camp-david/ (retrieved April 20, 2025).

White House. "On-the-Record Conference Call on the GCC Summit," May 11, 2015, https://obamawhitehouse.archives.gov/the-press-office/2015/05/11/record-con ference-call-gcc-summit (retrieved December 30, 2020).

White House. "Press Briefing by Press Secretary Jay Carney; Mike Froman, Deputy National Security Advisor for International Economics; and Deputy National Security Advisor for Strategic Communications Ben Rhodes," May 19, 2012, https://obamawhitehouse.arcives.gov/the-press-office/2012/05/19/press-brief ing-press-secretary-jay-carney-mike-froman-deputy-national-se (retrieved on December 30, 2020).

White House. "Remarks by President Biden, President Yoon Suk Yeol of the Republic of Korea, and Prime Minister Kishida Fumio of Japan in Joint Press Conference, Camp David, MD," August 18, 2023, https://bidenwhitehouse.archives .gov/briefing-room/speeches-remarks/2023/08/18/remarks-by-president-biden -president-yoon-suk-yeol-of-the-republic-of-korea-and-prime-minister-kishida -fumio-of-japan-in-joint-press-conference-camp-david-md/ (retrieved April 20, 2025).

White House. "Statement by President Obama at Closing of G8 Summit," May 19, 2012, https://obamawhitehouse.archives.gov/the-press-office/2012/05/19/state ment-president-obama-closing-g8-summit (retrieved December 30, 2020).

White House. "U.S. – Gulf Cooperation Council Camp David Joint Statement," May 14, 2015, https://obamawhitehouse.archives.gov/the-press-office/2015/05/14/ us-gulf-cooperation-council-camp-david-joint-statement (retrieved on December 30, 2020).

Wind, Herbert Warren. "A First Look: World's Most Exclusive Golf Course," *Sports Illustrated*, January 24, 1955, https://vault.si.com/vault/1955/01/24/a-first-look -worlds-most-exclusive-golf-course (retrieved on August 8, 2020).

Wirth, Conrad, "Parks, Politics, and the People (Chapter 7)," National Park Service, www.nps.gov/parkhistory/online-books/wirth/chap7c.htm (retrieved on November 16, 2020).

Wright, Robin, "Trump's Stunt with The Taliban Was Not About Negotiating Peace," *The New Yorker*, September 9, 2019, https://www.newyorker.com/news/our-column ists/trumps-stunt-with-the-taliban-was-not-about-negotiating-peace (retrieved June 12, 2022).

ARCHIVES

Franklin D. Roosevelt Library: https://www.fdrlibrary.org/archives.
Harry S. Truman Library: https://www.trumanlibrary.gov/library.
Dwight D. Eisenhower Library: https://www.eisenhowerlibrary.gov/.
John F. Kennedy Library: https://www.jfklibrary.org/archives/about-archival-collections.
Lyndon B. Johnson Library: http://www.lbjlibrary.org/research.
Richard M. Nixon Library: https://www.nixonlibrary.gov/index.php/research.
Gerald R. Ford Library: https://www.fordlibrarymuseum.gov/collections-library.aspx.
Jimmy Carter Library: https://www.jimmycarterlibrary.gov/research.
Ronald Reagan Library: https://www.reaganlibrary.gov/archives.
George H. W. Bush Library: https://bush41library.tamu.edu/.
Bill Clinton Library: https://www.clintonlibrary.gov/research.
George W. Bush Library: https://www.georgewbushlibrary.smu.edu/en/research.

FRANKLIN D. ROOSEVELT PRESIDENTIAL LIBRARY

FDR-43: Cost Estimate for Shangri-La (Hi-Catoctin Lodge), April 24, 1942
RG79 Records as Director Newton Drury, Box 4.
RG79 Recreational Demonstration Area Program Files 1934–47, Box 57, Reports.

RG79 Recreational Demonstration Area Program Files 1934–47, Box 59, Surplus Supplies.
RG79 Recreational Demonstration Area Program Files 1934–47, Box 61, Construction Projects File.

HARRY S. TRUMAN PRESIDENTIAL LIBRARY
Papers of Harry S. Truman Official File, OF 101-H (Shangri-La).
Wallace Graham Papers, Box 29, Chapter 22 Shangri-La.
David Stowe Papers, Box 10.

EISENHOWER PRESIDENTIAL LIBRARY
Robert Anderson Papers, Box 26, Miscellaneous.
Evan Aurand Papers, Naval Aide to the President Series, Box 7, W (1).
Edward Beach and Evan Aurand Records, Box 17, Eisenhower-Khrushchev Conference at Camp David-Movies.
Edward Beach and Evan Aurand Records, Box 17, Eisenhower-Khrushchev Conference at Camp David-Music.
Edward Beach and Evan Aurand Records, Box 17, Eisenhower-Khrushchev Conference at Camp David-Operation Plan.
Edward Beach and Evan Aurand Records, Box 17, Eisenhower-Khrushchev Conference at Camp David-Schedules (1).
Edward Beach and Evan Aurand Records, Box 17, Eisenhower-Khrushchev Conference at Camp David-Schedules (2).
Edward Beach and Evan Aurand Records, Box 17, Eisenhower-Khrushchev Conference at Camp David-Press.
Edward Beach and Evan Aurand Records, Box 25, Painting at Camp David.
Dwight D. Eisenhower's Papers, Ann Whitman Diary Series, Box 10, Diary March 1959 (1).
Dwight D. Eisenhower's Papers, Dulles-Herter Series, Box 12, Herter October 1959 (2).
Dwight D. Eisenhower's Papers, Name Series, Box 18, Hazlett 1953 (1).
Dwight D. Eisenhower's Post-Presidential Papers, Augusta-Walter Reed Series, Box 2, Kennedy 1960–61 (1).
Dwight D. Eisenhower's Post-Presidential Papers, 1965 Signature File Series, Box 7, PR-3 Public Relations-Interview.
Dwight D. Eisenhower's Records, Alphabetical File, Box 503, Camp David.
Dwight D. Eisenhower's Records, President's Personal File, Box 60, PPF 1-F-127.
James C. Hagerty Papers, Box 21, Khrushchev Visit—Camp David.
White House Office, Office of the Staff Secretary Records, International Trips Series, Box 9, Khrushchev Visit (3).
White House Office, Office of the Staff Secretary Records, International Trips Series, Box 9, Khrushchev Visit (4).
White House Office, Office of the Staff Secretary Records, International Trips Series, Box 9, Khrushchev Visit (5).

White House Office, Office of the Staff Secretary Records, International Trips Series, Box 9, Khrushchev Visit (6).
White House Office, Office of the Staff Secretary Records, Subject Series, DoD Subseries, Box 4, JCS (8).

GERALD R. FORD PRESIDENTIAL LIBRARY
Philip Buchen Files, Box 48, folder "President—Personal Camp David."
Richard B. Cheney Files, Box 1, folder, "Camp David."
Ron Nessen Papers, Box 23, "Press Office—Improvement Meeting, 6/28–29/75 (1)."
Ron Nessen Files, Box 25, folder "10/26/1974—Harry Reasoner, ABC News."
Eric Rosenberger and Douglass Blaser Files, Box 1, "Camp David—Background, 1969-1973 (1)."
Eric Rosenberger and Douglass Blaser Files, Box 1, "Camp David—Background, 1969-1973 (2)."
Eric Rosenberger and Douglass Blaser Files, Box 1, "Camp David—Background, 1969-1973 (3)."

RONALD REAGAN PRESIDENTIAL LIBRARY
Elizabeth Board Files, Camp David Maryland Public Television, Box 8.
Joseph W. Canzeri Files, Protocol/State Visits: Background on Camp David Jackets, Box 11.
Marlin M. Fitzwater Files, Camp David Chapel, Box 14.
Office of Correspondence Records, AVH-078 Donations for Construction of Chapel at Camp David, Box 5.
Office of Correspondence Records, AVH-081 Donations for Construction of Chapel at Camp David, Box 5.
Office of Media Relations Records, FLOTUS/PITUS Camp David 11/14/1986, Maryland Public TV, Box 52.
White House Office of Press Secretary, Press Releases and Briefings: Records, 06/05/1981, #773a Fact Sheet—Camp David, Box 5.

ORAL HISTORIES
Harry S. Truman Presidential Library
George E. Allen
Admiral Robert L. Dennison
Robert B. Landry
Rear Admiral Donald J. MacDonald
Robert G. Nixon
Gerald Paul Pulley
William M. Rigdon
John W. Snyder
Harry H. Vaughan

Eisenhower Presidential Library
Evan P. Aurand, oral history #127.
Wiley T. Buchanan, oral history #238.
John S. D. Eisenhower, oral history #543.
Clifford Roberts, oral history #266.
George Tames oral history #547.
Clyde A. Wheeler Jr., oral history #515.

Lyndon B. Johnson Presidential Library
Jack Brooks by Joe B. Frantz, February 1, 1971, interview I.
Ellsworth Bunker by Michael L. Gilette, October 13, 1983, interview III.
Dr. George Davis by Dorothy Pierce McSweeny, February 13, 1969, interview I.
Willard Deason by Michael L. Gillette, April 6, 1988, interview VII.
Billy Graham by Monroe Billington, October 12, 1983, special interview.
Peter Hurd by Elizabeth Kaderli, April 6, 1969, interview I.
Jake Jacobson by Michael L. Gillete, June 7, 1984, interview II.
Lady Bird Johnson by Michael L. Gillette, February 20–21, 1981, interview XX.
Arthur Krim by Michael L. Gillette, May 17, 1982, interview II.
Joseph Laitin by Michael L. Gillette, June 19, 1967, interview IV.
Lawrence E. Levinson by Joe B. Frantz, August 18, 1972, interview VI.
David G. Nes by Ted Gettinger, March 25, 1983, interview II.
Lawrence O'Brien by Michael L. Gillette, September 18, 1985, interview I.
Sir Keith Waller by Joe B. Frantz, December 1, 1969, interview I.
Lew Wasserman by Joe B. Frantz, December 21, 1973, interview I.
Lee White by Joe B. Frantz, February 18, 1971, interview II.
June White by Michael L. Gillette, February 17, 1976, interview I.
William S. White by Dorothy Pierce McSweeny, March 10, 1969, interview II.

www.ingramcontent.com/pod-product-compliance
Lightning Source LLC
Chambersburg PA
CBHW051728260326
41914CB00040B/2017/J